AGING

A Natural History

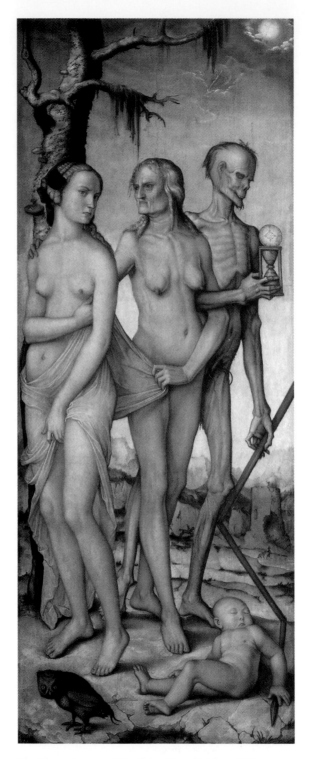

The Three Ages and Death by Hans Baldung Grien

AGING

A Natural History

Robert E. Ricklefs

Caleb E. Finch

**SCIENTIFIC
AMERICAN
LIBRARY**

A division of HPHLP
New York

Library of Congress Cataloging-in-Publication Data

Ricklefs, Robert E.
   Aging : a natural history / Robert E. Ricklefs, Caleb E. Finch.
      p.   cm.
   Includes bibliographical references and index.
   ISBN 0-7167-5056-2
   1. Aging — Physiological aspects.   2. Evolution (Biology)
I. Finch, Caleb Ellicott.   II. Title.
QP86.R525 1995
612.6'7 — dc20   95-2334
                                                         CIP

Printed in the United States of America

Scientific American Library
A division of HPHLP
New York

Distributed by W. H. Freeman and Company,
41 Madison Avenue, New York, NY 10010
20 Beaumont Street, Oxford OX1 2NQ, England

1 2 3 4 5 6 7 8 9 0   HAW   9 9 8 7 6 5

This book is number 57 of a series.

To my mother, Marian
    — Robert E. Ricklefs

To my wife, Doris
    — Caleb E. Finch

Contents

Preface

Aging is one of the universal human experiences. In our youth, we witness the growing frailty and passing of older family members. Later, we see such changes in our own generation, perhaps, above all, in ourselves. Aging and death seem as natural and ongoing as breathing, and just as inevitable.

Aging may be an intrinsic, fundamental aspect of life, but scientific research is transforming our knowledge of its sources and our ability to intervene in its processes. A new perception of aging is emerging, as on the one hand we are making breathtaking progress in understanding the genetic and biochemical bases of disease processes, while on the other we are learning from experimental studies on aging in a variety of animals and gaining important new insights from evolutionary biology. This scientific headway is well timed to address the increasing societal problem of caring for the growing numbers of elderly in the population, surely one of the most revolutionary changes in the character of human life during this century. Indeed, many of us are now reaching 100 years or more, truly advanced ages that were once perceived as extreme curiosities. Yet the desire to attain even greater human life spans continues to grow, and the evidence is strong that biomedical advances will delay or even eliminate many of the afflictions of advanced age.

The graying of human society raises important issues touching on all aspects of our lives: the medical challenge of improving the quality of life for the elderly; the economic challenge of supporting a growing population of retired, dependent men and women; the ethical challenge posed by the terminally ill; the societal challenge of balancing the needs of the old and the needs of the young. Society's ability to resolve many of these issues will depend in part on how well its members understand the underlying biology of aging.

This book considers the nature of human aging from our perspectives as biologists. We wanted to convey some impressive new insights from laboratory and clinical studies, but we also wanted to bring into general discussion some illuminating perspectives offered by the evolutionary biology of aging, which confronts the fundamental issue of how factors in the environment influence the genetic bases of aging patterns differently in different species. We will try to provide answers to several general questions:

- What are the causes of aging?
- Is aging universal among all kinds of organisms?
- Why do different organisms exhibit different patterns of aging?
- How much do individual people differ in manifestations of aging?
- Do individual differences result from heredity or environment?
- How may the human life span evolve in the future?
- What precedents in evolution may help us make wise choices about the allocation of resources needed to maintain increasing numbers of elderly?

Our approach is to place human aging in its broader biological context, emphasizing both the mechanisms of physiological deterioration and the origins and maintenance of aging as an evolved phenomenon.

The two of us come from very different areas of biology that do not mingle often these days. Caleb (Tuck) Finch has had a career-long interest in mechanisms of aging in the nervous and endocrine systems. Most of his studies are molecular analyses of tissues from laboratory rodents and post-mortem human brains. Robert Ricklefs is an ecologist interested in species diversity and the age-group structure of natural populations. Most of his work is based on field studies and quantitative modeling. The merger of these interests has stimulated us to ask questions about the nature of aging in humans that are not usually considered by our separate disciplines. In particular, patterns of aging in human populations are but one example from among a greater variety of such patterns exhibited both within and between species in nature. The study of these patterns from the perspectives of physiology, evolution, and population biology provide many insights into our own mortality.

We began to consider the present book when one of us (Finch) contacted the other (Ricklefs) in 1987 for advice on questions in ecology and population genetics during his writing of *Longevity, Senescence, and the Genome,* published in 1990. As that book evolved, Tuck found himself seeking a broader perspective in which to view mechanisms of aging in humans and thus began contacting scholars outside the biomedical mainstream. In fact, the two of us had crossed paths and pens much earlier in our careers. We were both surprised when Tuck found in his files a long-forgotten exchange of letters from 1968, when we were just beginning our scientific careers. Such is the nature of aging as the brain records it: traces of the past are layered over with the new and are not always revealed quickly. And so it may be with the evolution of life spans.

This book has been truly a group effort from the beginning. In its preparation, we have enjoyed a wonderful relationship with the editorial and production staff at the Scientific American Library. Senior Editor Jonathan Cobb was very helpful in developing the basic concept for the book. Susan Moran was the kind of editor that authors always wish for, persistently but pleasantly encouraging and cajoling, setting a high standard for writing, and through her own perceptions helping us to maintain the focus and continuity of the text. Travis Amos has done a tremendous job of ferreting out striking and informative photographs, and Tina Hastings ably supervised the stages of proof for both art and text. We also appreciated the many insightful and helpful suggestions from Donald Ingram, Donna Holmes, and David Reznick.

Robert E. Ricklefs
Rose Valley, Pennsylvania

Caleb E. (Tuck) Finch
Altadena, California

February 1995

AGING

A Natural History

Aging is a natural consequence of living for complex organisms like ourselves, although its typical course in our own species is only one of many patterns of aging in nature. Of course, an individual's own portrait of aging is unique.

*N*one of us can live forever. Even if we didn't age, the many dangers in life—accidents at home and on the road, contagious disease, violent crime—would eventually cut our lives short. The safest age for human beings is around puberty; 10- to 15-year-olds have the lowest risk of dying, and about 1 in 2000 adolescents, or 0.05%, die per year in North America and Europe. Then, throughout the world, and regardless of the adolescent risk of dying, the death rate begins to increase steadily soon after puberty as we begin to experience the slow physiological decline called aging. By the time we reach 100 years of age, our capacity to deal with disease and injury has diminished so much, and wear and tear has taken such a toll, that the risk of dying reaches 50% per year.

For the moment, consider a fantasy world without aging, in which individuals have a constant lifelong risk of death at the low adolescent rate of 0.05% per year. In such a world, we would have an immensely better outlook for

1

Patterns
of
Aging

attaining longevity. Indeed, we would be, potentially, immortal. Even so, just the roll of the dice each year, at an odds of 1 in 2000 of striking out, will lead to gradual attrition. Still, if not for aging, 95% of us would celebrate our centenaries and 50% of us would reach the seemingly astonishing age of 1200 years.

Returning now to the real world, it is clear that for most of us the age of death will be mainly determined by the processes of aging, rather than by any accident of fate. Most of us will not experience our centenaries, not because of bad luck, but because, even under the best of circumstances, we cannot avoid some consequences of living that cause our bodies to age. The same appears to be true of most other species of animals and plants.

Next to the miracle of life itself, aging and death are perhaps the greatest mysteries. We may wonder whether death is an inevitable consequence of life. Does the body deteriorate in the same way as the machines we build, or do living systems have special attributes that make them vulnerable to time? Why

does the collection of cells that is the body age, while the lines of germ cells leading from parent to child to grandchild persist indefinitely? Do different individuals among us age faster or slower? Do other species? Can aging be modified, and, most importantly, can life be extended?

These questions are important to your authors because we are both middle-aged and moving along, but also because we are both biologists interested in the causes and consequences of aging. Although many aspects of aging remain enigmatic, biological research has provided tentative answers to the questions most often asked about aging. In this and the following chapters, we will lead you through our present understanding of aging and shed some light on prospects for the future.

As a first step in thinking about this complex subject, let's check our assumptions: How do we know that most or all plants and animals must inevitably "age" with the passing of time? Certainly all species seem to have a maximum life span beyond which no individual lives. Humans as a species, for example, appear to live longer than any other mammal. The *Guinness Book of World Records* recognizes Shigechiyo Izumi, a Japanese man, as having lived a record 120 years. While there are doubts about the authenticity of his birthdate, there are none for Madame Jeanne Calment, who was born on February 21, 1875. At the time this book is published she will have just celebrated her 120th birthday.

The mammals closest to humans in life span may be orangutans, whales, and elephants, which live to at least 70 years. Many other large mammals survive to 20 to 30 years, whereas smaller mammals tend to have shorter life spans. Ten to 15 years is a normal life span for a dog, and the Virginia opossum is as short-lived as a laboratory rat or mouse, animals that under the best circumstances may survive 5 years. Birds show the same range of life span as mammals and, at the upper end, may rival humans in longevity, since there are reliable records of individual parrots living to 90 years. In contrast, flies have among the

Madame Jeanne Calment of Arles, France, photographed in 1994 at a party to celebrate her 119th birthday. At this writing, Madame Calment is the oldest person of confirmed age.

shortest life spans found in animals—typically 2 months in the genus *Drosophila*. The single-celled yeasts, which we use to brew beer and leaven bread, are even shorter lived—they survive but a few days.

The maximum life span for any species is often a hard number to come by because we have so few records of age at death. As more data accumulate, the maximum age can only increase. In general, we have a good idea about the maximum life spans for only a few species that have been domesticated or raised in the laboratory, and for which we have recorded the birth dates of large numbers of individuals. In the human population, only within this century has individual identification through birth records and fingerprints become reliable enough to prove life spans of 100 years or more. Appearances alone can be deceiving.

These examples do not prove that all species must experience aging. Even if organisms were potentially immortal, none would live forever and the maximum recorded life span would fall short of infinity. To find out whether aging, as opposed to death, is truly universal, we need to examine more closely what aging is, then look for signs of its presence.

What Is Aging? What Is Senescence?

Aging and *senescence* are words that can be used to characterize an extremely broad range of phenomena, affecting biological entities from molecules to populations of organisms. These terms may even be used to describe changes that happen over time to nonbiological entities such as machines and stars. Both words convey the idea that things change with age, but obviously there is more to their definitions than this.

Aging may colloquially refer to changes that are good, bad, or indifferent. In fact, common usage

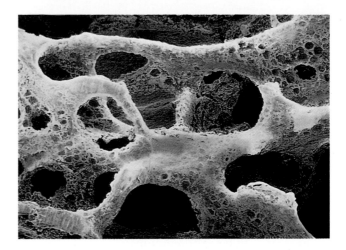

Aging bones often become spongy in structure from the loss of minerals, a form of deterioration called osteopenia. The resulting increase in osteoporotic fractures is one of the dangerous consequences of aging.

does not allow us a precise definition of aging. Fine wines are often left in the bottle to age. Babies become older (that is, they age) and learn to speak. We are not going to talk about aging in this sense. Moreover, organisms experience many changes in molecules and cells that are purely healthy. For example, millions of cells in our skin and intestines die every day as part of the continuing renewal of these tissues. While the turnover of these cells could be considered a form of aging at the cellular level, it has nothing to do with the individual's risk of mortality.

By *aging*, we refer to progressive changes during the adult years that often, but not always, reduce an individual's viability. Not all manifestations of aging are bad; for example, men grow bald and hair turns gray without any risk of disease or dysfunction. For a more precise term to describe specific loss of function in older individuals, we turn to the word *senescence*. As blood vessels age, for example, they undergo the gradual loss of elasticity known as arteriosclerosis, or hardening of the arteries. Arteriosclerosis is part of a more complex set of changes in blood vessels that can be life threatening if the blood vessel becomes too narrow. Thus, at older age, cells in the brain and heart are at higher risk of being irreversibly damaged because the blood vessels that supply these organs, when narrowed, are more likely to become blocked, leading to heart stroke or brain stroke. To give another example, mutations may accumulate over time in certain genes in cells of the reproductive system, as is quite common in the breast or prostate, and become a factor in the increase of cancer with aging. In both cases, these processes of aging lead to an increase in the risk of mortality, giving us a straightforward way to observe the progress of senescence in large populations.

How Biologists Measure Senescence

One way to characterize aging is to trace the increase in mortality rate with chronological age in populations of organisms. The mortality rate is the probability that an individual who is alive at a particular age will die during the following age interval, that is, before his or her next birthday. For humans, the age interval is generally chosen to be 1 year. Remember from the beginning of the chapter that the annual mortality among adolescents in North America and Europe at the age of 15 years was about 0.05%, or 1 in 2000 per year. At the age of 105, mortality has increased a thousandfold to about 50% per year. As in most other species of animals and plants, the mortality rate of humans increases gradually and progressively during aging. Actuaries often describe these changes by an exponential curve named after Benjamin Gompertz, the British actuary who in 1825 first described the exponential growth in mortality rate with age, now called the Gompertz formula, or "law of mortality."

Mortality in a population can be depicted either as the fraction of the population surviving to a particular age or as the mortality rate at a particular age. In the human population, the proportion of individuals surviving decreases gradually up to about 60 years of age and then drops off sharply like a steep ski slope. As you might imagine, the annual mortality rate and the survival curve are related to each other mathematically. For example, about 65% of the individuals who reach 15 years will survive to 50 years of age, but only 64% will survive to 51 years of age. The drop from 65% to 64% represents a loss of 1% of 15-year-olds but about 1.5% of 50-year-olds. Thus, the mortality rate at age 50 is about 1.5% per year, which is already 30 times greater than that of a 15-year-old. At later ages, progressively larger proportions of survivors die, so that the mortality-rate curve soars up sharply, with the slope getting steeper year by year. When the mortality rate is rescaled to its logarithm, we see that it increases as a straight line from about 15 to about 90 years. This "semi-logarithmic" plot helps us to compare rates of aging because, according to the Gompertz formula, the logarithm of the mortality rate tends to increase as a linear, or straight-line, function of age.

The slope of the straight line describing the semi-logarithmic relationship tells us how rapidly the logarithm of mortality rate increases with age, or the rate of acceleration of mortality. This number, which is called the Gompertz acceleration parameter, can also be expressed as the time required for the mortality rate to double. In most human populations, mortality rates double about every 8 years. The faster organisms in the population show signs of aging, the shorter the mortality rate doubling time (MRDT). When Gompertz plots are used to compare different human populations, a remarkable feature emerges. Despite big differences in average life spans between populations, the slopes of the Gompertz curves are all about the same. The differences are in the mortality rates of adolescents and young adults.

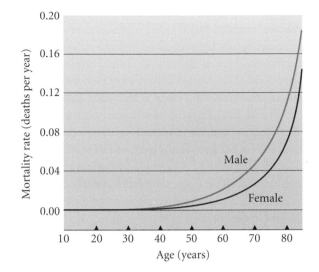

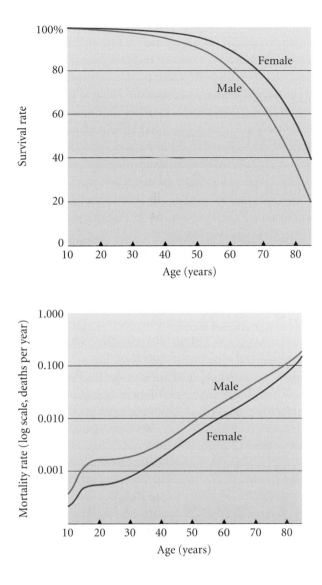

Top left: Survival curves based on the United States population show the percentage of individuals, male or female, in each age group who were still surviving in 1985. The scale begins at 100% puberty, when the population of each sex was about 100 million. The curves reveal the poorer survival of men during aging. Top right: These mortality curves are based on the same data as the neighboring survival curves. To construct the curves, someone calculated the percent loss of life for each 5-year interval, or the odds of dying for that 5 years. The curve for men shifts upward earlier than the curve for women. Bottom left: The mortality curves have been transformed to a logarithmic scale. The generally parallel slopes of the lines for men and women are interpreted to suggest a difference in the onset of degenerative changes during aging.

An MRDT of 8 years seems to be a general characteristic of humans as a species. But now we come to a real puzzle: How is it that the MRDT can be the same in countries that have very different levels of risk in the population of young adults or the diseases of aging? In Japan, for example, the risk of breast cancer is 10-fold less than in the United States, yet the MRDT is the same. Men and women differ greatly with respect to risk factors such as cancer, yet their MRDTs are also the same. We will come back to these interesting observations in later chapters.

Among mammals, mortality rate doubling times and maximum life spans vary widely, and yet there is reasonable correspondence between these numbers. For example, laboratory mice have maximum life spans of about 4 years and their mortality rates dou-

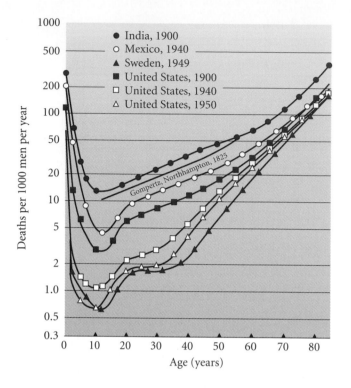

Human populations may differ 25-fold in the mortality rate at puberty, yet by later years the slopes of their Gompertz curves are about the same. Notice how plotting the mortality rate on a logarithmic scale emphasizes relative differences, making comparisons easier. At even older ages than shown here, mortality decelerates and may actually become constant.

mortality may actually *decrease*. Studies in progress by James Vaupel of Duke University and Odense University, Denmark, indicate that, after the age of 105 years, those one in a million still alive may have a greater chance of reaching 106 than individuals aged 104 had of reaching 105. These few may have very special genes or were lucky in their exposure to life's hazards. The recent trend for more people to survive to advanced ages strongly implies that the record human life span may soon be broken. Other species have shown similar slowing of the mortality risks at advanced ages. A clear example is the Mediterranean fruit fly, or medfly, in which the mortality rate slows down to a steady constant risk after about 90% of the population has died.

Not all changes in mortality rate with age are connected to processes of aging. In many cases, the risk of death increases when an individual matures because of dangers linked to reproduction. For example, male red deer fight fiercely with other males to keep their harems, and their increased mortality has nothing to do with senescence. Female red deer are also at higher risk during birthing and nursing.

ble every 3 months, a ratio of about 16 to 1. In humans, the numbers are proportionately larger: the maximum life span is about 120 years and the MRDT is about 8 years—a ratio of 15 to 1. At the short end of the scale are laboratory populations of flies and nematodes, whose mortality rates double every 5 to 10 days. Such rapid acceleration of mortality is paralleled by proportionately rapid manifestation of senescence and correspondingly brief life spans.

At ages beyond 90 years in humans, the slope of the Gompertz curve decreases. People who survive to these advanced ages appear to be special: their risk of

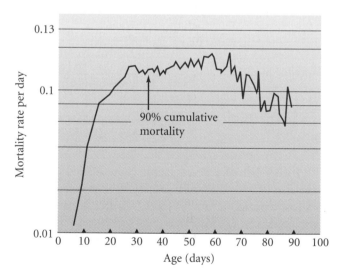

The medfly mortality rate shows a Gompertz-like acceleration until age 15 days, when the rate flattens out.

Chapter One

6

These variations in mortality rates should caution us not to view the Gompertz curve as a precise law of nature. Even so, it is useful for comparing aging between different species and populations because it provides a simple and reasonably accurate description of mortality rates in most populations.

Aging in the Natural World

In the human population, the mortality rate begins to increase shortly after puberty and continues increasing through the child-bearing years. We tend to think that most people end their reproductive lives decades before the deterioration of aging seriously affects them, but the Gompertz curve tells us that this cannot be true for all individuals: aging can definitely diminish a person's lifetime reproductive success. The same is true in many natural populations. If aging cuts down the reproductive rate, then the possibility arises that aging affects evolutionary fitness.

We all appreciate that species change over time in both their physical characteristics and behavior. It was Charles Darwin who explained the mechanism by which such changes happen. Evolution is possible because no two individuals are genetically identical—they will vary in body size, sharpness of eyesight, susceptibility to disease, and countless other ways. Individuals with certain traits will be favored in their environment: they will live longer and produce more offspring. Accordingly, the representation of the genes for these traits will increase in the population as a whole.

The variety of aging patterns in animals and plants has prompted many biologists to ask whether senescence can be modified by evolution. A pattern of aging, though, is not a simple trait, determined by a single gene, that can be favored or not. Rather, evolution acts by favoring modifications in the physiological mechanisms of aging, the processes that lead to cancer or heart attacks or other forms of degener-ation. Differences in the mechanisms of aging would also be evidence of evolution's hand at work.

To some degree all mammals experience the same types of degeneration with age. Cancers and other abnormal growths are one of the most universal signs of aging. Cancers arise when cells proliferate out of control, typically in organs and tissues with cells that continue to divide: the bone marrow, lymphatic system, skin, and reproductive tract. In most species of mammals, proliferating cells also thicken the walls of aging arteries, as a part of the process of arteriosclerosis.

These shared manifestations of aging notwithstanding, there are also many differences among species. For example, about 50% of humans alive at the age of 90 years will show loss of short-term memory and degeneration of nerve cells in particular brain regions—symptoms that are associated with Alzheimer disease. However, although Alzheimer symptoms appear in the mouse lemur by 10 years and in the rhesus monkey by 30, no laboratory rodent has shown any hint of Alzheimer-type changes at even the most advanced ages of 4 or more years. Conversely, although the prevalence of pituitary tumors increases strikingly in aging rodents—most female mice and rats have some pituitary enlargement by 2 years—the incidence of pituitary tumors does not rise during aging in men and women. We thus recognize a great deal of diversity in age-related diseases. The smoothly accelerating risks of mortality experienced by all these species during most of the life span are the results of all their different diseases of aging combined.

Birds may have patterns of aging and mortality that equal those of mammals in diversity. Chickens, quail, and turkeys (all domesticated birds in the evolutionary grouping *Galliformes*) rarely live longer than 10 to 15 years. However, condors, macaws, ravens, and parrots may live to at least 70 years and possibly much longer. Gulls, fulmars, and other marine birds fly between these extremes, but longevity records are very sketchy. The pattern of aging be-

comes very interesting when we turn to certain of these marine birds. While mortality accelerates during aging in such birds as quails and turkeys, a lifelong study of the fulmar by Scots ornithologist George Dunnet has yet to show any increase in mortality rate or decline in female reproduction up to at least the age of 40 years. Certainly no female of a similarly sized species of mammal is known to maintain her fertility at a comparable age. Do these birds avoid aging altogether?—we do not yet know. Polly, a pet yellow-naped parrot, did gradually become decrepit in her later decades, when she was as old as most humans ever get.

Some reptiles, which as a group are more closely related to birds than to mammals, also show remarkably few signs of aging. Although the records are a bit sketchy, it is plausible that one specimen of Marion's tortoise died accidentally at 150 years of age in a British fort on Mauritius. Studies in progress on several other turtle species suggest that they remain fertile throughout life and that their mortality rate remains low, as in some birds.

The obvious question arises, if some birds and reptiles can live for a long time, why don't all? Surely long-lived animals would be able to leave more off-

George Dunnet has aged, but the fulmar he is with has not. The photographs show Dunnet with the same bird, identified by the band on its leg, in 1950 (top) and 1992 (left).

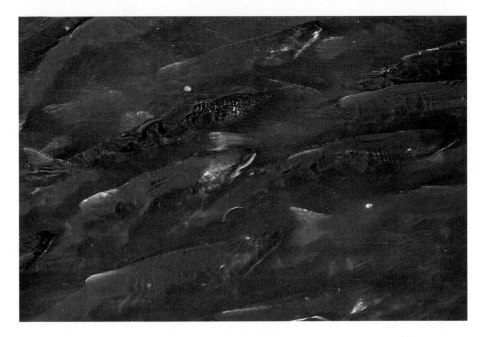

Spawning sockeye salmon in the Wood River Lakes Region of Alaska.

spring and thus more copies of whatever genes determine their longevity. We may ask why a trait seemingly so harmful as aging has not been eliminated by evolution altogether. Of course, one might pose the same question of any genetic defect, but in the case of senescence several evolutionary theories of aging suggest intriguing explanations. Although these must wait for a later chapter, the example of Pacific salmon gives some idea of the trade-offs between longevity and number of offspring that a particular environment may require, and also show the influence of evolution on one particular mechanism of aging. Pacific salmon show spectacularly rapid senescence and death after their first and only spawning migration. These fish are anywhere from 2 to 8 years old at that time, depending on the species and location. As spawning approaches, levels of corticosteroids in the blood skyrocket. Corticosteroids, which are produced by the adrenal gland, are a class of hormone released in times of stress that acts to mobilize metabolic reserves. In our own species, when hyperactive adrenal glands produce excessive corticosteroids, the

hormones can damage tissues throughout the body and produce a syndrome known as Cushing's disease. Corticosteroids have equally devastating effects on salmon. The muscles and tissues of the gut and immune system atrophy, and spawning fish often develop coronary artery disease. To top it off, the salmon don't eat during this strenuous time of mating, during which they may swim hundreds of miles upstream to a spawning site, and they gradually waste away.

This behavior is not so senseless as it seems. The rivers in which the salmon spawn are safe places for their fry, as their newly hatched offspring are called, and have plenty of small food items, so the young fish can grow rapidly. The adults, by contrast, are open-ocean feeders, and the small rivers cannot support their hordes on the return to the spawning grounds. Under the circumstances, it would seem these fish have little choice but to forgo feeding and put all their bodily resources into an exhausting and consuming effort to breed: females lay huge numbers of eggs and males fight viciously among themselves

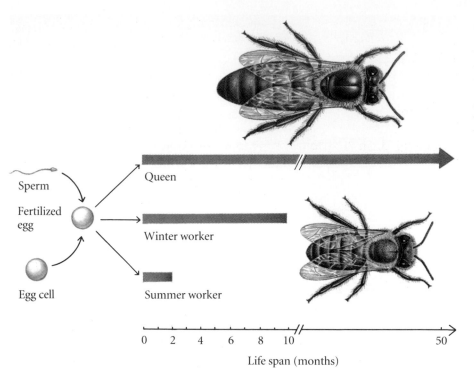

Honey bee castes have greatly different life spans, even though a queen or a worker can be formed from the same egg and members of different castes can have the same genes. If workers hatch in the early summer, they live only 2 months; but if they hatch later, they stay with the queen over the winter and add 8 months to their life spans.

for the best spawning sites and for the opportunity to mate with females attracted to these sites to lay their eggs.

In contrast to the Pacific salmon, Atlantic salmon spawn repeatedly, up to six times. Although they too undertake long migrations, they set aside bodily reserves for the round trip and come back year after year. Their corticosteroid levels are lower, and this difference might be a factor in their longer survival. Nonetheless, coronary artery disease in Atlantic salmon progresses further with multiple migrations than it does in Pacific salmon. The longevity of Atlantic salmon in the face of coronary artery and other chronic diseases is an example of the rugged resiliency of vertebrates to physiological deterioration. Our bodies, as well, have many built-in safety factors that allow reproduction to continue despite the accumulation of damage over the life span.

Many fish can live and reproduce for decades. The longevity records are held by rock fish and stur-

geon, which may approach 150 years of age, according to the number of rings on their scales. A few very old individuals of the rock fish *Sebastes aleutianus*, examined by Bruce Leaman of the Pacific Biological Station of Fisheries, produced normal egg masses and showed no sign of the usual tumors and other pathological lesions found in mammals at advanced ages. Many fish, broadly including sharks and rays, do develop tumors, of course, but it is safe to say that rock fish, sturgeon, carp, and others show the effects of aging much more slowly than do salmon.

When we turn to the invertebrates, we also find a wide range of life spans and patterns of senescence characterizing many groups of these animals, including insects. The fruit fly *Drosophila melanogaster*, which is a favorite subject for genetic investigations, shows a marked acceleration of mortality, but the signs of aging are different from those in mammals. Flies do not develop tumors, for example. The absence of cancerous growths is not surprising, because the body tissues of adult fruit flies undergo no cell division—adults have all the cells they will ever need before they emerge from the pupa. Another difference between flies and most vertebrates is that injuries to the brittle cuticle and wings of insects are not repaired and damage accumulates over time. Flies wear out as they collide with objects in the environment or, if they are males, fight among themselves. The chemosensory receptors on the legs that flies use to recognize food also suffer from wear. Because the wings and the outer coverings (exoskeleton) of the legs and antennae have no living tissue, cellular processes cannot repair damage the way our wounds heal themselves. Old flies can become very tattered indeed. Unlike birds, which replace their worn feathers, insects are given only one coat to wear for their adult lives.

The damage that flies and many insects suffer during aging is sometimes called mechanical senescence. We mammals also suffer mechanical senescence. Wear and tear on heavily used joints may cause irreparable damage and arthritis; after years of chewing and grinding, teeth may wear down to the point that they become useless for chewing. These examples suggest that the design of the body may influence the outcome of aging. Joints seem to be particularly difficult to engineer well, and, especially in such bipedal animals as humans, tremendous stresses on these moving parts inevitably lead to wear and damage.

Honey bees provide a wonderful example of how alternative life styles may lead to widely differing life spans in animals that are genetically alike. Individual honey bees from the same batch of fertilized eggs can grow up to become either long-lived queens able to survive for 5 years or short-lived workers with life spans only a tenth as long. A queen or a worker may arise from the same egg, depending on the amount and type of food given the larvae by nurse bees. Larvae destined to become queens receive large meals that stimulate the secretion of juvenile hormone. When this hormone is not present at a critical time in development, the larva's ovaries degenerate and the bee develops into a sterile, but genetically female, worker.

Honey bee queens fly only once, during their famous nuptial flight taken shortly after they emerge as adults. During this flight, they mate and acquire sperm that they must store in the reproductive tract to last a lifetime. Queens lead a mostly sedentary life within the hive, where they are fed and cared for by workers. Although they produce prodigious numbers of eggs each day in season, queens show no signs of wearing out from this extraordinary reproductive activity. Unlike *Drosophila*, honey bee queens do have some dividing cells in their intestinal linings, which they probably need to repair the wear on this organ from intense feeding. It is not known why honey bee queens eventually die. In some species of termites, the long-lived queens are killed by the workers following reproductive failure, when they are no longer useful to the colony.

Just after emerging as adults, worker bees remain in the hive, where they feed and groom the queen. At some point in their adult lives, the hive bees abandon

Like honey bee queens, termite queens outlive their workers. Some termite queens last more than 20 years.

their safe domestic activities and begin to forage outside the hive. This switch in behavior is caused by an increase in juvenile hormone secretion. Miles of flying each day, and frequent bumping into plants, cause mechanical senescence; most worker bees simply wear out and die within about 2 months. Honey bees show how the same set of genetic factors can result in dramatically different life styles and longevities, depending, in this case, on differences in nutrition during development.

Mayflies (Ephemeroptera) live on the short end of the life-span spectrum. Adults of a single species hatch together in a group, mate, lay their eggs, and die, all within a few hours or days. Adult mayflies altogether lack mouth parts and intestines; these degenerate during the last stage of development of the aquatic larva, when feeding ceases. Eggs and sperm are also fully formed before the adult emerges from the pupa. Thus, although the larval mayfly may live several years, the adult is programmed to die soon after it reproduces and thereby completes the life cycle.

The ancestors of modern mayflies, which lived 300 million years ago in the vast swamp forests of the late Paleozoic Era, evidently were voracious feeders as adults, with robust chewing mandibles. Some, like *Bojophlebia*, which had a wing span of 18 inches (46 centimeters), were gigantic. Thus, the adult mayfly's lack of working mouth parts and curtailed life span appear to be derived traits in the evolution of the mayfly lineage. Short adult life spans have apparently evolved many times in other orders of insects, showing how life histories, including patterns of senescence, continually evolve and diversify.

One of the most important organisms in the study of aging is an invertebrate: the tiny nematode worm *Caenorhabditis elegans*. These nearly microscopic worms live about 1 month from egg to grave. In laboratory cultures, their mortality rate doubles every 5 days, like that of *Drosophila*. Like the adults of most insects, the adult *C. elegans* have no dividing cells. Why these worms die is still a mystery, but the causes of death must differ from those of flies or

The adult golden mayfly (*Hexagenia* sp.) emerging from its pupa. This fragile insect may take 3 years to develop, but lives only a few days, unable to feed, as an adult.

More than 200 million years ago, adult mayflies were fierce predators with fully functional mouthparts that ate much better than their descendants. The giant that left this fossil had a wingspan of 18 inches.

mammals because they show no evidence of mechanical senescence or tumors. Studies of *C. elegans* have recently stirred some excitement because scientists have found genetic mutants in laboratory cultures of the worms that live longer than nonmutant individuals. One of these genetic factors, a mutant of the *age-1* gene, was found by Tom Johnson of Colorado to slow the acceleration of mortality in adults. Other mutants add to the total life span by retarding larval development. How these genes work is not yet understood, but they hold great promise for enlightening us about the causes of senescence.

Vegetative Reproduction and the Proliferation of Cells

Although many plants grow, set seed, and die within a single growing season, the extraordinarily long life spans of some plants provide meaningful clues to the basic causes of aging. Many species of hardwoods

and conifers live for 1000 years or more, producing seed year after year. The greatest individual life spans are found in the bristlecone pine (*Pinus aristata*): the ages of some trees have been estimated from annual growth rings to exceed 4500 years. There is no hint of senescence in these long-lived trees.

Certain plants, like strawberries, are well known for their ability to propagate vegetatively by runners; the new shoots that sprout from these runners are genetically identical to the propagating plant and are really just part of the same individual. Propagating in this manner, some plants appear to be potentially immortal. Wine lovers may be amused to read that clones of the Cabernet Sauvignon grape have been propagated by cuttings for at least 800 years. Moreover, the banana has never formed viable seeds during the hundreds and probably thousands of years it has been cultivated vegetatively. Some clones, as the lineages of vegetatively produced plants are called, are huge. Clones of creosote bushes in the Mojave Desert may be 11,000 years old and cover an acre or more.

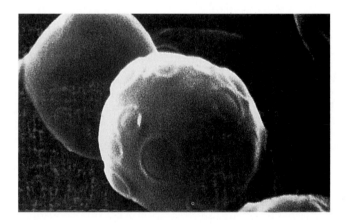

Yeasts are also organisms that make use of asexual reproduction. The yeast cell forms a limited number of buds, from which its offspring arise. The circles on the surface are scars from previous buds.

The bristlecone pine, shown here in its stark habitat in the White Mountains of California, seems to live forever. By ring dating, life spans approach 5000 years.

What's significant about vegetative propagation is the continual proliferation of cells at the growing shoot, whether that shoot produces a runner, root, leaf, flower, or other shoots. This continual cell division, and the fact that the important living parts of plants are close to the growing tips, seems to put off senescence. Aging takes the largest toll mostly in organisms with fixed adult sizes, in which most cell proliferation has stopped: roundworms, flies, humans.

Many animals with simple body plans can also reproduce vegetatively. Although their life histories include sexual phases, sponges and corals also reproduce vegetatively and may live to great age.

Certain remote relatives of the vertebrates—the tunicates—retain the capacity for asexual reproduction. These marine invertebrates often produce large colonies of genetically identical "individuals" by this process. Although tunicates share a number of vertebrate traits—their tadpolelike larvae have a noto-chord, or rudimentary backbone—no adult of any vertebrate can equal the tunicate's ability to produce a new organism with a two-chambered heart and an intestine from a single, nonsexual cell budded off the body wall. Like plants, such vegetatively reproducing animals as corals and tunicates show no apparent limit to the ability to produce generation after generation of new individuals. Although individuals may also reproduce sexually to start a new clone, and although each individual ages and dies, the clone's genetic identity can continue through sexual reproduction.

The Immortal Germ Line and the Mortal Soma

In sexual populations, an individual grows from a cell that is formed by the union of an egg and a

The ring of bushes is actually a single clone of a creosote bush. This bush, in the Mojave Desert of California, is the largest known creosote ring and, at possibly 11,000 years of age, the oldest living plant clone anywhere. The circular growth is presumably from the expansion of a small clump.

sperm. Each egg and sperm is a single cell, the result of the successive divisions of a lineage of ancestral cells. The lineages of cells that produce the eggs and sperm are called germ lines. The germ cells of most animals are set aside early in embryonic development from those of the rest of the body, which is called the soma. It is said that the germ line is potentially immortal because it persists between generations, whereas the soma is mortal because its cells die with the individual. The distinction between the immortality of an individual's germ line and the finite life span of the individual's soma or body was first articulated by the great nineteenth-century biologist August Weismann.

The continuity of cells between generations can, in principle, be traced to the first organisms on earth. All organisms, from bacteria to humans, share many of the most fundamental attributes of life, including the genetic code and the basic biochemical reactions of cellular metabolism. From these common bonds, we can deduce that all of life on earth most likely descended from a single germ line that originated several billion years ago. If there were organisms with different origins in the past, their lineages have disappeared without a trace.

Development and Aging

Developmental biologists have long been fascinated by organisms with different patterns of early development, and have searched for connections between development and aging—the beginning and the end of life. Two very different patterns of development are displayed by the nematode *C. elegans* and any vertebrate such as ourselves. The adult *C. elegans* has a precisely fixed number of cells, including number of germ cells. This precision results from a mechanically invariant process of cell division beginning with

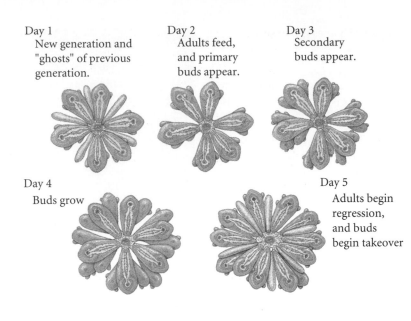

Day 1
New generation and
"ghosts" of previous
generation.

Day 2
Adults feed,
and primary
buds appear.

Day 3
Secondary
buds appear.

Day 4
Buds grow

Day 5
Adults begin
regression,
and buds
begin takeover

Above: Part of a colony of a tunicate, or sea squirt (*Botryllus schlosseri*). The six long, foot-print-shaped structures radiating from the bottom center are the genetically identical individuals. Between them are semi-transparent "footballs," the asexual buds. Right: A colony grows as the adults bud. Roughly every week, all the adults are reabsorbed into the colonial matrix, and a new generation of buds matures rapidly.

the fertilized egg. Indeed, prospective germ cells are identifiable as distinctive regions within the egg itself, even before the first cell division.

Vertebrates show far less rigidity in their cell numbers. Vertebrates "know" when to stop growing not by counting the number of cell divisions, but because interactions among the cells convey information about size and the stage of development. The germ-cell lineages of mammals do not become clearly established as distinct from the soma until after many cell divisions, and they cannot be traced back to particular zones of the egg. By the time the ovary or testes are formed in the embryo, the germ-cell lines have been formed, although the processes by which the germ lines are set aside from the soma are not well understood. In plants, mechanisms of development are even less well understood. Germ cells in vascular plants do not appear in the developing flower until just before they are needed.

The time needed for development, from fertilized egg to fully formed organism, can be days to more than a century, depending on the species. The adult phase can also vary widely in its duration and in the expression of senescence. There appears to be little relationship between the duration of adult and embryonic phases of life. Either can be short or prolonged. A bird might live 17 years as a reproducing adult after only a few months as a chick, whereas a periodical cicada may live only a few days as an adult after 17 years as a larva. Thus, the evolution of different life spans appears to proceed rather independently of the body plan and physiological attributes of the organism, whether single- or multicelled. If there is a connection between development and aging, it is that the capacity for regeneration or repair of body parts that become damaged during aging is a result of development.

Aging is one of the truly great biological mysteries. How can mechanisms that lead to death be such an integral part of life itself? How do germ lines avoid aging? Why do some species tend to die at an early age when close relatives may live decades longer? To tackle these questions, we shall first explore the actual physiological changes that accompany aging and describe some of the causes and mechanisms of physiological decline, focusing on what we know about humans and other mammals. Then we shall compare patterns of aging among plants and animals and see how they agree with the predictions of evolutionary theories about aging. In this way, we shall attempt to explain why aging differs so much between different species, as well as why it should occur at all. In the end, we shall see that aging and death are natural consequences of life for complex organisms such as ourselves. It may be possible to retard aging up to a point, but we should not expect dramatic gains in maximum life expectancy. Instead, we should make the best of what we have and rejoice in the regenerative act of procreation, for therein lies our immortality.

Albrecht Dürer, the artist who created this drawing, noted that its subject was 93 years old and yet healthy and cheerful to talk to.

*T*heories that explain aging are of two types: the "how" theories and the "why" theories. This chapter describes some of the "how" theories of aging that are beginning to illuminate the various mechanisms that cause organisms to age. These theories have arisen from experiments, performed on a remarkable range of species, that attempt to find the causes of aging in particular body systems. Later, in Chapters 6 and 7, we discuss the "why" theories of aging, which seek to explain why aging occurs. The "why" theories are the attempts of evolutionary biologists to give a type of existence proof for the pervasiveness of biological aging—to deduce that aging is a necessary consequence of life itself.

Our focus here is on the changes that aging causes in the somatic tissues of the body, including the reproductive organs that produce the eggs and sperm of the germ line. As we have seen, while individual life spans must be finite, germ lines continue back to common ancestors in the dis-

2

Theories of Aging

tant evolutionary past and are as close to immortal as can be imagined. When we speak of reproductive organs that show aging, we are including these organs as part of the soma of a mortal individual, rather than viewing them as the next step in the germ line's progress through generations of individuals.

Living organisms are often viewed as having a hierarchical organization, built up from molecules to cells to organs, and various theories of aging have suggested that mechanisms of aging act at one or the other of these levels. This hierarchy represents a sort of reverse order in the history of theories of aging, since molecular theories of aging are most recent. Indeed, we know that changes during aging are not confined to any one level, but can extend their influence up and down the hierarchy, from molecule to organ to molecule.

Spontaneous Mutations

One of the first serious attempts to explain how we age goes under the name "the somatic mutation hypothesis." This theory proposes that the crucial events in aging are mutations, changes in the DNA of a living cell that are passed on to the next generation of cells when the cell divides. Mutated DNA can create havoc with the body's proteins, since it is the function of each gene to direct the synthesis of a different protein. Proteins are the body's workhorses: some proteins, called enzymes, control the body's chemical reactions, including the metabolizing of food to create energy; other proteins form muscle and various structural parts of cells and tissues. Special proteins of a recently discovered type, the transcription factors, bind to DNA and regulate the individual activities of genes themselves. When a mutation in a gene alters a protein, the protein may not work as well or it may work normally, depending on where the mutation appears in the DNA.

It was well documented earlier in the century that both x-rays and radioactivity from radium can induce mutations. For example, in H. J. Muller's classic studies of the 1920s, he exposed male fruit flies to x-rays before mating and showed that their offspring had lethal mutations in direct proportion to the dose of x-rays their fathers had received. Obviously, the offspring had inherited their fathers' mutated genes. Earlier in this century x-rays were used liberally to treat many types of medical conditions, and the subjects of this treatment often showed an increased risk of developing leukemia. For example, one study found a threefold increase of leukemia in women given pelvic x-radiation for nonmalignant gynecological problems. Survivors of the atomic bombs dropped on the cities of Hiroshima and Nagasaki in Japan also showed an increase in leukemia, but contrary to expectation their children did not. Although mutations can occur in any cell throughout the body, they will only be carried by the next generation when they appear in the eggs and sperm of the germ line. Presumably, most of the embryos inheriting mutations from the atomic bomb survivors' germ cells died early in development and were rarely brought to term.

A DNA molecule is formed of two separate strands that intertwine to form the famous Watson-Crick "double helix"; each strand is a chain of four chemically distinct subunits, called bases, that have been named adenine, guanine, thymine, and cytosine. The best-studied types of mutation are the so-called point mutations, in which one DNA base is substituted for another at one site in a single gene. Such mutations can be caused by ionizing radiation or by exposure to certain chemicals. Sources of radiation give off highly energized particles that collide with DNA and knock off atoms haphazardly. As the cells attempt to repair the damage, they often substitute a different DNA base, creating a point mutation. Additionally, radiation can cause chromosomes to break, and such breaks are frequently lethal to a cell the next time it replicates. The results of exposure, whether to radiation or chemicals, are hit or miss: only a tiny fraction of the exposed cells will have any mutation, and almost none of these will have the same point mutation, simply because humans and mice, say, each have *twelve* billion different DNA bases that can be hit in each of their cell nuclei.

Mutations are also known to arise spontaneously, but at very low rates when there has been no exposure to radiation. Because most mutations are harmful, in theory the accumulation of spontaneous mutations could ultimately cause dysfunctions that kill the individual. Thus mutations in genes were proposed as a cause of aging by the physicist Leo Szilard and the biochemist Denham Harman.

The hypothesis was suggested in part by the abbreviated life spans of mice that had been exposed to sublethal ionizing radiation. By 1937, it was recognized that lightly irradiated mice showed a slowly emerging "generalized atrophy" that was considered premature aging, at least in part because the hair grayed. In fact, hair graying is not a usual outcome of aging in laboratory mice. Because radiation can also cause mutations in sperm and eggs, which show up as abnormalities in the next generation (that is, aging in the germ line), the proponents of this mutation-accumulation theory called it the somatic mutation hypothesis to keep the focus on somatic tissues.

Once the somatic mutation hypothesis had been proposed, it stimulated scientists to undertake an intensive search for proteins with altered functions in old individuals. This search was not very successful for many years because the techniques used were not sensitive enough. Eventually, as we shall describe in the next section, it was proved that many proteins did undergo chemical changes during aging, but the hypothetical somatic mutation of genes was not responsible.

Scientists have recently had better luck in demonstrating that DNA itself is chemically modified during the course of life. For example, with highly sensitive techniques of chromatography, Kurt and Erika Randerath have found unusual modifications of DNA bases, called I-spots, that increase progressively during aging. The I-spots appear in the

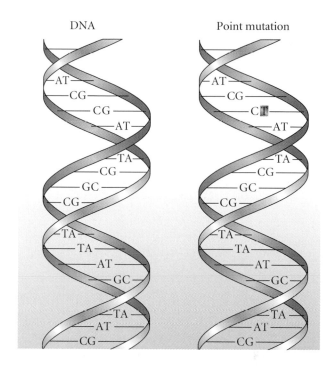

A schematic representation of the DNA double helix, showing a point mutation from guanine (G) to thymine (T) that disrupts the normal pairing of cytosine (C) and guanine inside the helix.

DNA of cells in many tissues in all species of mammals so far examined. While the chemical identity of most I-spots is unknown, Bruce Ames of the University of California, Berkeley, has identified another modified base whose presence in DNA strands also seems to increase during aging as 8-hydroxyguanine, formed by the addition of an OH group (an oxygen atom and a hydrogen atom) to the base guanine. How these changes come about remains unclear, yet we do know that we can induce similar changes by exposing susceptible tissues to mutation-causing chemicals, including some that are found in tobacco smoke. Although we do not yet understand what effects these chemically modified bases may have, it is likely that many more kinds will turn up as further techniques in the biochemistry of DNA are developed.

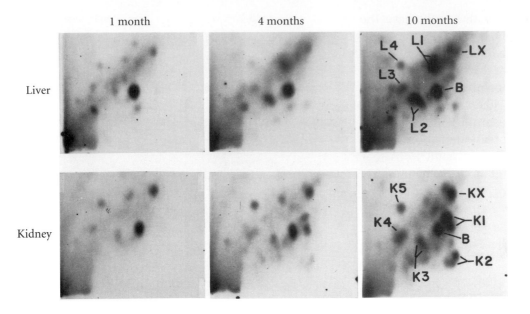

Chromatograms of DNA taken from the liver and kidney of male rats show that six or more modified bases ("I-spots") increase in amount as the rats age through 10 months (early middle age). The letter B identifies a spot that did not change with age.

While great progress has been made in the chemistry of mutations, we still do not have good estimates of the spontaneous frequency of mutation in most tissues of the body, because when mutations arise, they can be quickly corrected by the cell's own enzymes.

Genetic mutations play an unquestioned role in the development of some cancers. Many cancers and other abnormal growths appear with markedly greater frequency as we age. The steps leading cells to malignancy are still largely obscure, but somatic mutations may be necessary in many cases. Recently, mutations of two genes, called *p16* and *p53*, have been found in many human cancers. These genes are known as tumor suppressors, and normally encode proteins that slow cell proliferation. When certain mutations occur in the *p16* and *p53* genes, these proteins no longer function properly, and, as though a brake were released, cells with these mutations begin to grow and divide rapidly.

There are hints that mutations have yet another consequence for the aging body. Very occasionally a molecule of DNA loses a single base, a sequence of bases, or even an entire gene through spontaneous deletion. Structures inside the cell called mitochondria seem especially vulnerable to such DNA deletions.

Mitochondria are the main sources of energy within cells, and they have their own DNA, called mtDNA, which allows them to be self-replicating. The mtDNA encodes some of the enzymes found in mitochondria that participate in the production of ATP, the molecule in which cells store energy. During aging in humans and mice, there is a progressive increase in the frequency of abnormal mtDNA molecules that have lost large pieces of their DNA. In some cases, however, the deletion does not prevent the mitochondrion from replicating, and so the abnormal mitochondria persist or even increase in proportion. mtDNA deletions are most common in brain, muscle, and other tissues having little cell division. In certain parts of the brain, as much as 3% of the mtDNA may be abnormal by the end of the life span. We might expect that the presence of these abnormal mtDNA molecules would make the mitochondria themselves defective in energy production, but this has not been proved directly.

It is of interest that the survivors of the atomic bombing of Hiroshima and Nagasaki have shown no acceleration of aging, nor any shortening of life. The somatic mutation hypothesis thus seems most likely to explain higher cancer rates, but its importance to the other changes that come with age remains to be shown. In sum, there is no doubt that changes in DNA do occur during aging, but the consequences are not clear.

Damage from Free Radicals

In looking for agents that could cause DNA mutations, Denham Harman was struck by the high chemical reactivity of free radicals. By its chemical definition, a free radical is a fragment of a molecule or an atom that contains at least one unpaired or odd electron; free radicals can be produced from almost any molecule through the removal of an electron from one or more of its atoms. Unpaired electrons are unstable, and, when they are present, atoms have a strong tendency to attract the electrons of other atoms or molecules to regain their resting states, in which all electrons are paired. Thus, in trying to grab additional electrons, free radicals attack and modify other molecules. Harman proposed that the activity of free radicals could account for the DNA damage that he believed led to aging. Again, the idea came from studies of radiation, which is known to generate free radicals. Free radicals can be formed when atoms collide with one another, as happens during radioactive decay, and they are also formed by the impact of x-rays and even the ultraviolet radiation of sunlight.

Once a free radical is formed, it can propagate a chain reaction, as atoms and molecules steal electrons from one another. The process of transferring electrons from one molecule to another is known as oxidation. This term, coined early in the history of this type of chemistry, does not nowadays imply that oxygen is involved. However, in many cases in living systems, the end result of the transfer of electrons is that the free radical combines with oxygen. Thus, the combining of hydrogen with oxygen to yield water

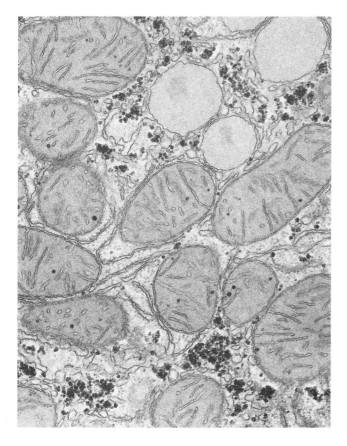

An electron microscope image of mitochondria, the powerhouses of the cell where ATP is made. The ribbed structures inside, called cristae, are the sites of the ATP-producing reactions.

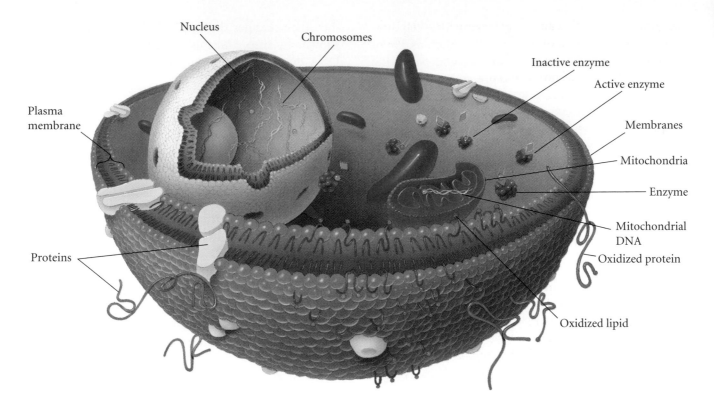

Nucleus

Chromosomes

Inactive enzyme

Active enzyme

Membranes

Mitochondria

Enzyme

Mitochondrial DNA

Oxidized protein

Plasma membrane

Proteins

Oxidized lipid

Free radicals can attack and oxidize molecules that constitute the cell, including proteins, lipids, and DNA. According to one theory of aging, such attacks—indicated schematically by attachment of a small, bright blue sphere—cause the body to deteriorate through molecular damage.

and the conversion of the ferrous iron ion (missing two electrons) to the ferric iron ion (missing three electrons) are both oxidative reactions. DNA molecules that are drawn into such reaction sequences can be damaged, and, significantly, so can other molecules. Free radicals do much of their damage directly, rather than through disrupted genes.

Fortunately, our bodies are not completely helpless against the attacks of free radicals. Antioxidants such as vitamins E and C can soak up free radicals and thereby slow the propagation of chain reactions. Besides these vitamins, a number of other enzymes break up free radical reactions by removing molecules formed in the middle of the reaction sequence. Nevertheless, free radicals are thought to be an important continuing source of chemical damage to vital macromolecules, particularly DNA, proteins, and the fatty lipids of cell membranes. However, free radicals are not the only cause of oxidative damage. This type of damage from other processes may also contribute to aging, but the chemistry of these processes is very complex and understood only in part.

There is abundant evidence that proteins and lipids sustain oxidative damage during aging in mammals and some invertebrates. For example, many proteins in tissues taken from older individuals contain additional carbonyl chemical groups

$$-\overset{\displaystyle \overset{O}{\|}}{C}-$$

that have been produced in the process of oxidation. The key point is that when a protein becomes oxidized, it usually becomes inactive. Early studies by David Gershon revealed that a fraction of the enzyme molecules were inactive in aging fruit flies, nematodes, mice, and humans, and their inactivation has recently been traced by Earl Stadtman to oxidative damage. The oxidation of lipids may reduce the resiliency and fluidity of the membranes surrounding cells and cellular structures such as mitochondria. Because oxidized lipids in the blood promote abnormal thickening of arteries, they are thought to contribute to many vascular diseases.

Free radicals are also part of normal metabolism and cannot be totally avoided. Indeed, oxidative reactions that involve free radicals are found in many tissues of all organisms. For example, the free radical nitric oxide (NO) appears to serve as a neurotransmitter or neuromodulator, a chemical signal used for communication between nerve cells in the brain. Moreover, during infections and inflammation, free radicals are produced by tissue macrophages—specialized cells of the immune system—presumably to disable or kill invading cells that cannot tolerate these highly active chemical agents.

While macrophages can act like benign Buck Rogers ray guns, they can sometimes also damage innocent bystanders—the vital molecules and cells that the body needs to maintain normal functions.

A false-color scanning electron micrograph of a macrophage cell moving over a surface. Wandering macrophages are cells made in the bone marrow that circulate in the blood. Macrophages migrate to tissues, notably the lymphatic system and lungs, to defend the body against invasion by foreign organisms and at sites of infection. In an active state, as here, the cell spreads out using its frilly cytoplasm as arms to draw itself along the substrate to seek and engulf particles.

This may be why chronic inflammations can increase the risk of cancer in certain tissues. In some diseases of aging, the presence of activated macrophages in an injured tissue leads to further recruitment of other macrophages, and the result is a chronic inflammation of the kind common in aging joints plagued by arthritis. It is likely to be the macrophage activity that causes the bulk of the damage in joint diseases such as rheumatoid arthritis, for which anti-inflammatory drugs are widely used.

In the brain, the neurotransmitter dopamine is degraded by enzymes that produce free radicals during the removal of dopamine from the synapses (connections) between neurons. It is thought that damaged mitochondrial DNA accumulates during aging in brain regions with high levels of dopamine as an indirect consequence of the presence of these free radicals. One of the regions high in both dopamine and damaged mtDNA is the basal ganglia, a part of the brain that helps control movement. The tremors of the disease of aging called Parkinson's disease arise from damage to dopamine-transmitting neurons in the basal ganglia and are thought by some scientists to be triggered by oxidative damage.

We have cited only a few of the diverse sources from which free radicals continuously arise during the body's normal activity. Free radicals are intimately involved in many common changes and chronic diseases of aging. But there is one type of free radical reaction that seems to have especially wide-ranging effects: free radical oxidations consisting of the spontaneous chemical addition of glucose to proteins throughout the body, especially in diabetics.

A Free Radical Reaction with Glucose

Most older people show a tendency to have mild hyperglycemia, or elevated blood sugar, particularly after meals. Our levels of blood sugar are determined in part by the rate at which energy-demanding organs like muscle remove the sugar glucose from the bloodstream. The rate of removal, in turn, is regulated by the hormone insulin, which binds to receptors on cell surfaces and increases the uptake of glucose by the cell.

As we age, insulin becomes less effective in promoting the uptake of glucose by muscle and other organs, and hyperglycemia becomes more common. We say that we develop insulin resistance, a common condition that may involve altered insulin receptors on the surface membranes of target cells. Doctors classify more severe cases of elevated blood sugar as non-insulin dependent (maturity-onset) diabetes, which, unlike juvenile-onset diabetes, is not caused by insufficient secretion of insulin. The criteria for diagnosing type II diabetes must be adjusted for age:

using the blood sugar criteria applied to young adults, more than 50% of those older than 65 years would otherwise be classified as diabetics.

When diabetes goes untreated, the excess glucose in the bloodstream reacts with hemoglobin in a free radical oxidation, through a process called nonenzymatic glycation. The reaction creates a chemically modified hemoglobin, called HbA_{1c}. The amount of HbA_{1c} gives doctors an estimate of the level of hyperglycemia prevailing during the previous month. When the blood-glucose levels of diabetics are brought back to normal, HbA_{1c} gradually disappears through the normal turnover of red blood cells, which have life spans of about 3 months.

This type of glycation has powerful consequences for how we age. Besides hemoglobin, other, longer-lived proteins also may become glycated, particularly collagen and elastin, molecules that compose the connective tissues in our joints and elsewhere. Unlike HbA_{1c}, glycated collagen and elastin are typically not replaced; individual molecules of these substances may be as old as the individual. Again, unlike HbA_{1c}, which continues to function properly to bind oxygen in the red blood cells, many other glycated proteins stop functioning as they should.

The chemistry of glycation is highly complex, as shown by the pioneering work of Anthony Cerami, but the result is that highly diverse compounds called advanced glycosylation end products (AGEs) become attached to many types of proteins. Two of the newly created AGEs may be the chemical groups pyrraline and pentosidine, chemical groups that are not normally formed. Similar oxidizing mechanisms account for the browning of freshly cut fruit and the toasting of bread. The formation of AGEs can also lead adjacent molecules to become cross-linked. In the case of collagen and elastin, cross-links diminish the flexibility and elasticity of structures made up of these molecules, such as the lens of the eye and connective tissue in the joints. It may not be overstating the facts

Insulin is released into the bloodstream when blood glucose rises above its normal level. The attachment of insulin to receptors on a cell surface signals the cell to take in glucose. As soon as the blood glucose falls sufficiently in level, insulin stops being released and cells stop taking in glucose. If the uptake mechanism is faulty, as in diabetes, glucose remains in the bloodstream, where it causes damage by reacting with other molecules.

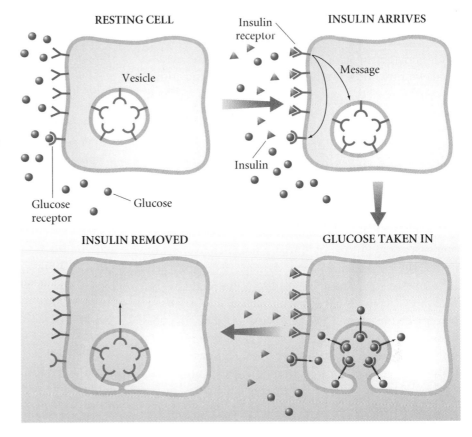

RESTING CELL

Vesicle

Glucose receptor

Glucose

INSULIN ARRIVES

Insulin receptor

Message

Insulin

INSULIN REMOVED

GLUCOSE TAKEN IN

to say that these chemical changes are among the most universal of aging processes.

Bruce Kristal and B.-P. Yu have recently outlined a general theory of free radical oxidation that treats it as a universal mechanism in aging. Their key point is that once glycated proteins are formed, these proteins can further catalyze damage by interacting with free radicals from other sources. There is evidence that free radicals from many sources accelerate the formation of AGEs, both directly by oxidizing molecules or indirectly by inactivating molecules that act as scavengers of free radicals. Thus, there are many ways that molecules can age through wear and tear.

Many laboratories are studying how vitamins and nutrients, as well as new drugs, can slow the cumulative effects of glycation and oxidation during diabetes and during the more general aging processes that damage vital functions. We caution that there are many unknowns in these extremely complex biochemical reactions: a drug could provide short-term improvements and yet provoke unexpected adverse consequences later. As we shall see in Chapter 6, some evolutionary theories of aging predict a similar outcome from many normal processes: processes that favor vigor in young adults can have long delayed dire effects in the aged.

The Mortal Cell

After considering aging mechanisms at the molecular level, we now move to the next level of organizational complexity, the cell. There we find operating a whole new set of mechanisms that have been proposed by various theories to cause aging. One group of cellular theories addresses the body's capacity to replace cells that have become worn or damaged.

By the beginning of this century, it had been recognized that many of the organs tending to fail during aging had only limited capacity to replace or regenerate their cells. Among these organs, the most obvious are the heart and the brain, which as most of us know are vulnerable to damage from blocked blood vessels. Neurons in the brain and cells in the heart muscle are as old as each individual and cannot be replaced by new cells if damaged or killed. In contrast, cells in the bone marrow, gut, and skin are continuously being turned over; these tissues restore losses and repair injuries readily, even at advanced ages.

The modern concept of cell aging stems from a seminal discovery made by Leonard Hayflick in 1961. He found that fibroblast cells will divide only a finite

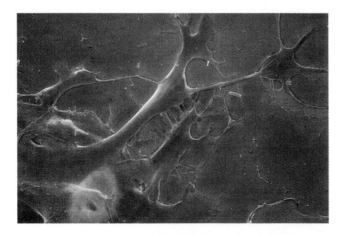

A scanning electron microgram shows most of a fibroblast.

number of times in cell cultures maintained in the laboratory. Fibroblasts are cells found in connective tissues throughout the body, where they produce collagen, fibronectin, and other fibrous molecules that hold our organs together. Fibroblasts from the skin can be stimulated to accomplish about 60 doublings, or cell divisions, in cell culture.

Hayflick's method is to plate a sample of cells in a culture dish under sterile conditions and let the cells grow out until they fill the dish. Normal cells will cease proliferating when the dish is filled with a single layer of cells. Then, a portion of these cells is used to inoculate a fresh culture dish. After about 50 population doublings there is a point at which the cells no longer grow out vigorously when replated, and the surviving cells remain blocked in their progress through the cell division cycle at the stage just before DNA is synthesized. This phenomenon is called in vitro cell aging, the *in vitro* referring to the use of glass (vitreous) culture dishes. Although no longer dividing, the cells do not necessarily die, since some stationary cultures have been kept for a year or more. Many other somatic cell types grown in sterile conditions appear to eventually cease dividing as well.

Now we encounter a real puzzle: How do we explain the contradiction that, in many types of invertebrates and plants with "vegetative" reproduction, these somatic cells may continue to divide virtually indefinitely, while cultured mammalian cells stop proliferating after a well-defined number of divisions? There are in fact mammalian cells that do continue to divide indefinitely: cancer cells are well known for their out-of-control proliferation, which is demonstrated when tumors are transplanted from one animal to the next, or cultured cancer cells are transferred from one laboratory dish to the next, like the famous HeLa cells. Such "serial," or repeatedly transferred, cultures show no limit to propagation. Tumor cells may be special cases, however, because unlike normal cells they are commonly not *diploid;* that is, they do not have normal numbers of chro-

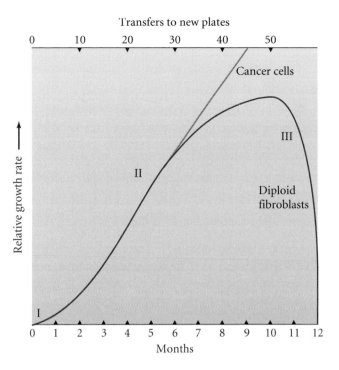

Hayflick's own graph, somewhat modified, showing the cessation of growth in fibroblast cells after about 50 doublings. The growth becomes ever more luxuriant in phase II, but then slows as the culture becomes senescent (phase III) until the final doubling. A cancer "cell line," in contrast, has infinite potential life.

mosomes, one set from each parent. Rather, cancer cells often lose chromosomes or gain extra copies. When normal cells are cultured from the skin, lungs, or bone marrow, these diploid cells undergo a limited number of divisions and then stop.

The "Hayflick limit" of fibroblast cultures varies with the age of the donor, and in our own species it typically ranges from 40 to 60 population doublings for fetal cells and 20 for adult cells. The number of potential doublings appears to decrease progressively as the age of the donor rises, although individual variation is large at all ages. The number of doublings has also been related to the typical life span of a species: Hayflick limits of fetal fibroblasts are 14 to

28 doublings for mice, 15 to 35 for chickens, 40 to 60 for humans, and over 100 for tortoises.

Exactly what the Hayflick limit means for how we age is often debated. Most agree that even the oldest living person has plenty of fibroblasts and other cells that can divide when they need to. Furthermore, cells do not die after they stop dividing, as one might expect of a culture that has become "senescent." We argue that the terms *senescence* and *aging* can be misleading and that there may not be a general meaning that can be broadly applied to describe changes over time in atoms, molecules, cells, organs, organisms, populations, or societies.

Some of the same genes that are altered in cancerous cells may in unaltered form play a role in the Hayflick limit. As cells approach the Hayflick limit, we see many changes: in particular, the concentrations of particular molecules rise or fall by highly

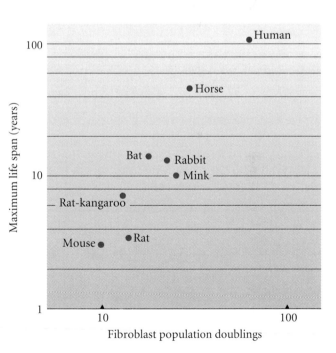

The fibroblasts of longer-lived species undergo more doublings before ceasing to grow.

specific amounts. Such changes are similar to those that take place early in development, as the at-first identical cells of the embryo begin to differentiate into neurons, skin cells, muscle cells, and so on. Thus, the Hayflick limit may represent a normal process of cell differentiation.

The developing embryo initially consists of a group of quickly dividing cells that are not very distinct from one another. We can view the embryo's development as the propagation of a series of cell lines, each derived from one or a few of the cells present in the embryo's earliest stages. As the days and weeks pass, the growing cell lines become progressively more distinct, or differentiated: they take on distinctive appearances and specific functions. Future nerve cells send out long fibers, through which they will send electrochemical signals to their neighbors; while the precursors of red blood cells develop a thick, platelike shape well suited to the task of transporting oxygen. All these cells start off and finish having the same complement of genes; their eventual form and function are determined by which of these genes are turned off or on. The turning off and on of specific genes also determines whether cells of a certain type stop dividing early in life, like brain cells, or continue to divide rapidly, like the cells of the skin and bone marrow.

The limits of proliferation discovered by Hayflick may prove to be set by some of the same genes that cause neurons to stop dividing during development, yet allow skin and bone marrow cells to continue proliferating throughout life. Stem cells contained in the bone marrow constantly divide and differentiate to produce new red blood cells, needed to keep the supply of these short-lived cells replenished. The immediate precursors of red blood cells, the erythroblasts in the bone marrow, are genetically programmed to undergo a finite number of divisions, after which the nucleus is expelled to yield the circulating red blood cell. Lacking a cell nucleus, our red blood cells lack the genetic information they need to replace their proteins as they age and last

only about 3 months before they are removed. We may now understand how vegetative reproduction is possible in some species but not others: in one case certain genes controlling cell proliferation are expressed, and in the other case they are not.

Although many cell types stop proliferating after a limited number of divisions, most researchers do not view the Hayflick phenomenon as a fundamental limitation in the design of somatic cells, but rather as a limit that is programmed when cells differentiate. Just how the cell shuts off proliferation is being investigated by Judith Campisi at the University of California, Berkeley, and at Baylor University by the renowned husband-and-wife team James Smith and Olivia Periera-Smith. These researchers are finding that certain genes become more active only as cells approach their last division (*sdi1*, for senescence-derived inhibitor), while others are less active (*c-fos* and *p53*). Some newly active genes may shut down other genes that are needed for the cell cycle to progress. If mutated, *p53* and other cell cycle genes can have the opposite effect: the uncontrolled cell division of cancer.

Aging cells in culture undergo another molecular change that links differentiation to aging. As cells "age" in culture, Calvin Harley and Carol Greiden discovered that they lose DNA from the ends of their chromosomes, the so-called telomeres, which contain highly repetitive DNA sequences but few genes. Significantly, the immortal germ line seems to be protected against the loss of telomere DNA by a complex enzyme called telomerase, found in the testes and ovary. Telomerase may also be active in cancer, since malignant cells do not appear to have lost any of their telomere DNA. Since the telomeres contain few genes, it is unclear whether the loss of telomere DNA is a cause of the limited numbers of in vitro cell divisions.

Is there evidence that a similar limit brings cell division to a halt in the living organism (in vivo)? Yes, although that evidence is indirect and merely suggestive. First, we have seen that among the few

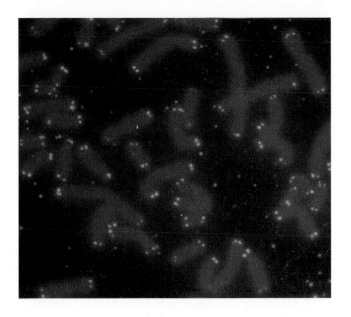

Telomeres (yellow) at the ends of chromosomes shrink as human cells age and divide. Telomerase, a complex enzyme that maintains the telomeres, may make germ-line and tumor cells immortal.

heart muscle cells are nearly two decades since their last division. And they serve us well for many decades more. Barring damage from stroke or Alzheimer disease, the vast majority of our brain neurons will be with us the rest of our lives. The popular wisdom that "we lose a million neurons each day during usual aging" is not supported by many careful studies.

As scientists continue to study cell proliferation, they are likely to achieve greater insight into the mechanisms that cause cancer, a disorder that increases strikingly with age, as well as those that cause vascular disease and other, more subtle changes in cells that divide during their normal course of duties. However, we do not anticipate that a global theory that can explain *all* the details of aging will emerge from studies of cell proliferation. Clearly it isn't inevitable that somatic cells stop dividing, as proved by the success of many invertebrates and plants in reproducing from their somatic cells by asexual or vegetative reproduction. The halting of proliferation in certain cells may, however, explain the faltering of the immune system as we age.

mammals examined so far, cells from longer-lived species undergo a greater number of divisions in vitro. In addition, fibroblasts from the skin of older individuals reach their Hayflick limit in vitro after fewer divisions. Since diabetes and other, related metabolic disorders reduce the capacity of cells to continue dividing, metabolic changes during aging could be indirect factors. However, David Harrison has showed that bone marrow cells that produce red blood cells do not exhaust their capacity to proliferate during the life of the mouse and that the erythrocyte precursors in the bone marrow of mice are equally able to replicate in the very old and the very young.

The fact that many cells in our body are in a nondividing state does not mean that they are senescent. By the time we first vote, our brain neurons and

Wear and Tear

Wear and tear occurs during aging of organs as well as of molecules. Many mechanical objects wear out through constant use, and certain parts of the body may suffer in an analogous manner. Many scattered examples of the changes that come with aging are best explained as wear and tear. Some body parts are formed once during development and cannot be replaced. Such irreplaceable cells and organs wear out as they are subjected to mechanical friction or, even more so, gross injury.

Old lions become tooth worn and must feed on prey caught by others in their pride. The extensive tooth wear of grazing animals like deer and elephants is so regular in its progress that it gives field biolo-

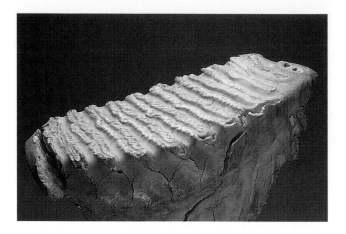

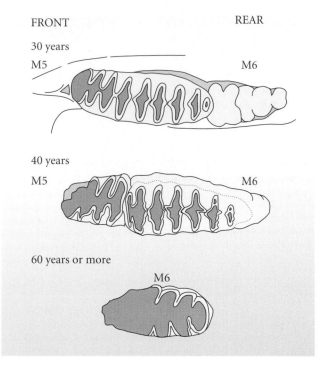

FRONT   REAR

30 years

M5   M6

40 years

M5   M6

60 years or more

M6

Elephants have six sets of molars (M1 to M6), which emerge in succession, about 10 years apart, as the enamel ridges of the previous molars wear out. At the age of 30 years (top panel), M6 is just emerging on the right, as M5 comes into full use. By 60 years (bottom panel), M5 has disappeared through use, while M6, the last molar to develop, will soon meet the same fate. When the last molar is gone, the tooth-poor old elephant will starve to death. The photograph on the left shows a full tooth, in which the enamel ridges are becoming a bit worn.

gists a convenient estimate of age. Elephants provide a particularly interesting example of the importance of delaying tooth wear if long life is to be achieved. These animals have evolved a striking modification of the schedule of tooth development to reduce the consequences of tooth wear during their long life spans. Unlike other mammals, elephants go through six sets of molars in their lifetimes. In both African and Asian species, the molars are doled out set-by-set, so that new molars emerge at approximately 10-year intervals. Each set inevitably erodes under the extreme demands of chewing abrasive vegetation more or less continuously during the animal's waking hours. But as one set of molars wears down, the next is growing in. The last set typically wears out at 70 years, close to the maximum life span. It remains unanswered whether tooth wear limits the elephant's life span or is adjusted to correspond to a life span determined by other factors. Indeed, this chicken-or-

egg riddle would have no answer if both wear and other manifestations of aging proceeded apace as different facets of a completely general phenomenon.

Until very recently, most humans lost all their teeth by middle age (remember the line from Shakespeare's *As You Like It:* "Sans teeth, sans eyes, sans taste, sans everything"). However, many teeth did not wear out but were pulled out to cure infections or abscesses. Nowadays, it is common to arrive at the later years with a full bite, an achievement that is a tribute to the many programs, private and public, that have attended to the dentition of children.

The joints of our knees, hips, shoulders, fingers, and hands are also targets of wear and tear during their many years of usage. Before so many of us adopted a basically sedentary life style and we developed social institutions that could care for the disabled, impaired movement would have put a life at great risk. Still, nearly everyone's joints become damaged to some degree during aging. The most common form of deterioration is osteoarthritis, in which the cartilage pads that cushion the joints degenerate and calcium deposits accumulate in areas of irritation within the joint. The result can be painful and disabling. The worn-out ankles of dancers and fingers of cotton pickers provide convincing evidence that heavy use accelerates these changes, yet the role of wear and tear in the degenerative changes of joints in mammals is still unclear. At least in humans, ordinary nontraumatic use is not a strong factor in the extent of arthritis at later ages. Similarly, there is little evidence that repeated beating (3 billion times during the human life span) wears out the heart muscle; rather, the heart as a pump is most threatened by narrowed blood vessels and calcified valves.

Degenerative problems seem to plague all mammals late in life, whether large or small, from elephants to laboratory mice. While these conditions are rarely lethal to our own species, wild animals would become more vulnerable to predators as they lost mobility and the ability to react quickly to possible dangers.

Most of the muscle atrophy observed in older people results from lack of use, since older people who were largely sedentary have improved their muscle strength remarkably through exercise. Our capacity to add mass to existing muscles is well preserved throughout life. The taking of regular exercise in later years is gaining in popularity, and the trend is anticipated to delay many disabilities of aging and could greatly lower the costs of health care. Charles Evens has identified the levels of muscular strength needed for various activities of daily life, such as dressing and climbing stairs, and has determined the amount of muscular training needed to reacquire these activities at advanced ages. Nevertheless, even athletes who have trained continuously from an early age gradually decline in performance. This is easily seen in the progressively slower times for swimmers

and runners in the Masters' competitions and in the lower maximum heart rates of endurance athletes. These declines have been attributed in part to a loss of elasticity in the heart, lungs, and blood vessels, caused primarily by the reduced elasticity of connective tissue, and to a gradual thickening of the walls of blood vessels, which restricts blood flow.

Insects put a different spin on wear and tear. Their brittle and irreplaceable wings and exoskeletal parts are easily damaged by flying, fighting, mating, and other rough activities during their month or so of life. The delicate sensory organs of an insect's exoskeleton may also be damaged, so that the insect can no longer feed and navigate.

At a molecular level, the accumulation of so-called aging pigments (lipofuscins) is sometimes considered a phenomenon of wear and tear. Lipofuscins are fatty aggregates that accumulate progres-

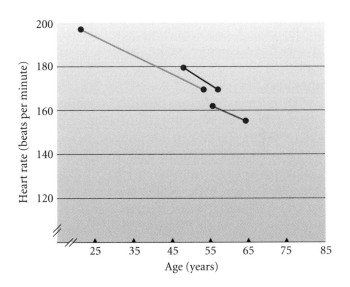

The maximum heart rates of endurance athletes, as recorded in several studies, decline from a little less than 200 beats a minute at age 25 to less than 160 beats a minute at age 65.

sively in cells with age, particularly in nondividing cells. The aging pigments are found in many organisms, but do not seem to be toxic by themselves. For example, the amount of aging pigment present seems unconnected to the loss of neurons that we experience in several parts of the brain as we age. The composition of aging pigments is complex and difficult to characterize, but they contain oxidized lipids. One hypothesis is that lipofuscins are undegradable waste products created during free radical and other oxidative chemical processes.

The Body's Defenses Weakened

The flu that a young person shakes off after a day or so may be a serious threat to the very aged. The immune system becomes weakened as we age, and less able to defend us against an array of pathogens, yet paradoxically it also becomes more likely to attack the very body it was evolved to protect. Its declining strength is the basis for another theory of aging at the cellular level.

The immune system patrols the body for novel antigens, foreign molecules that are most typically present on the surface of invading organisms, like viruses or bacteria. Through marvelously subtle and complex mechanisms, novel antigens stimulate the production of antibodies that circulate in the blood and can neutralize the invaders or signal other immune factors to do so. These antibodies are secreted by a special class of white blood cells (lymphocytes) called B-cells because, in mammals at least, they are made in the bone marrow. Some bacteria and viruses slip inside host cells so quickly that antibodies cannot find them. As a second line of defense against these hidden pathogens, other lymphocytes become programmed to react to cells presenting novel antigens. Lymphocytes of this type are called T-cells, because they arise in the thymus gland.

The decline during aging is particularly striking in the response to antigens that are new to the individual (the primary immune response). Novel antigens are commonly encountered in the seasonal flu, against which we are not well protected by the immune response to earlier infections, because influenza viruses mutate and produce novel antigens at high rates. Consequently, older people are vulnerable to the new strains of flu that appear each season, and they are also more difficult to immunize. In fact, the success of inoculations against influenza decreases sharply after age 80, although the body maintains considerable resistance against pathogens it has already seen in earlier decades (the secondary immune response). Thus as we become very old, we are more susceptible to infectious diseases like influenza and more likely to die from them.

The decline in the primary immune response with age is explained by the progressively smaller numbers of available "virgin" T-cells. Richard Miller and Marc Weksler have shown that the stock of virgin T-cells dwindles over time as these cells encounter pathogens and other intruders and become "memory" T-cells committed to respond to particular antigens. The memory T-cells represent an individual's cumulative exposure to infectious organisms, allergens, and other sources of new antigens. In a sense, the immune system becomes "overeducated" by exposure to myriad antigens during life. The regulation of the immune system is very subtle, and it is possible that the total number of T-cells is determined at an early age. If so, it may be possible to fool the body into producing new virgin T-cells at later ages.

Antibodies are sometimes made against the body's own proteins. Ordinarily, this does not

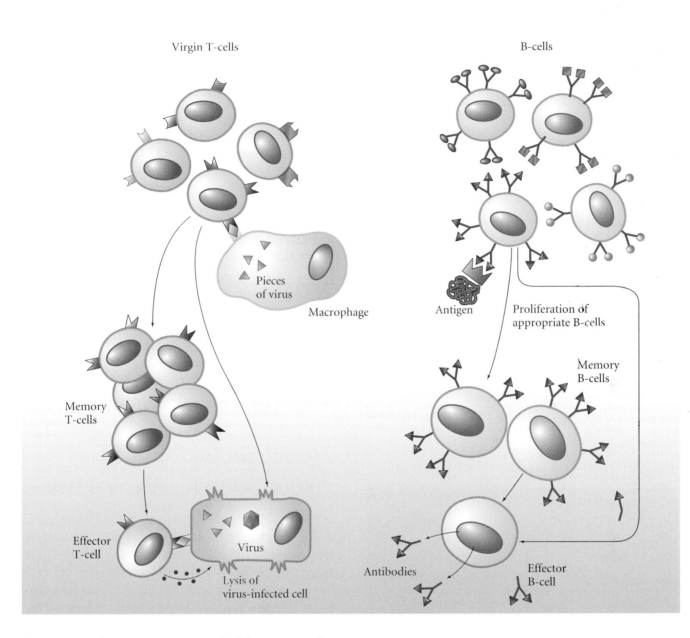

Virgin T-cells

B-cells

Pieces of virus

Macrophage

Antigen

Proliferation of appropriate B-cells

Memory T-cells

Memory B-cells

Effector T-cell

Virus

Lysis of virus-infected cell

Antibodies

Effector B-cell

The two types of immune response. On the left, a virgin T-cell recognizes a viral antigen on the surface of a macrophage that has digested a virus. That T-cell is then activated to divide, producing many T-cells able to recognize and destroy virus-infected cells. On the right, a B-cell with the appropriate receptor recognizes an antigen floating freely in solution, and receptor and antigen bind. The activated B-cell divides to form cells that secrete antibody proteins, which are soluble forms of the receptor.

happen much, except in autoimmune diseases such as lupus erythematosus and multiple sclerosis. However, as the body ages it has an increasing tendency to produce low levels of auto-antibodies, and these may destroy vital molecules. For example, Howard Fillit found that 35% of Alzheimer patients had auto-antibodies to a protein (heparin sulfate proteoglycan) in the cerebral blood vessels. Conceivably, these auto-antibodies could attack and injure blood vessels, which might then release blood into the brain. Auto-antibodies have been observed in at least 25% of individuals by 80 years, although they may be harmless in most people. Still, their presence is another sign of the immune function's tendency to become "overeducated" during the long human life span.

In contrast to the declining responses of T- and B-cells, some other cells of the immune system show little or no change. Macrophages, which scavenge foreign antigens that they later present to T-cells for destruction, show no impairments in function. On the contrary, during normal aging and, especially, in people stricken by Alzheimer disease, macrophages appear to become hyperactive in the brain (the brain has specialized macrophages that are known as microglia).

Macrophages show signs of becoming activated elsewhere in the aging body as well, often causing inflammation and swelling. The most familiar of these joint inflammations is rheumatoid arthritis, which in a mild form is very common after 70 years of age, although not necessarily disabling. Why the various types of macrophages become so active is unclear. Possibly, they are reacting to the oxidized or glycated proteins that accumulate during aging.

In summary, aging brings change to the immune system that proceeds in two directions. While the ability of B- and T-cells to respond to new antigens declines, the various macrophages seem to become more aggressive. The diversity of these changes illustrates again how difficult it is to fit the processes of aging to a simple model or concept.

Hormonal and Neuroendocrine Theories

When a child reaches puberty, the pituitary gland sends a signal to the ovaries and testes to step up their production of sex hormones—estrogens and progesterone in women and androgens in men. These hormones in turn stimulate the sexual organs to mature and continue to regulate how they behave, until in women, at least, the disappearance of sex hormones from the ovaries brings on the onset of menopause. The loss of childbearing ability is a significant consequence of aging, but the contribution of hormones to aging goes well beyond that.

The pituitary, ovaries, and testes are part of a more extensive system of glands that secrete hormones into the bloodstream, called the neuroendocrine system because these glands are controlled

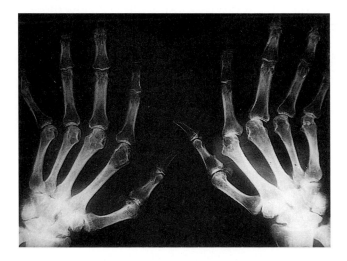

An x-ray reveals the deformity of hands afflicted with rheumatoid arthritis.

by the brain. Reciprocally, the brain listens carefully to the chemical signals made by the glands it controls. Recent evidence shows that changes stimulated by these hormones are far more general than had been recognized. Hormones, speaking generally, regulate many aspects of development in most multicellular plants and animals. In many cases, some of the same hormones that control maturation and reproduction also influence how we age.

For striking examples of hormones that have a role in both reproduction and senescence, we look at organisms that die after their first season of reproduction. The abrupt senescence of these "semelparous" organisms is mainly the doing of hormones. The best-known case is that of Pacific salmon, described in Chapter 1, which die when levels of corticosteroids in the blood become sharply elevated. High levels of blood corticosteroids are also responsible for the rapid senescence of male marsupial mice of the genus *Antechinus*. However, no placental mammal has a semelparous life history or ages rapidly because hyperactive adrenal glands are releasing too much corticosteroid. In fact, most mammals are perennial breeders, and, in humans, corticosteroid levels actually decline in later years. Nonetheless, corticosteroids may damage some especially sensitive cells, particularly those in the hippocampus region of the brain. We emphasize that there is no evidence for a "death hormone" in humans or other mammals that compares with corticosteroids in Pacific salmon.

Female mammals, however, experience a characteristic hormonal change at menopause. Among aging patterns, human menopause—or the shutting down of the female reproductive system between 45 and 55 years of age—is perhaps the most enigmatic aspect of aging—particularly inasmuch as human males have no comparable post-reproductive life stage. Menopause is in fact the most recognized universal trait in human aging. The record maternal age for childbirth of 59 years (>60) now has been broken by in vitro fertilization, but such late childbirth is not likely ever to become a natural feature of any human population.

Menopause comes as the result of the loss of estrogen- and progesterone-producing cells in the ovary. The ovary has a finite number of eggs and a finite number of their accompanying hormone-producing follicles. From birth onward in all mammals that have been studied, the ovary gradually loses its egg cells, or oocytes, and when enough are lost, so too are regular menstrual cycles and fertility. Thus, mammalian ovaries are built before birth to age irreversibly.

The number of oocytes may be finite, but it is still vastly greater than the number of eggs that are available for fertilization. More than half of the initial million oocytes are lost before puberty and less than 0.05% will ever be available for fertilization.

Many other mammals share this pattern of excessive oocyte production and wastage. This trait is widely distributed among mammals that evolved from a common ancestor a hundred million years ago. Most likely, this common ancestor also produced a finite number of oocytes because this trait is unlikely to have evolved independently in so many different branches of mammals. In other vertebrates, especially fish, there is evidence that the ovary can make completely new sets of oocytes during adult life. Whatever the case for females, males in all vertebrate groups continue to produce sperm at very late ages.

Some of the oocytes ordinarily lost are probably defective, although defective oocytes can sometimes be fertilized. That this is so is suggested by the high incidence of aberrant chromosome numbers in spontaneous abortions: about 50% of spontaneously aborted fetuses at all maternal ages have abnormal numbers of chromosomes.

Just as not all defective oocytes remain unfertilized, so not all defective fetuses are aborted. As menopause approaches, there is an alarming increase in birth defects such as Down syndrome and other problems resulting from abnormal numbers of chro-

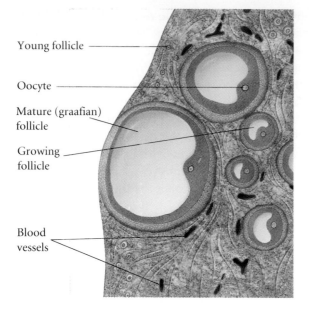

This cross section through part of a human ovary shows each oocyte surrounded by a layer of hormone-producing cells; oocyte and surrounding cells together constitute the follicle. Each month several follicles mature, while many other growing follicles degenerate. The egg enlarges and the surrounding cells proliferate.

Young follicle

Oocyte

Mature (graafian) follicle

Growing follicle

Blood vessels

mosomes. One in 700 infants overall is born with Down syndrome, but the incidence rises sharply before menopause to a dreadful 10% among the offspring of women giving birth in their late 40s. The father's age makes little or no contribution to birth defects that appear ever more frequently among the offspring of older women, perhaps because the male's sperm is produced shortly before fertilization. The incidence of Down syndrome adds greatly to the burden of aging in society because, of those born with the syndrome who survive to adult life, *all* will develop Alzheimer disease if they live long enough.

Down syndrome is caused by an extra copy of chromosome 21 that appears early in the developing fetus or even in the mother's egg before fertilization, when imperfections in chromosome movements occur during cell division. These chromosomal abnormalities are completely different from mutations, since the genes themselves are normal—there just happen to be extra copies of them on the extra chromosome. Of particular interest, chromosome 21 carries the gene for beta-amyloid, a protein that ac-

cumulates in the brains of people stricken with Alzheimer disease.

The egg cell is itself a remarkable example of arrested cellular aging and as a cell is almost as old as the mother. All germ-line cells undergo a special type of cell division, called meiosis, that reduces the number of chromosomes by half to produce a so-called haploid set. At fertilization, a haploid set of male chromosomes joins the haploid female set in the egg nucleus, and the normal, diploid number of chromosomes is reconstituted. By the time the future mother has reached the midpoint in her development as a fetus, her oocytes, or potential eggs, have grown as far as the first stage of their meiotic cell division. At that point they stop developing. This arrested stage of egg formation, which is called the prophase of meiosis, persists until just before ovulation, up to 60 years later in women with late menopause.

In the prophase stage, the chromosomes are condensed and the meiotic spindle is formed: that is, a set of microtubules is attached to the chromosomes. The spindle will eventually pull matched sets of

Chapter Two

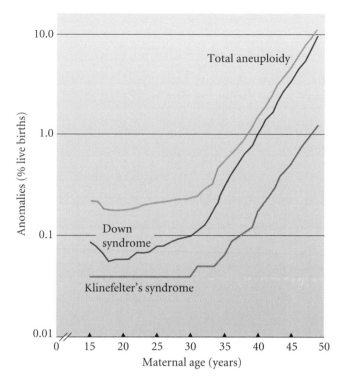

As women approach menopause, the risk accelerates that they will bear offspring with birth defects caused by abnormal numbers of chromosomes (aneuploidy). The most common birth defect is Down syndrome, due to an extra copy of chromosome 21. The less common Klinefelter's syndrome, found in males with an extra X chromosome, causes sterility and the development of breasts resembling those of a woman.

chromosomes to opposite points in the oocyte. For the oocyte to survive the very prolonged prophase intact, special mechanisms must exist to maintain and repair both the chromosomes and the spindles that move the chromosomes apart. No molecular repair mechanism is perfect, however, and damage to the spindle or to the chromosomes themselves can cause the chromosomes to move improperly during the final phases of meiosis, so that different numbers go to each pole of the spindle.

Are menopause and its consequences inevitable? There are hints that it may be possible to slow

down the aging of the ovary, at least in rodents. Studies show, for example, that middle-aged mice have more oocytes and greater fertility if the number of calories they eat is reduced by 40%. A good possibility is that a restricted diet acts by affecting the hormones of the neuroendocrine system, because removing the pituitary also slows the loss of oocytes in mice.

Strangely enough, removing one of the two ovaries seems to accelerate the aging of the other:

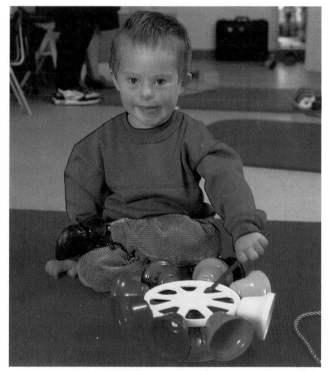

A young boy with Down syndrome (also known as trisomy 21), a form of mental subnormality caused by the presence of an extra number 21 chromosome. The main physical signs are slightly slanted eyes, round head, flat nasal bridge, fissured tongue, and generally short stature. Those with the syndrome normally attain an I.Q. in the range 50 to 60, equivalent to a 5-year-old child. With the help of family and social support, a person with Down syndrome can gain considerable social independence.

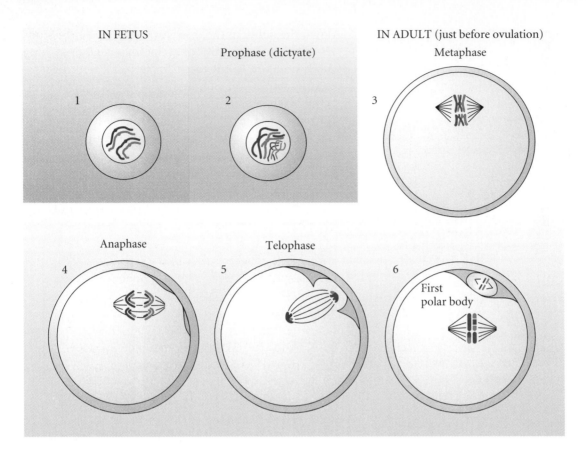

IN FETUS

Prophase (dictyate)

1

2

IN ADULT (just before ovulation)

Metaphase

3

Anaphase

4

Telophase

5

6

First polar body

During meiosis in the egg cell, matching chromosomes pair (1), then at prophase (2) the chromosome pairs replicate and the spindle is formed. The spindle will pull the sets of chromosomes apart to form two cells (3, 4, 5, 6), only the larger of which will fulfill its function as an egg. Meiosis begins in the embryo, but comes to a stop at prophase and will not proceed to completion until years later, just before ovulation.

Roger Gosden has shown that removing an ovary in young mice *increases* the likelihood of abnormal chromosomes appearing in the fetuses they carry. This experiment is important because it removes the effect of maternal age and draws our attention to the stock of oocytes in the ovary as a main factor. Thus, even the ovarian clock of aging can be reset in either direction. Perhaps in the future we will be able to control the loss of oocytes and the risk of Down syndrome by finding the right mix of sex hormones.

A woman can track her fertility cycles by the event of menstruation, which is a consequence of lowered secretions of estrogen and progesterone about two weeks after ovulation. When ovulatory cycles are lost during aging, menstrual cycles cease, whence the term *menopause*. Ovulation is stimulated at midcycle when the brain instructs the pituitary gland to release a burst of hormones, the "gonadotrophins" luteinizing hormone (LH) and follicle-stimulating hormone (FSH). The gonadotrophins

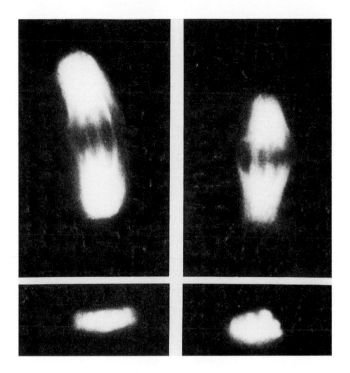

The chromosomes and spindles of oocytes during meiosis, taken from 4-month-old (left) and 9-month-old (right) mice. The equatorial views at the bottom show that the chromosomes have become spread out and misaligned in the older mouse. Such changes may cause the chromosomes to move improperly, producing an egg with an abnormal number of chromosomes.

travel through the blood to the ovary, where they stimulate the maturation of oocytes and ovulation, but also stimulate a new crop of follicle cells to begin making estrogen. During menopause, then the ovary is running out of its supply of follicles, the brain and pituitary sense the resulting estrogen deficits and attempt to compensate by increasing the production of LH and FSH.

The dramatic loss of sex steroids during menopause has consequences for many areas of health. Both types of ovarian steroids, estrogens and progesterone, decrease after menopause to the same low levels found in girls before puberty and in women whose ovaries have been removed surgically. One consequence is that tissues that developed at puberty tend to atrophy. But the most immediate manifestation of estrogen loss is usually the "hot flash," an unwelcomed feeling of warmth caused by a transient rush of blood to the skin of the upper body.

Hot flashes are actually triggered in the brain. They are that organ's response to the reduced levels of estrogens that appear in the bloodstream as the ovaries become exhausted of sex hormone–producing follicles. Hot flashes are a clear example of how exposure to sex hormones influences the nervous system during aging, and particularly of how hormones may have irreversible effects on adult brain cells, a phenomenon that is not widely recognized. The replacement of estrogens (hormone replacement therapy) prevents hot flashes from occurring. Now consider this puzzle: If estrogen deficits cause hot flashes, why don't girls have them before puberty? Moreover, what about men, who also have low estrogen levels?

A clue to this puzzle comes from women born with defective ovaries. This problem is common in women with Turner's syndrome, a condition in which only one copy of the female sex chromosome (the "X" chromosome) is present (represented as XO). While XO women are born with normal external female genitalia, their ovaries are usually defective. Lacking sufficient estrogens, these women never enter puberty. Many women with Turner's syndrome seek treatment as adults and are given estrogens to develop breasts or prevent bone loss. If estrogen treatments are suspended, hot flashes begin soon after.

Adult men treated with estrogens also develop hot flashes when the estrogen therapy is ended. This seemingly bizarre circumstance arises in men who have been treated for prostate cancer with estrogens, which can suppress the growth of androgen-dependent cancer cells. The root cause of hot flashes is certain neurons that regulate blood flow in the skin; in some way, exposing these cells to estrogen makes

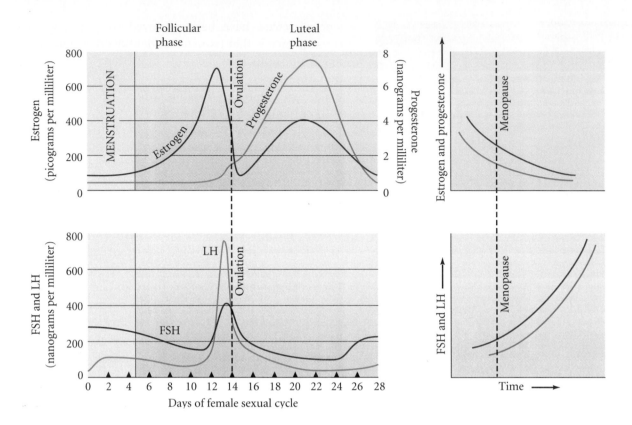

Left: The blood levels of reproductive hormones vary during the course of the menstrual cycle. Ovulation is induced when the hormones LH and FSH are secreted by the pituitary. Right: As menopause approaches the ovary shuts down production of estrogen and progesterone, while the pituitary tries to compensate by increasing its production of LH and FSH.

them sensitive to a subsequent estrogen deficit. As S. S. C. Yen puts it, some neurons become addicted to estrogens.

Hot flashes may be unpleasant, but they are fairly harmless. Over time after menopause, however, more dangerous risks emerge. One of these is the loss of compact bone, a process called osteoporosis. Mild, progressive bone loss is apparent in almost every man and woman by the age of 40, but this degenerative condition accelerates in women after menopause, because they have an estrogen-depen-

dent pathway of bone-mineral metabolism not present in men. When the loss of bone reaches a certain threshold, bones are no longer strong enough to support ordinary body weight. As a direct consequence of osteoporosis, then, there is an increase in spontaneous fractures. Such fractures are a major cause of disability and increase the risk of death by about 50% in older men and women. As more and more men live to greater ages, they too will increasingly experience the consequences of osteoporosis. Fortunately, hormone replacements and other mea-

The cross sections at the top show the normal loss of bone as a person ages. The bones of an aged osteoporotic person (shown in cross section bottom right) become thinner and more porous compared to the bones that person enjoyed in youth (bottom left).

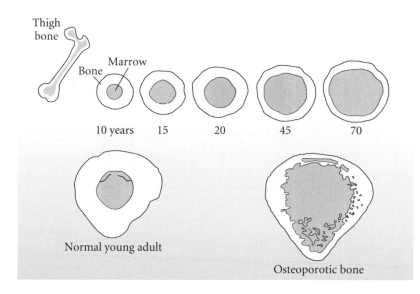

Thigh bone

Marrow
Bone

10 years   15   20   45   70

Normal young adult

Osteoporotic bone

sures are proving effective in slowing osteoporosis and reducing its risks in women.

There is no exact equivalent of menopause in men, because cells in the testes continue to produce sperm and androgens throughout adult life. Nevertheless, men are at an increasing risk for reproductive dysfunctions in old age. While paternity has been documented at an age of 94 years, full sexual activity becomes increasingly rarer at later ages. The male population as a whole exhibits increased numbers of abnormal sperm, increased incidence of impotence, and increased incidence of lower testosterone production with progressive age. The daily rhythm of testosterone secretion also flattens out; this is a striking example of a neuroendocrine change in men that arises as age alters the pacemakers of daily activities in the hypothalamus of the brain.

The male quail undergoes a particularly dramatic reproductive senescence. Mary Anne Ottinger at the University of Maryland has found that by 4 years of age, most of these birds have lost interest in

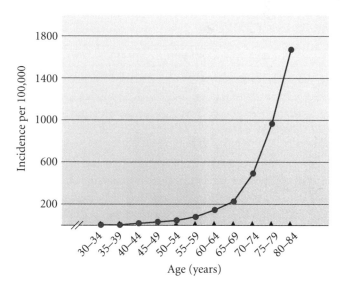

A woman's risk of spontaneous fracture from osteoporosis increases exponentially as she ages. The sharp increase in risk after menopause may in large part be caused by the loss of estrogen. Men do not show a comparable rate of fracture until later ages.

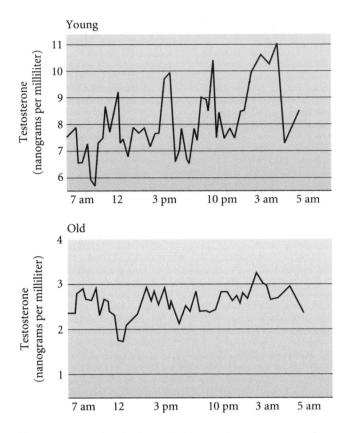

Young

Old

The testosterone levels of two healthy monks were measured every 20 minutes. The testes of the younger, 35-year-old man secreted the hormone in strong, fast pulses, whereas secretion of the hormone had slowed considerably in the older, 65-year-old man.The pulses of testosterone are driven by signals from the brain that act on the pituitary to release its hormones (LH and FSH), and these hormones in turn act on the testes. Thus, the age change in testosterone can be traced to the brain.

the opposite sex or in fighting for a mate. Their blood testosterone has become low, their testes shrunken, and their gonadotrophin levels, particularly of FSH, elevated as at menopause. Since even shots of testosterone will not reactivate malelike behavior, the brains of aging quail must become less sensitive to steroids. Waning virility is not the older quail's most serious problem, however: about 10% of aging male quail develop testicular tumors, an inci-

dence more than 200 times higher than in human men. The quail is a particularly strong example of how differently the organ systems of other species may be affected by aging.

Many hypotheses based on hormones other than the sex hormones have been developed to explain aging, but these have little supporting evidence. The various endocrine hormones other than estrogen do not show major declines with age in any species of mammal.

Speaking more widely, it is clear that the timing of events in the life histories of virtually all plants and animals is regulated by hormonal mechanisms. When an organism hatches or is born, its rate of growth, its sexual maturation, and the duration of its adult reproductive phases are *all* controlled by hormones. In turn, the timing of hormone secretion is controlled by the nervous system or, in the case of plants, by some equivalent mechanism that incorporates environmental information about temperature, light, and nutrient availability and produces hormonal signals at advantageous times. If we consider the life span from the embryo onward, it is clear that hormones are major mechanistic determinants of the life span and patterns of aging.

The Elusiveness of a Universal Theory of Aging

None of the theories of aging are able to explain all of the changes observed in any organism, nor do any attempt to. Even within a species, we do not understand how specific changes in molecules, cells, or organs influence the risk of mortality in populations described by Gompertz plots. Merely having a dysfunction or disease does not predict when an individual might succumb. People with cancer or AIDS, for example, may live for years.

The challenge of understanding aging is even more daunting when we begin to comprehend the enormous diversity of aging processes throughout the animal and plant kingdoms. We still do not know of mechanisms that can explain why life spans vary among mammals by a factor of 30. Moreover, it is in the nature of aging that it begets changes across all levels of biological organization. An equivalent task might be to deduce from the laws of physics of sub-nuclear particles how the brain works, a challenge few physicists could imagine taking on. Even within biology, theories of aging cannot compare in mechanistic detail to the exquisitely explicit hypotheses we have to explain how the details of development are at the opposite end of the life cycle.

Nonetheless, we do have hypotheses that explain particular features of aging in particular species, so long as the focus remains on a small domain, such as oxidative damage to proteins. As we shall see in Chapter 7, the manifest diversity of aging processes is consistent with evolutionary theories of why aging should occur at all. In anticipation of those arguments, we close this chapter by saying that aging has to do with the declining force of natural selection on characteristics expressed later in life. Before developing this evolutionary theme further, however, we shall examine in more detail the course of aging in human populations and the variety of patterns of aging in the natural world.

A common sight on beaches is skin damage from years of exposure without proper protection. Overexposure to the ultraviolet rays of sunlight also leads to a high risk of skin cancer.

By themselves, many of the changes that occur with age may make us less active, but they are not life threatening. The climbing mortality rate as we age results primarily because various specific diseases become more frequent and more severe. Cancer, vascular disease, and Alzheimer disease increase with aging in all human populations, although few of us become the victims of *all* these assaults on our health.

Why do our bodies succumb to these diseases? The last chapter provided some possible answers—mutation, damage from free radicals, wear and tear. But as we dig a little deeper, we find that these answers raise still more questions. If aging is inevitable, why do some people develop cancer or heart disease and not others? One possibility is that victims of cancer or heart disease were exposed to environmental risks such as tobacco smoke, which can promote these diseases. But it is also true that individuals differ genetically in their risk to certain environmental hazards. As an example,

3

Environmental

Risks

some people carry genetic defects in the enzymes that repair DNA. Such people are at very high risk of developing a form of skin cancer called xeroderma pigmentosum from exposure to the ultraviolet radiation encountered in normal doses of sunlight. Evidently, differences in both environmental factors and genetic makeup influence aging.

The range of environmental influences on aging is extraordinarily broad and extends manyfold the well-known examples of smoking and ultraviolet radiation. Moreover, a host of infectious organisms cause diseases, some of whose effects are magnified in the aged, that may also accelerate aging. Individuals may respond differently to each of these environmental influences, because their genes vary in ways that make them more or less resistant to these risk factors. We want to show in this chapter how widely the environment can alter the outcomes of aging, with a few examples of how genetic factors can also influence these outcomes. We will also consider the

difficult question of whether aging is accompanied by other changes that cause environmental hazards to have a greater impact.

Most simply, the "environment" refers to the surroundings at a particular moment. In our usage, we intend the term to encompass the external environment outside of the individual, including such obvious factors as our exposure to sunlight and tobacco, but also the food we eat and the drugs we take. Thus, the external environment quickly penetrates inside us. Moreover, because of changes to our immune and hormone systems during aging, the cells and molecules *within* our bodies are also subject to changes in their own local environments, such as hormones, nutrients, and the free radicals produced by macrophages. All of these meanings of the term *environment* are crucial to understanding the processes of aging.

A major finding of molecular biology has been that environmental cues control the genes within our somatic cells—these genes are normally turned on,

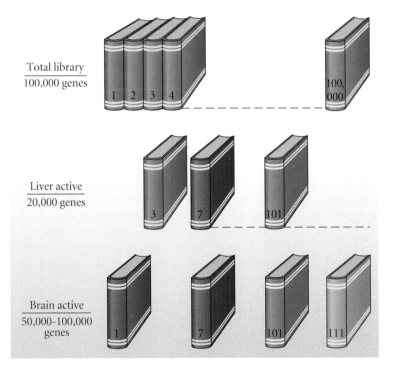

Total library
100,000 genes

Liver active
20,000 genes

Brain active
50,000-100,000 genes

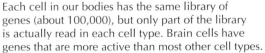

Each cell in our bodies has the same library of genes (about 100,000), but only part of the library is actually read in each cell type. Brain cells have genes that are more active than most other cell types.

or turned off, by hormones, factors in the diet, changes in temperature, and so on. We can take quite literally the concept of a genetic library, in which all cells have the same set of books, each book representing a gene. However, not all cells have the same active reading shelf of books that are right at hand for easy reference. And if we wanted copies of a book, the rate of copying might vary from cell to cell. At any one time, some genes are producing proteins at a high rate, others more slowly, and others not at all, depending on the needs of the cell. Certain genes are easily activated, while others produce proteins only in very special circumstances if ever. Sometimes, it takes a long time to get into the basement of the genetic library and get that book out of its storage crate! The control of which genes are active and at what rate is called gene regulation, and special proteins, called transcription factors, do the job.

During development, this dynamic process of gene regulation is the basis for cell differentiation, the process that decides whether a cell in the embryo becomes, say, a muscle cell or a neuron. Although each cell has the complete gene library with copies of genes present in the zygote, these genetic factors are controlled differently in each cell type. Some genes may be silent (repressed), while others are always active (expressed), and yet others can be expressed or not depending on the environment of the cell or of the organism. We have seen an example in the social insects, in which the same eggs can be programmed to develop into short-lived worker bees or long-lived queens.

The body has a variety of mechanisms for controlling which genes in a cell are active and which are not. The transcription factor proteins may bind to particular places in the DNA sequence of a gene and either promote or shut off its transcription to a molecule similar to DNA called messenger RNA (mRNA). Messenger RNA is an intermediary between DNA and the protein it produces; its task is to carry the gene's instructions to the protein-synthesizing machinery. The parts of a gene that regulate the extent of its transcription are called the *promoter*, and they are usually located just upstream of the start site of the messenger RNA transcription. These are the sites where transcription factors bind to the DNA. Another mechanism regulates the rate at which proteins are synthesized from the mRNA templates.

The life spans of particular messenger RNA molecules and proteins are not fixed, because there are special enzyme systems that degrade each type of molecule. It is as if the copies from the genetic library are printed on paper that ages quickly, to fall apart into shards and shreds so that information is removed from circulation when it is not needed any longer or becomes obsolete. Thus, gene expression is controlled at many levels in a cell. There is no general rule about which mechanism is more important in any particular tissue or organism.

These processes are particularly clear during the female reproductive cycle. At one stage in the menstrual cycle, the body gets rid of the lining of the uterus if pregnancy has not begun. All this is controlled by sex steroids acting on genes in cells of the uterus in such a way to set the cell life spans. When the cells die, the uterine lining is shed, causing the menstrual discharge.

How is gene expression effected by environmental causes of aging? While it is clear that many environmental factors directly alter proteins and other biological molecules by oxidation, others indirectly promote aging by influencing the activities of genes. Some of the DNA of most cells is active throughout life, either in replicating cells or controlling the turnover of proteins. This active DNA has to be kept in good repair, and for that to happen the genes that control the repair mechanisms must continue to function. The shutdown of those genes could promote aging, as could the shutdown of genes that control cell proliferation and tissue growth.

The definition of environment becomes even more profound when we consider the entire life of an organism, because environmental influences be-

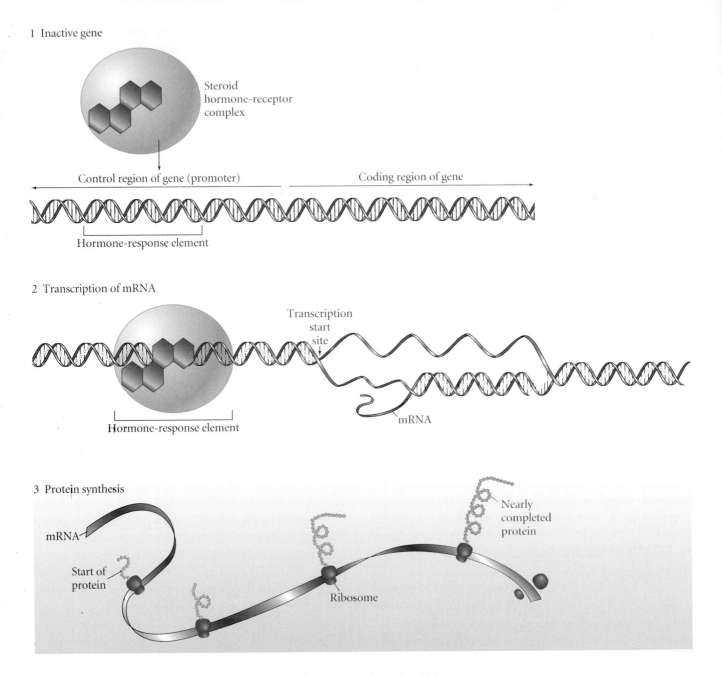

1 Inactive gene

Steroid hormone-receptor complex

Control region of gene (promoter)

Coding region of gene

Hormone-response element

2 Transcription of mRNA

Transcription start site

mRNA

Hormone-response element

3 Protein synthesis

mRNA

Start of protein

Ribosome

Nearly completed protein

A steroid hormone, acting as a transcription factor, simulates gene activity. Steroid hormones like cortisol enter a cell from the blood, after first binding to a special receptor protein on the cell surface. This hormone-receptor complex then binds to the hormone-response element, a special short sequence of DNA found on some genes. When this connection is made, yet other proteins can fit into place that activate mRNA transcription. The mRNA reaches and binds to ribosomes that make more of the protein coded by the gene.

gin to act on the individual from fertilization onward. The sperm and egg that, when united, will produce a new individual are subject to their own special environments inside the body. Consider further that an embryo's developing ovary contains *all* the eggs for the next generation when still in the uterus of its mother: this means that the diet, smoking habits, and many other factors in the life of a pregnant woman might have a direct impact not only on her children but on the grandchildren that will be produced from the egg cells that are forming in her embryonic daughter. Thus, the effects of the environment can potentially be transmitted across generations.

Aging and the Fetal Environment of Mice

The mammalian fetus is sensitive to many factors in the maternal environment, factors that can have profound effects on the future adult, including how it ages. A striking example concerning rodents was discovered by Fred vom Saal of the University of Missouri, who found that the sex of the fetal neighbor determines how long the future adult will remain fertile. Pregnant mice and rats typically have four to six fetuses in each horn of their uterus. A female fetus might be flanked by neighboring fetuses that are

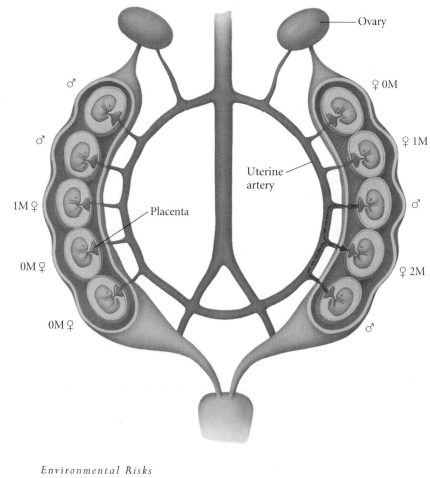

The hormones that a rat or mouse was exposed to in the uterus affect its adult sexuality. Females surrounded by males on both sides (2M females) are exposed to higher levels of testosterone than embryos that do not develop next to a male (0M females). Adult 2M females are more aggressive and behave more like males than adult 0M females.

either male or female. Vom Saal found surprising differences in reproductive aging when he compared individuals whose fetal neighbors were both males and individuals whose fetal neighbors were both females. When a female fetus is flanked by males on both sides, this "2M-female" continues reproduction to a later age than an "0M-female," which has female neighbors on both sides.

Just what causes these differences in reproductive aging is not well understood. One clue pointing to the influence of hormones comes from observing the responses of older females that have been injected with testosterone. These injections induce more malelike behaviors in aging 0M-females than in 2M-females: the 0M-females become more aggressive in fighting and in exploring new territory, behaviors that are typical of male rodents. One hypothesis is that, while still in the uterus, 2M-females were exposed to male hormones transported by placental blood connections from one fetus to its neighbor. It is likely that as a result 0M- and 2M-females have slightly different numbers of neurons in brain regions that regulate reproduction and behavior—that is, in particular subregions (nuclei) of the hypothalamus. These subtle differences are part of the continuum of sex differences in brain circuitry that develop in rodents and probably all mammals through exposure of the developing brain to subtle differences in the sex steroids present in the maternal environment.

As in rodents, female human fetuses can be masculinized if they are exposed to androgens. This sometimes happens when the mother has an adrenal tumor that secretes androgens during pregnancy; consequently, a genetically female fetus develops the genitals of a male. This condition, known as the adrenogenital syndrome, is usually surgically corrected at birth or soon after. In contrast to rodents, there is no evidence in humans that the adult sexual behavior of such individuals is modified. While we show many differences from rodents in how sex behaviors are regulated, most neurobiologists consider it likely that some similarities will be eventually uncovered.

Cancer, Diet, and Hormones

Any type of cell that is still capable of dividing is also capable of becoming launched on the unending cycle of cell division that constitutes cancer. For this reason, most cancers are found in tissues that have large numbers of dividing cells, such as the gut, bladder, bone marrow, and lymphatic system, as well as the reproductive organs. Cancers are very rare in the adult brain, but when they do occur they do not originate with neurons, which are nondividing cells.

In cancerous growths especially, the initiation of rapid cell division has been linked to mutations in genes that regulate cell divisions, such as the *p53* gene that acquires mutations in many types of tumors; many of these mutations lead to cancer by breaking the inhibitions that prevent cells from replicating. Some of these mutations may be spontaneous, but many are obviously exacerbated by various factors in the environment, including disease organisms. Although we do not fully understand the chains of events leading from environmental risk factors to cancer, many seem ultimately to lead to alterations in gene expression that in turn alter how the cell carries out its functions.

Breast cancer can be considered a disease of aging since a woman's chances of developing it are negligible before puberty and climb steadily afterward. The risk usually stabilizes after menopause and remains level for the rest of a woman's life, and may even decline. As for what causes the increased risk, a good possibility is that cells are stimulated to divide by their cumulative exposure to the actions of sex hormones during the reproductive years.

Like many other hormones, estrogens act by influencing gene expression. Depending on the type of cell, estrogens may either stimulate or inhibit cell division. The balance between estrogen and progesterone, the other main sex steroid produced by the ovary, often determines whether a cell divides or not. For example, in the breast, most tumors originate in the special epithelial cells that are found in the terminal ducts of the lobular units from where milk is secreted. These cells have low rates of division during the follicular phase (the first half of the reproductive cycle before ovulation), when estrogens are high and progesterone is low. A few days after ovulation during the luteal phase, the ovary increases its production of progesterone, and there is a doubling in the rate at which breast epithelial cells divide. However, in the uterus, progesterone inhibits cell division. Thus, parts of the reproductive tract react differently to particular sex steroids, which is part of the puzzle in designing oral contraceptives and postmenopausal hormone replacement therapies that may reduce the overall risk of breast and uterine cancer with aging.

The risk of developing breast cancer may vary tremendously from one country to another—a strong sign that environmental factors are also at work. For example, women in Japan are only about a tenth as likely to develop breast cancer as caucasian women of the same age in North America. In both countries, women show parallel accelerations in the risk until about 50 years of age, followed by parallel decelerations of the risk after menopause to a constant rate of risk. However, here we come to a major puzzle: women of Japanese descent born in Los Angeles appear to acquire the 10-fold higher risk of breast cancer found among caucasian women in Los Angeles.

The causes of these remarkable differences are not known. Because the traditional Japanese diet contains little fat, some medical researchers have hypothesized that dietary fat promotes breast cancer. Differences between Japanese and North American

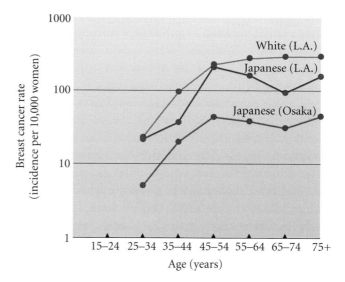

Japanese women in Osaka have only a tenth the risk of developing breast cancer as both Japanese and white women in Los Angeles, although the cancer's rate of increase slows in all three populations after menopause.

diets certainly influence patterns of body growth. For example, American girls tend to enter puberty earlier and American women achieve greater height as adults. Of course, dietary factors other than fat could be important, since the Japanese diet has constituents like soy bean products that are not eaten regularly by most people in North America. Almost certainly, however, the genetic differences between Japanese women living in Osaka and Japanese women living in Los Angeles are negligible compared to the genetic differences between Japanese women and caucasian women, all living in Los Angeles. The example illustrates how a major disease of aging that affects 10% of North American women may be sensitive to environmental factors.

That diet may play a role in breast cancer doesn't mean that hormones don't as well. Diet may somehow affect the production of hormones and they in turn could trigger the onset of cancer. The leveling off of the risk of breast cancer after menopause gives us a hint that hormones, particularly estrogens and progesterone, have a place in the chain of causation between environmental factors and cancer. These sex steroids decline sharply after menopause as the ovary becomes depleted of its hormone-producing follicles. But that doesn't mean that estrogen is no longer stimulating breast cells to divide, for fat cells are another source of the hormone. For example, obese women have a higher risk of developing cancer in the endometrium (lining of the uterus) because their fat tissue produces estrogens. Even after menopause, when the ovary has ceased to make estrogens, the adrenal cortex secretes the steroid androstenedione, which can be converted to estrogens by enzymes in body fat cells.

The potential ability of female sex steroids to cause cancer may raise warning flags about the use of hormone replacement therapy to prevent osteoporosis and other problems of a woman's postreproductive life. Fortunately, recent studies by Malcolm Pike and Brian Henderson of the University of Southern California suggest that the risk of breast cancer, as well as other reproductive tract cancers, may actually be lowered through the use of combinations of estrogens and progesterone (the so-called combined oral contraceptives). Within a decade, oral contraceptives may be designed to provide a lifelong protection against cancer in the reproductive tract. In anticipation of our discussion of ethical issues in the last chapter, we wonder if the doctrinal opposition to oral contraceptives by some religious authorities may give way to rationalization of their use to prevent cancer.

To verify the hormone-cancer connection, scientists have turned to studies of laboratory animals. And indeed, many studies have shown that rats treated with estrogen have a higher incidence of tumors in the pituitary gland, an organ that in the rat is especially likely to develop malignant growths. Moreover, it seems that estrogen actually causes changes in the DNA of the rat's pituitary gland and other organs that are at high risk for tumors. This raises the possibility that under some circumstances estrogen may cause cancer by creating mutations rather than by its usual mechanism of turning genes off or on.

Pituitary tumors do not seem much affected by age in humans, but the incidence of these tumors increases progressively during aging in rats and mice. Ovarian steroids may be the primary cause of pituitary tumors, since removing the ovary in young females prevents their occurrence. Pituitary tumors often secrete high levels of prolactin, a hormone that induces lactation, and prolactin in turn stimulates the development of mammary tumors in old female rats. Thus, in the rat, there is actually a chain of tumors set off by one hormone and continued by another. The differences between rodents and humans in the locations of spontaneous reproductive tract tumors emphasize again the many ways that patterns of aging diverge during evolution.

Some types of cancer develop only in women and other types only in men, as a consequence of obvious anatomical differences in the reproductive tracts of the two sexes. Women have no equivalent, for example, of benign prostatic hypertrophy (BPH), the slow enlargement of the prostate gland that is considered to be virtually universal in men who reach 65 years.

While prostatic hypertrophy is considered benign by contrast with malignant and metastasizing (invasive) cancers, the consequences are not so benign. When the prostate has swollen enough to block the flow of urine, this condition quickly leads to kidney failure and death, unless there is surgical intervention. Moreover, men are also subject to the risks from active hormones: the hormone testosterone stimulates cell division in the prostate, which is especially likely to develop cancer at later years. Nearly 10% of all men in the United States will be diagnosed with the cancer, although postmortem studies suggest that the real incidence may be much higher. Fortunately, most nests of cancer cells appear to die out spontaneously, without invading other tissues.

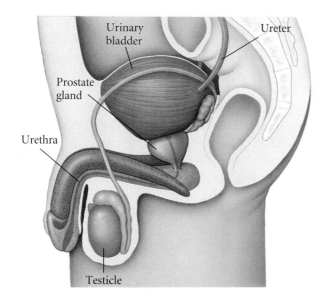

The prostate gland lies below the urinary bladder and surrounds the urethra—the tube that carries urine from the bladder, through the penis, and out of the body.

The fundamental link between cell division and cancer, on the one hand, and cell division and hormones, on the other, may be bad news for us: it implies that the risk of cancer stimulated by our own hormones may be built in to our systems. Whereas we expect the forces of natural selection to weed out built-in risks as our species evolves, the risks of breast and prostate cancer may be tolerated by evolution because they are statistically balanced by the effectiveness of the reproductive system in propagating our species. Trade-offs like this one are a common theme in the workings of evolution.

Skin Cancer, Aging, and Sunlight

A man or a woman runs a higher risk of skin cancer the more he or she has been exposed to ultraviolet (UV) radiation from sunlight. Thus, abnormal growths of the skin tend to appear in body regions that are the most exposed, like the face and neck, rather than in regions that are usually covered. The link between sunlight and skin cancer is demonstrated by the high incidence of cancers and other abnormal skin growths in fair-skinned people. Indeed, more than 50% of fair-skinned people may have such growths by the age of 70 years. In contrast, the incidence of skin cancer is estimated to be much less in darker-skinned people living in the same climate zones. For example, in the United States, the lifetime risk of being diagnosed with invasive melanoma is more than 12 times higher for white women than for black women.

For comparison, the lifetime risk of *breast* cancer differs much less between races: although there is a 30% greater risk of breast cancer in white women than black women, it may be that white women have better access to medical care and are more likely to be diagnosed. Other noncaucasian races also have a low incidence of skin cancer, even in equatorial regions. Unlike many other cancers, skin cancer tends to be an affliction of the well-to-do among the fair-

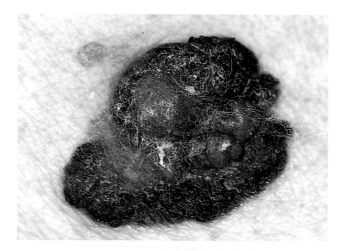

A tumor of melanin cells, the cells carrying skin pigment, can form on the skin, eyes, or mucous glands of persons with malignant melanoma, an especially dangerous form of skin cancer.

skinned population. Members of this group are thought more likely to be weekend or summer beach goers, who receive a heavy dose of sunlight without the protection of a tan built up through constant exposure.

UV radiation is thought to cause skin cancer by creating one or more mutations in cells that then escape the normal controls of growth. The radiation can produce breaks in DNA chains directly, or it can alter the chemistry of the cell in such a way as to cause mutations indirectly. Among the genes commonly mutated in malignant melanomas is the *p53* gene.

We can trace historical trends in skin cancer to show how cultural changes in behavior influence patterns of aging. The incidence of malignant melanoma in white males nearly doubled between 1970 and 1990 in the United States; the years of the worst increase were from 1975 to 1979, when the number of white men with skin cancer increased by 5% each year. Since 1986, the rate of increase has slowed remarkably to 0.1% per year. In earlier decades, many people aggressively exposed themselves to sunlight, but as the public became aware of this hazard, people tempered their exposure to UV radiation by applying sunscreens and reducing the time they spent tending their tans. There is hope that the increase will cease altogether: the consequences of continuous overexposure to sunlight are very slowly manifested and cancers do not appear until several decades later, so we are still seeing the results of earlier carelessness.

Exposure to sunlight is far from an unmitigated evil, though, and is even necessary to our health, because UV irradiation chemically transforms a substance in the skin (ergosterol) to vitamin D2, one member of the vitamin D complex. This vitamin was once called the sunshine vitamin because irradiation of the skin can protect against rickets, the abnormal bone development caused by vitamin D deficiency. Ironically, the same fair skin that increases the risk of cancer also yields more vitamin D2 for pale-skinned people of the sun-starved northern latitudes.

Besides the often disfiguring consequences of skin cancer, dermatologists recognize that many signs of "premature" aging in skin are the result of cumulative exposure to sunlight. Left unprotected, skin ages faster as UV radiation damages irreplaceable molecules and alters DNA so as to promote cell growth. Small patches of skin wrinkle, thicken, or darken due to the proliferation of keratinocytes (callous-producing cells), as well as melanocytes (pigment-producing cells). Another mark of sun exposure is a roughening of small patches of skin, called senile keratosis, which occurs during aging in 50% of fair-skinned people throughout the world. These changes are also hazards of such outdoor occupations as fishing and farming. Thus, several generations of sun seekers have prematurely aged their skin, while enjoying the fleeting panache of an outdoorsy image.

These examples illustrate how prolonged exposure to different types of environmental agents can

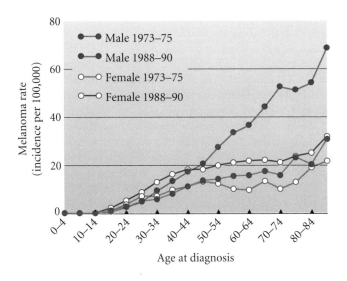

The incidence of skin cancer in white-skinned women and, especially, men in the United States was much higher in 1988 than in 1973. Fortunately, public awareness of the danger from excessive exposure to sunlight has helped slow the rate of increase in new cases per year since 1986.

lead to afflictions of aging. Reproductive tract tumors are promoted by hormones that stimulate cell division as part of normal reproduction. Similarly, exposure to UV radiation is a cause of cancer and premature aging of the skin. These two examples also emphasize that some unwanted outcomes of aging grow out of normal physiological processes. Both estrogen and UV radiation are necessary for our bodies to function normally but also increase the risks of abnormalities. Aging and living seem to go hand in hand.

The Thrifty *Genotype*

Success in reproduction depends on other hormones besides the sex steroids. The female must have adequate nutritional reserves to maintain pregnancy and then to nurse her infant. Ensuring the supply of nutrients and energy is the task of metabolic hormones, principally the hormone insulin that promotes the storage of energy reserves as fat.

In 1962, James Neel proposed that certain *thrifty* genotypes should be favored under conditions of fluctuating food resources because they result in the efficient storage of fat reserves. Looking back into prehistory, it is striking how often the Paleolithic art of Europe represents women with large buttocks and breasts. We wonder whether women who were able to store reserves of fat were more desirable as mates; such women might have enjoyed a greater potential for producing enough milk to nurse their children during long winters when food supplies were uncertain. Although fat storage may be beneficial for reproduction in young adults, excess fat and blood cholesterol also promote degenerative changes, particularly in the vascular system, during later life. Ironically, the health risks of *thrifty* genotypes increase as food supplies improve, because there are no periods of food shortage when fat stores might be depleted.

A stone carving of a woman, found in the Dordogne region of France. The carving was created during the Old Stone Age or Paleolithic Era, more than 10,000 years ago. Many Paleolithic images of women feature extensive fat deposits, which might have been desirable for pregnancy and nursing when food supplies were unreliable.

There is striking evidence that the adverse effects of the *thrifty* genotype can emerge quickly. For this evidence, we look at the rise in adult-onset diabetes, a condition that begins when the cells become less sensitive to insulin, the chemical that stimulates the uptake of glucose from the bloodstream. This condition, often present in the obese, is called non-insulin dependent diabetes (NIDD) to distinguish it from the rarer childhood diabetes that is caused by insulin deficiency. If NIDD continues for many years, then hyperglycemia typically ensues, in a condition known as diabetes mellitus. The excess sugar in the bloodstream leads to many degenerative changes, including blindness and an acceleration of vascular disease, along with the hypertension and increased risk of strokes and heart attacks that vascular disease brings with it. In part, these degenerative conditions are attributable to the accelerated glycation of proteins. Studies of twins and family pedigrees suggest that NIDD may have a genetic basis, although no specific gene mutations have yet been identified in persons with diabetes mellitus.

In recent decades the incidence of NIDD has increased sharply in some human populations. For example, NIDD is strikingly high in North American Indians and other ethnic groups who have recently adopted modern life styles and diets. Several habits of modern life predispose these groups to NIDD: they consume more energy-rich food (junk food, that is) than is typical of the traditional diet, and they are less active physically.

Is the diet of North American Indians actually worse than the average, or does some other factor especially predispose them to developing NIDD? Long periods of stable, high food abundance allow adults to survive into middle age and also promote obesity. Under these circumstances, nature would select against genotypes predisposing individuals to NIDD, and the frequency of such genotypes in the population would slowly be reduced. This situation may have emerged as town life developed in the Europe of the Late Stone Age (neolithic period of prehistory); in this way, caucasian and native Americans may have come to differ genetically in their predisposition to NIDD.

Quite recently, another important trend has emerged; namely, the incidence of NIDD has *declined* in the Naurans, a Pacific Island people. Possibly, many Naurans have changed their diets in response to the broad public recognition of the risks of obesity, or gene selection may have occurred, or both.

Eat Less and Live Longer

For decades, it has been known that rodents will live longer if they are kept on a diet that is reduced in calories by 40%, but nutritionally sufficient in amino acids, vitamins, and trace elements. The spare diet not only improves their health by reducing chronic diseases after mid-life, but also increases their life spans by about 30%. Both the average and maximum life span are increased, and consequently both the slope of the Gompertz curve and the mortality rate doubling time are decreased. The figure on the next page shows survival curves for mice allowed to feed freely and mice on a calorically restricted diet: the mortality rate doubling time is about 50% slower in the calorically restricted rats. Yet the two survival curves remain parallel, further support for the interpretation that mortality rate accelerations are a good index to fundamental processes in aging. This is the clearest example of how an environmental change can alter the rate of aging and the rate at which the mortality rate increases.

Restricting the number of calories delays or even suppresses a remarkably broad range of age-related diseases, including nearly all of the usual changes that come with aging in rodents. The benefits of the diet range from reducing the incidence of tumors and kidney degeneration to enhancing immune responses. The one drawback is that the severe reduction in calories considerably reduces fertility.

Just how restricting calories has its healthy effects is not well understood. At first, one possibility seemed to be that eating less reduced the rats' metabolic rate—that is, the rate at which their bodies converted food to energy. A more gradually produced energy supply might force all life processes to

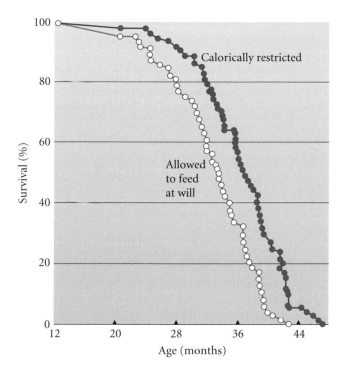

Survival (%)

100

80

60

40

20

0

Calorically restricted

Allowed
to feed
at will

12   20   28   36   44

Age (months)

When males of two long-lived mouse strains were put on calorically restricted diets at 12 months of age and given nutrient supplements, their life spans increased by 20 percent.

run at a slower pace, so that the animals were somehow "living" more slowly. Most investigators agree, however, that the metabolic rate per gram of body mass is not greatly affected by a reduction in calories, although this conclusion is controversial. Because rodents on calorically restricted diets are smaller, however, the total metabolic output is also smaller, as it must be when less food is consumed. These rodents have lower blood glucose and a lower incidence of glycated proteins late in life than do rodents allowed to feed freely. In addition, insulin acts more efficiently in glucose transport, an improvement that reduces the incidence of NIDD symptoms. Because laboratory rats usually overfeed themselves and cannot exercise freely, they provide a good model for the experience of human populations that recently in

their evolution somewhat abruptly adopted "modern" high-calorie life styles.

These intriguing studies are still inconclusive about the role of diet in raising or lowering the risks of disease for people who are not obese. Glucose cannot be completely eliminated from the blood—we would die quickly of hypoglycemia. As was true for sex steroids, we must live with the built-in risks of our blood glucose, which our bodies depend on to function normally, but which appears to slowly eat away at some of our proteins by forming chemical additions that themselves propagate free radical damage. Life is a biohazard!

There is another evolutionary reason for the rodents' response to a low-calorie diet. Although the reproductive system matures normally, the diet suppresses fertility (estrous) cycles and female fertility decreases sharply. Similar changes occur in women during starvation or those who suffer from anorexia nervosa. Even mild starvation suppresses reproduction to avoid having to satisfy the high food requirements of pregnancy and nursing. The species would benefit because individuals would be expending energy on reproduction only when the food supply was sufficient to ensure that infants survived. One final effect of diet restriction is that it slows the loss of ovarian oocytes, suggesting, perhaps, that reducing the intake of calories alters the neural centers that control the ovary via the pituitary. We might wonder whether a longer-lasting supply of egg cells would delay menopause, but we do not know whether slimming diets prolong the period of fertility in humans.

Robin Holliday has proposed that the response to calorie restriction is an important adaptive strategy among species that must adjust their reproduction to uncertain and fluctuating food supplies. Human populations evidently vary in the frequencies of genetic factors that influence the sensitivity of fat storage to food supply. Many rodent strains also carry genes predisposing individuals to obesity and NIDD. We presume that these aspects of metabolism and reproduction are regulated ultimately by the hypothalamus, a part of the brain that contains centers for controlling reproduction, metabolism, and eating behaviors. Genetic studies of how the brain controls behavior, metabolism, and reproduction might provide insights into the related problems of anorexia and bulimia, eating disorders that afflict women especially.

Vascular Aging and Vascular Disease

Aging slowly brings about many changes in the blood vessels that make up the vascular system—changes often begun early in life. The least dangerous is a slight stiffening of the artery wall known as arteriosclerosis, or hardening of the arteries. As a consequence of arteriosclerosis, the systolic blood pressure tends to creep up with aging. This is the blood pressure felt as the heart is contracting and forcing the blood onward. The growing arterial stiffness also causes the pulse to leave the heart at a higher velocity, because the aorta and other large vessels do not expand quite as much when the surge of blood from the heart enters these vessels. Thus, during strenuous effort, the maximum pumping capacity of the heart decreases by about 25% over the life span.

Arteriosclerosis appears to be a usual outcome of the wear and tear that vessels experience through the pulsing of blood several billion times over the life span. By itself the condition is not necessarily dangerous, and because it is found to some degree at

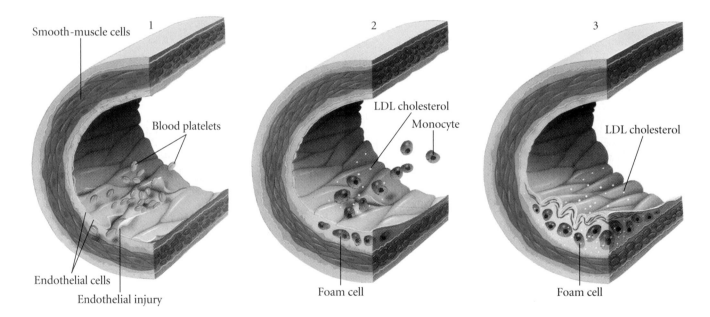

The formation of an atherosclerotic plaque begins when the thin layer of endothelial cells that lines an artery is damaged. According to one theory, blood platelets and particles of low-density lipoprotein (LDL) penetrate the damaged endothelium (1). In response, the damaged area is invaded by smooth-muscle cells from the layer below and by scavenging macrophages (2). Both types of cell ingest and degrade LDL, and cholesterol from the LDL accumulates with the transformed muscle and macrophage cells to form an atheroma.

later ages in most mammals, arteriosclerosis is best considered a normal, possibly inescapable feature of aging.

A more dangerous consequence of aging is the formation of atherosclerotic plaques, or atheroma. These are fatty cellular growths, raised like a callous above the blood vessel wall, which may sometimes become calcified. When autopsies were performed on U.S. soldiers killed during the Korean and Vietnam wars, the examiners were greatly surprised at the number of highly fit fighting men whose coronary arteries showed atherosclerotic plaques at an early stage. Atheromas can grow into the vessel and block flow, particularly if a blood clot becomes caught, causing immediate damage to tissues whose blood supply is cut off. The result is a heart attack if one of the coronary vessels is blocked, or a stroke if a cerebral artery is affected.

Many factors influence the rates at which arteriosclerosis progresses and fatty plaques develop. One factor is the relative amount of two major types of blood lipid, high-density lipoproteins (HDL) and low-density lipoproteins (LDL). The word *density* in the full names of the two types of lipoprotein refers to their rate of sedimentation when blood serum is centrifuged during laboratory analysis. Lipids are the significant molecules in fats and oils; they can be a source of energy for the body, but are also components used to build membranes in the body's cells. Lipids are carried through the bloodstream to cells

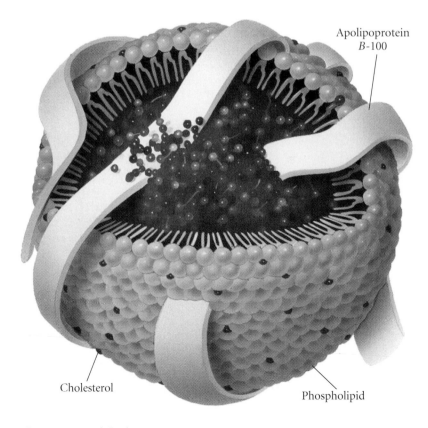

Apolipoprotein *B*-100

Cholesterol

Phospholipid

Low-density lipoprotein (LDL) is a spherical particle whose core consists of cholesterol molecules linked to single long fatty acid chains. The oily core is shielded by a surrounding coat formed of cholesterol molecules (red), phospholipid molecules (yellow), and one large protein molecule.

where they are needed by transporters having the form of lipoproteins, lipids joined to a protein.

The two lipoproteins HDL and LDL are distinguished by the different proteins and types of lipids they contain, although both contain in high proportion the notorious chemical cholesterol. Cholesterol is also used to make steroids in the adrenal glands and gonads—we can't do without it!

The HDL transporters tend to remove excess lipids from the circulation by delivering them to the liver for elimination. In contrast, LDL remains in the bloodstream much longer if not taken up by cells.

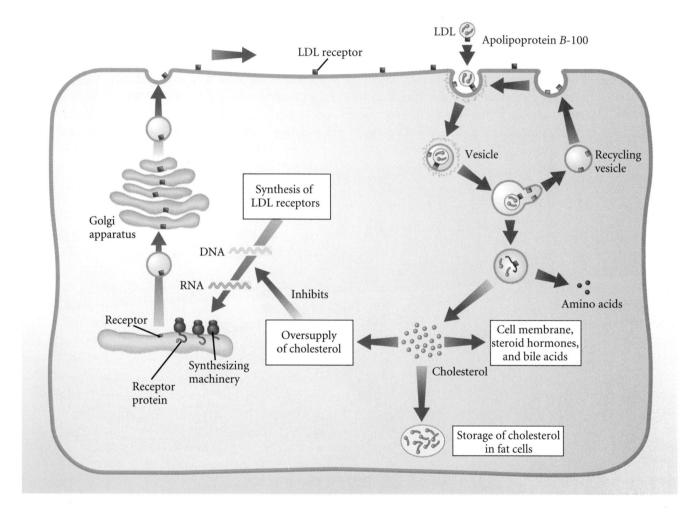

LDL attaches to a receptor and is taken into the cell. There, enzymes break down the LDL's protein molecule into amino acids and detach the fatty acid chains from cholesterol molecules to yield cholesterol that will be used to synthesize membranes, hormones, and other products. Should the cell experience an oversupply of cholesterol, it will store the excess and suppress the transcription of the receptor gene into mRNA, so that no more receptors are manufactured. Fewer receptors mean that more LDL remains in the bloodstream, where it can contribute to atherosclerotic plaques.

Thus LDL is an important risk factor of heart attacks and strokes, because its lipids can be taken up by a developing atheroma. Higher ratios of HDL ("good" lipoproteins) to LDL ("bad" lipoproteins) reduce the risk. To call these lipoproteins "good" and "bad" is an overstatement, of course, because we need some of each in the "right" amount.

When a lipoprotein reaches a cell where it is needed, a special protein on the cell membrane, called a receptor, recognizes the lipoprotein and brings it into the cell. The unlucky members of some families inherit defects in these LDL receptors. As a consequence, too much LDL remains in the bloodstream, where its lipids accumulate in atheromas and lead to a very high risk of premature death from heart attack. Indeed, a child with two copies of the defective gene may have a heart attack as early as the age of 2 and will almost certainly have one by the age of 20. Fortunately, these genes are quite rare and account for less than 1% of the deaths from vascular disease. With drastic modification of diet, it has been possible for these individuals to lower their cholesterol and slow the course of the disease, with a resulting increase toward normal life expectancy.

Diets high in cholesterol and saturated fats simulate the same defect in genetically normal persons. These diets signal the body to produce fewer LDL receptors in order to avoid overwhelming the cell with lipids. The result is predictable: more LDL remains in circulation and encourages the growth of fatty plaques. Whatever the individual's profile of HDL and LDL, some degree of vascular change seems to be inevitable as we age, even if we escape heart attacks or strokes. One study of 5,033 autopsies in Minnesota found that everyone older than 80 years had some degree of pathological change in their cerebral arteries.

Here again we come to an example of the sex hormone estrogen's widespread influence on aging. Estrogen decreases the amount of LDL and increases the amount of HDL. Consequently, vascular disease becomes more common after menopause because the loss of ovarian steroids increases the LDL:HDL ratio. As we might expect, estrogen replacement therapy tends to restore the blood lipid ratios of postmenopausal women to values typical of young adult women and reduces the risk of heart attack and stroke by about 50% compared to women who never took estrogen replacements.

The Dementias of Aging

Recent findings from research anticipate a merger of several longstanding ideas about brain aging. We may finally be able to reconcile two seemingly unrelated dictums: the cliché "A man is as old as his arteries" and the observation "Scholars grow wiser as they age, but the noneducated become foolish" (from a second-century Talmudic commentary). The key to this new synthesis lies in understanding several ways in which genes and the environment interact to produce dementias of aging, by which we mean the progressive loss of the ability to remember and to reason. Consequently, the dementias of aging, particularly the Alzheimer type, impair the performance of myriad activities of daily living that depend on our memory and problem-solving abilities.

The risk of dementia increases after 60 years of age in every human population that has been studied, and that risk doubles about every 5 years. This acceleration appears to exceed even the general acceleration of mortality, which doubles every 8 years between the ages of 60 and 90. The incidence of Alzheimer disease in particular accelerates continuously after 50 years. By the age of 85 years or older, almost half of us will show some signs of dementia. There is no indication of a "safe" age, after which the risk has passed, as exists for Huntington's disease, for example. Those who are from families with this genetic defect can feel safe if they remain healthy though 65 years of age, but no such reassurance is possible for dementia of the Alzheimer type. Worse, there is no recognized age when the risk may drop

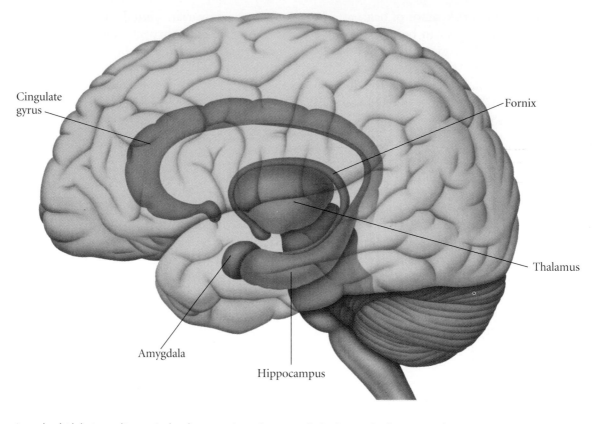

Cingulate gyrus

Fornix

Thalamus

Amygdala

Hippocampus

A mark of Alzheimer disease is the degeneration of nerve cells in the cerebral cortex and hippocampus, a structure buried within the brain that is vital to memory. A cluster of neurons that also shrink and die in Alzheimer disease is represented as the knob on the left side of the cingulate gyrus.

off, as happens with the risk of breast cancer after menopause.

At least two diseases are responsible for the rising risk of dementia during aging. The vascular changes that are a part of aging predispose us to multiple strokes that damage many parts of the brain when lack of blood kills off tissue in small patches, called infarcts. The result is often dementia, with loss of memory and impairment of many life activities. For example, if, as is common, the damaged parts of the brain control the movements of muscles, the victim will be unable to talk normally. This kind of dementia is called multi-infarct dementia.

In contrast, neurologists and pathologists agree that the dementia of Alzheimer disease is not a consequence of strokes or any other obvious cerebrovascular blockage. Nor is the blood flow in any way restricted. Rather, Alzheimer disease involves the degeneration of nerve cells in very restricted parts of the brain, notably in the cerebral cortex and hippocampus, both of which are particularly associated with memory. Unlike multi-infarct dementia, this

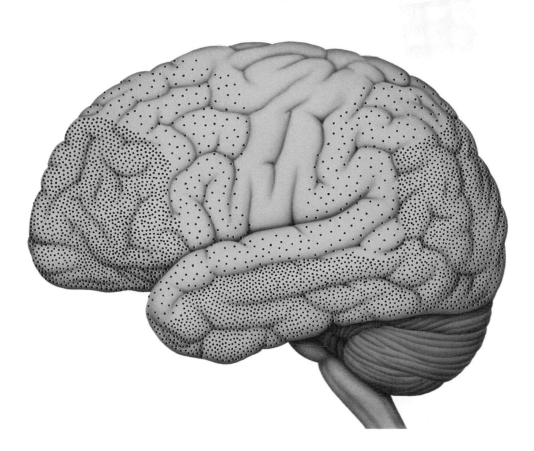

Amyloid deposits also form in the cerebral cortex of persons with Alzheimer disease, and are especially numerous in the areas indicated by shading. Increasing density of shading indicates increasing numbers of amyloid deposits.

disorder is less commonly associated with impairments of movement.

At postmortem examination under the microscope, tissue from afflicted parts of the Alzheimer brain is instantly distinguished by the presence of masses of a gluey extracellular material called the senile plaque, which contains a protein known as beta-amyloid or Aβ. Amyloid is an old term that historically refers to starchy deposits of proteins that become highly aggregated. A modern criterion is that amyloids show the special optical property of birefringence (double refraction) that is seen with Congo red and certain other dyes under polarizing light. Other types of amyloid that may accumulate with aging, however, are distinct from the beta-amyloid of Alzheimer disease, which accumulates uniquely in the brain.

Neurons affected by Alzheimer disease show another protein abnormality, the presence of dense bundles of fibers called neurofibrillary tangles inside their axons and dendrites (the long, tapering extensions of neurons). These tangles are formed from

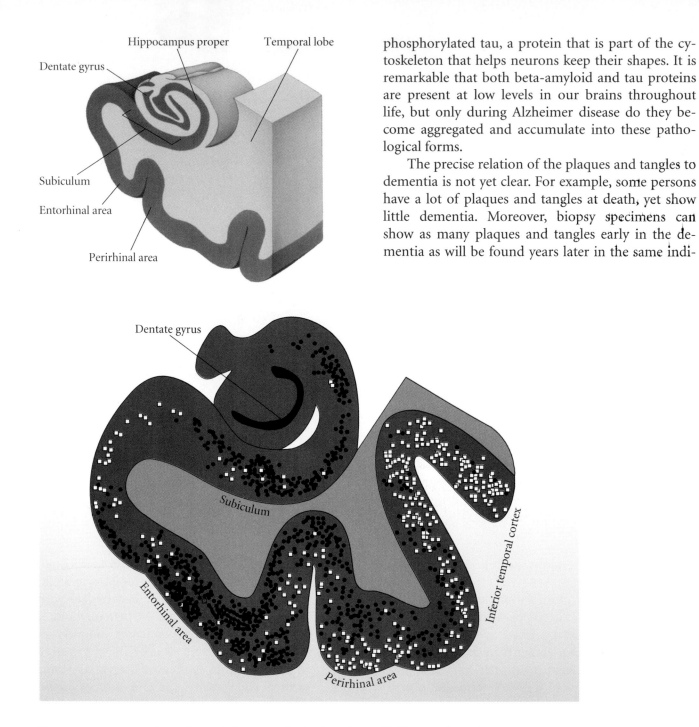

phosphorylated tau, a protein that is part of the cytoskeleton that helps neurons keep their shapes. It is remarkable that both beta-amyloid and tau proteins are present at low levels in our brains throughout life, but only during Alzheimer disease do they become aggregated and accumulate into these pathological forms.

The precise relation of the plaques and tangles to dementia is not yet clear. For example, some persons have a lot of plaques and tangles at death, yet show little dementia. Moreover, biopsy specimens can show as many plaques and tangles early in the dementia as will be found years later in the same indi-

The computer-generated map (bottom) shows the distribution of neurofibrillary tangles and senile plaques in the hippocampus and inferior temporal cortex (seen in a three-dimensional view top) of an elderly patient showing only mild signs of cognitive decline.

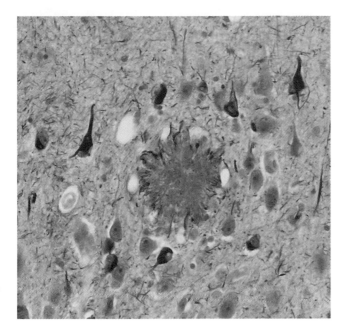

The dark globular mass in this stained image is a plaque of beta-amyloid protein in the brain of an Alzheimer patient. The plaque is surrounded by a halo of abnormal axons and dendrites and degenerating nerve cell bodies that appear darker than normal neurons.

vidual at his or her demise. One hypothesis is that the formation of plaques and tangles is an intermediate stage in Alzheimer disease. Once present, these abnormalities would go on to promote further events in nerve cell deterioration, leading to the disconnection of nerve cells from their neighbors and to nerve cell death.

The genetic basis of Alzheimer disease is rapidly becoming known. Some families carry dominant genes for the disease, and these have been located on at least three chromosomes. Particularly striking are rare families with early-onset dementia, which may be apparent in individuals in their 20s or 30s. This condition of presenile dementia had already been recognized in 1898 by Alois Alzheimer, a German psychiatrist who conducted detailed anatomical studies of patients at their deaths. Nearly 70 years would pass before neurologists became convinced

that the early- and late-starting diseases are the same, and that in both diseases the same brain regions are afflicted with plaques and tangles.

If we look at how often dementia is attributed to Alzheimer disease rather than stroke, we see that the most commonly cited cause of dementia differs among countries, a result that hints at environmental contributions to dementias of aging. Indeed, depending on the countries, the incidence of Alzheimer disease relative to that of multi-infarct dementia may vary severalfold. These differences between countries arise from many factors, including cultural biases. In some cultures, dementia by itself is considered to be a "bad" disease and shameful, whereas strokes and heart attacks are thought to be normal outcomes of aging. It is easy to see how in such cultures the cause of death cited on death certificates could be misleading, especially since examination of the brain is not routine on elderly deaths. Detailed postmortem examinations can rule out multiple strokes as the cause of dementia, but such examinations have not yet been performed for large samples outside of Europe and North America.

The extent of cerebrovascular disease and hypertension is another variable that differs between countries. Arteriosclerosis thickens the walls of the cerebral arteries in virtually everyone to some degree, but the typical course of cerebrovascular disease appears to differ among peoples of different nationalities, in large part because of differences in the incidence of hypertension. Hypertension at any age is well recognized to accelerate atherosclerosis and to increase the risk of brain stroke, as well as heart attack. The incidence of hypertension with age varies widely between populations, even within a country, depending on how much people smoke, exercise, and use salt. These behaviors alone, however, do not fully decide the course of vascular disease, for a person's genes also have a strong influence.

At one extreme are the relatively rare genetic disorders that cause atheromas, or atherosclerotic plaques, to appear at an early age. These are the in-

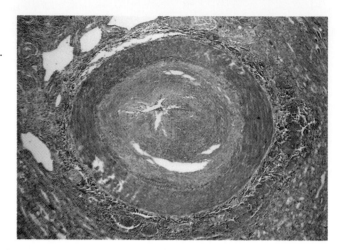

This artery is almost blocked by the growth of cells forming an atherosclerotic plaque in the arterial wall. Blood clots are often trapped in such constricted arteries, which become unable to deliver blood to the tissues, causing tissue death and, in the case of the heart or brain, a stroke.

herited blood lipid disorders caused by a variety of rare mutations in the LDL receptors. Far more common, however, are genetic variants of apolipoprotein E (apoE), one of the lipoproteins that transport lipids in the blood to LDL receptors. About 5% of caucasians carry a form of the gene called *apoE-4,* which increases the risk of stroke and heart attack. A recent discovery, made by Allen Roses and his colleagues at Duke University, is that there is a strong association between the number of copies a person has of the *apoE-4* form of the gene and the risk of developing Alzheimer disease. Remember, most genes are present in two copies that we received from each of our parents; someone could have one, both, or none of their two *apoE* genes in the deleterious form of *apoE-4.* Other copies of the *apoE* gene could be in the common forms *apoE-2* and *apoE-3,* which along with *apoE-4* are the three main "alleles" of the gene. Although the *apoE-2* and *apoE-3* alleles do not increase the risk of Alzheimer disease, 90% of individuals with two copies of the *apoE-4* allele (double-

dose *apoE-4* homozygotes) develop Alzheimer disease by 80 years of age. These individuals have about a 10-fold greater chance of developing Alzheimer disease than individuals with other combinations of the *apoE* alleles. Moreover, the double dose of *apoE-4* also carries with it a 1.4 times greater risk for coronary artery disease, and a 3-fold risk of multi-infarct dementia. One copy of the *apoE-4* allele from either parent brings a lower, but still considerable risk. Fortunately, the risk of having a double-dose of *apoE-4* is relatively low—about 1% of the total population.

The frequency of *apoE* alleles is not yet certain and may vary between ethnic groups. How the *apoE-4* allele acts to cause Alzheimer disease is still mysterious, and it may be acting through different mechanisms than those involved in vascular disease. We do know that as the risk of dementia associated with *apoE-4* alleles rises, so does the amount of beta-amyloid found both in the brain tissue and in the cerebral blood vessels. Nothing about beta-amyloid deposits seems to be good—more beta-amyloid brings more misery.

Although the *apoE-4* allele should be considered a risk factor of several life-threatening diseases, having that form of the gene does not absolutely doom someone to develop one of them. For example, several women aged 100 years and known to have double doses of *apoE-4* show no signs of dementia. On average, however, most people with two copies of the *apoE-4* allele die at younger ages, and so the allele becomes less and less common in individuals alive at progressively older ages. Interestingly, the *apoE-2* form of the gene is more common in centenarians than in younger individuals, as Daniel Cohen has found. Possibly, *apoE-2* acts as protection against vascular diseases.

Several other genes also lead to Alzheimer disease, but at much earlier ages in those families unfortunate enough to carry them. These genes, located on chromosomes 14 and 21, are even rarer in the general population than *apoE-4*. If yet more genes are discovered to be associated with Alzheimer disease,

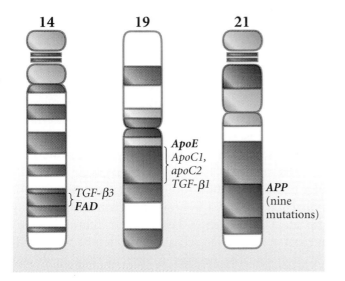

Three chromosomes carry genes that predispose to Alzheimer disease. On chromosome 21, rare mutations have been mapped to the gene for beta-amyloid protein precursor (APP). Chromosome 19 contains the apolipoprotein E (apoE) gene, which has an allele *(apoE-4)* that increases the risk of Alzheimer disease. At this time the *apoE* gene has been associated with certain types of Alzheimer disease, but has not been proven to be the general genetic determinant. The approximate location of another dominant gene that contributes to familial Alzheimer disease (FAD) has been found on chromosome 14.

plained by assuming the syndrome was caused by some now-vanished environmental factor. The factor at blame is most likely something in the diet eaten during World War II, when the extreme shortage of food forced the inhabitants of the island to make their bread using flour milled from a local plant, the cycad, which is known to contain toxins.

Medical researchers have lately recognized a surprising environmental risk factor in dementias of aging: lack of education. Very recently, six studies of different populations in Asia, North America, and Europe have found that higher education protects against dementia at later ages, whereas the lack of education above an eighth-grade equivalent increases the risk.

then this disease may turn out to be the most common genetic disease of adulthood, at least *50 times* more frequent than the much rarer familial lipid disorders responsible for premature death from heart attack.

A very strange neurological disease that shares with Alzheimer disease the presence of excess beta-amyloid and tangles has intrigued investigators because it seems to be associated with some mysterious environmental factor. This dementing illness was discovered in a particular group of men and women on the island of Guam and was given the hefty name Guamian Parkinson–dementia–amyotrophic lateral sclerosis syndrome. The syndrome is disappearing rapidly from Guam, a development most easily ex-

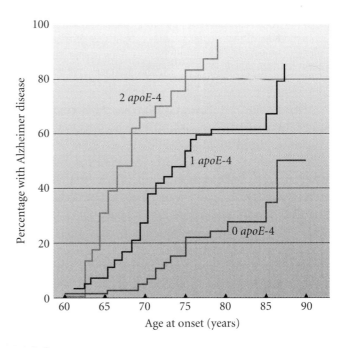

The risk of Alzheimer diseases is higher the more copies of the *apoE-4* allele are on chromosome 19. Nearly all persons born with two copies of the allele die before 80 with Alzheimer disease. Even so, a few individuals more than 90 years old have this genetic risk factor but show no signs of dementia.

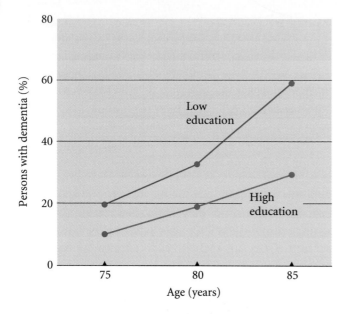

Higher education appears to protect against dementia in later years, as concluded by studies of elderly in China, North America, and Europe. The basis for this strong effect is mysterious. One hypothesis is that higher education builds up reserve synapses and circuits in the brain that are a buffer against the neuron damage during Alzheimer disease.

How could education influence Alzheimer disease? There are two possibilities. On the one hand, education could be a proxy for the absence of other factors, such as exposure to occupational hazards, head trauma, and hypertension, all of which promote vascular deterioration. The better educated, and thus better placed socioeconomically, a person is, the less likely he or she is to encounter these environmental risks of dementia.

On the other hand, education could stimulate the development of additional synapses between neurons in the brain. The increased numbers of synapses might serve as a reserve or buffer against losses that occur progressively during Alzheimer disease. Based on the results of experimental studies with laboratory animals, neurobiologists agree that the number of synapses can be influenced by the presence of environmental cues that stimulate the

senses over a long period. For example, rats placed in sensually impoverished environments—bare cages with only food and no cage mates—tend to lose synapses in the cerebral cortex, by about 20%, compared to rats maintained in cages with other rats and toys to play with. Stimulating the central nervous system has its strongest benefits when the additional stimulation is begun before puberty, but it can also be initiated with much success later in adult life.

The clear implication is that the greater demands of a higher education induce the formation of additional synapses in the brain, which may then delay the onset of dementia. Perhaps our Talmudic commentator was not so self-serving when he wrote that the noneducated became foolish as they aged. But then how can we view the dictum that "a man is as old as his arteries"? Both statements can be revisited in light of the insight that vascular changes have an important influence on two types of dementia: multi-infarct dementia and Alzheimer disease that arises from the *apoE-4* genotypes. In other words, if vascular disease becomes prominent during aging, whether because of genetics or environmental factors, then dementia is a likely outcome. Clearly, dementia has at least several causes, originating in both the genes and the environment. The race between wisdom and dementia may be begun early in life through our access to education.

Stress and Aging

As our last example of how factors in the environment can influence aging, we describe some remarkable observations on laboratory rats. These observations link three apparently separate biological activities to how we age: early social experience of newborns, resistance to stress as adults, and loss of brain neurons in old age. We caution that these findings cannot yet be firmly extrapolated to humans, although some other data suggest that they eventually may be.

Newborn mammals respond intensely to social contact, with consequences that can last a lifetime. A striking example was discovered by Robert Sapolsky of Stanford University in collaboration with Michael Meany of McGill University, both scientists who study the major hormone released during stress and its interactions with the brain. This hormone is the steroid cortisol in humans and the steroid corticosterone in rats; in both animals the hormone is secreted by the adrenal cortex, a gland located just above the kidney, and has numerous roles in regulating energy metabolism during stress. Because cortisol and corticosterone raise the level of glucose in the blood, they are known as glucocorticoids.

When newborn rodents are picked up and put in unfamiliar cages for 30 minutes each day for 20 days (until weaning), this social experience leads them to become less sensitive to stress as adults. Right after an animal is exposed to stress, the levels of stress steroid shoot up in the blood as the adrenal cortex pumps out the hormone corticosterone. Sapolsky and Meany measured how long corticosterone remained elevated after their rats were subjected to psychological stress by brief (and nonpainful) physical restraint. Adults that had been handled as neonates had briefer periods of elevated hormone and recovered faster from the stress. Moreover, when examined at later ages, the rats that had been handled as neonates had also lost fewer nerve cells from the hippocampus than had controls. The hippocampus, recall, is one of the brain regions that is devastated by nerve cell loss during Alzheimer disease.

The rationale for looking for nerve loss in the hippocampus had come from earlier experiments on rodents and monkeys. Philip Landfield, then at University of California, Irvine, as a postdoctoral fellow with Gary Lynch, had found that more nerve cells had degenerated in the hippocampus of old rats

Robert Sapolsky and Hideo Uno found that vervet monkeys suffering from gastric ulcers, a strong sign of excessive stress, also showed signs of nerve damage in the hippocampus. In these monkeys, more nerves had degenerated in the hippocampus (right) compared to monkeys serving as controls (left).

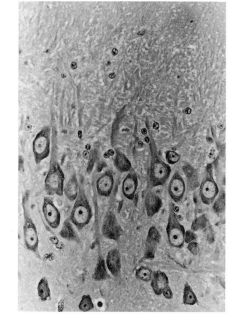
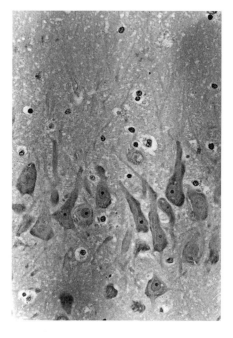

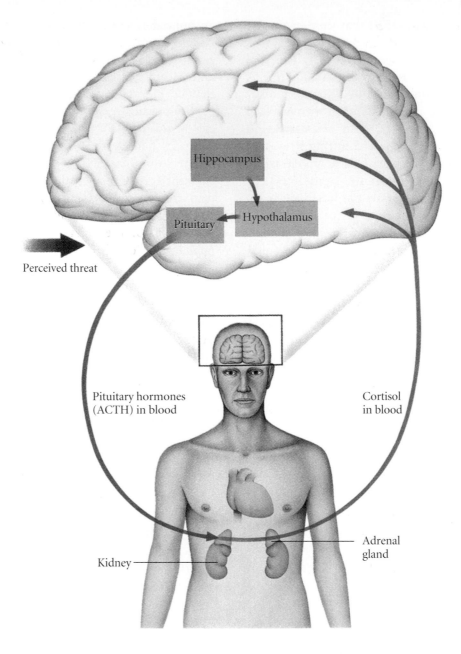

Hippocampus

Hypothalamus

Pituitary

Perceived threat

Pituitary hormones
(ACTH) in blood

Cortisol
in blood

Kidney

Adrenal
gland

The adrenal glands and stress centers in the brain form a feedback loop. The perception of a threat stimulates the hippocampus and hypothalamus, among other brain areas. The result is a hormonal signal sent from the hypothalamus that tells the pituitary gland to release the hormone ACTH into the bloodstream. When ACTH reaches the adrenal gland, the gland will respond by releasing the stress hormone cortisol, which has a variety of effects throughout the body, some of them influencing the very brain centers whose original stimulation leads to the hormone's release.

having high blood levels of corticosterone and that removing the adrenal gland, the source of this hormone, slowed the loss of these nerve cells. Moreover, the hippocampus was found by Sapolsky to be similarly damaged in vervet monkeys that had experienced profound stress when they were removed from their normal habitat in east Africa. Other studies with rodents have shown that, under many stressful circumstances, the risk that neurons will be irreversibly damaged is heightened by elevated levels of glucocorticoids. These and other findings have suggested that stress, elevated levels of glucocorticoids, or both if sustained for too long, will cause injury to nerve cells in the hippocampus.

The hippocampus has a role in regulating the amount of glucocorticoids released during stress. When the hippocampus is damaged surgically by experimenters, rats that are subsequently subjected to stress show a slower return to resting levels of blood corticosterone. Thus, there may be a vicious cycle, in which damage to the hippocampus from whatever cause leads to greater exposure to corticosterone and thence to more damage to the neurons of the hippocampus. This possibility is being considered to explain why people with Alzheimer disease have both high levels of cortisol in the bloodstream and high levels of damage to the hippocampus. The hippocampus is at high risk to damage from stroke, and any such damage might accelerate the elevation of cortisol in the bloodstream and, thereby, further the loss of neurons.

The Sapolsky-Meany study demonstrates how the experiences of newborns can program the brain to respond differently to stress years later. These findings give powerful precedents for seeking similar phenomena in humans. Stresses from retirement, the death of a spouse, or other changes in social environment are practically universal experiences after midlife. Indeed, people undergoing the stress of bereavement have a higher than average mortality rate for their age group. This psychophysiological vulnerability may last several years. Just why individuals should respond differently to stress is unknown, but early experiences could quite conceivably have an influence on how the brain regulates stress steroids.

Population Differences in Aging

The examples in this chapter of environmental influences on aging illustrate only a few of the many idiosyncracies and local details that distinguish the aging process in different regions and cultures. Throughout the world, the genes we inherit interact with the environment in different ways to powerfully affect the outcome of aging. With the exception of the relatively rare blood lipid disorders that cause premature death from vascular disease and the *apoE-4* gene of Alzheimer disease, few other genes have been identified that influence how we age. Thus, the relative roles of heredity and environment in creating the variation we see in aging are not well understood.

The incidence of many types of cancer can differ remarkably between populations, as the incidence of breast cancer differs between women in Japan and women in Los Angeles. Such differences suggest that it should be possible to reduce the risk of each type of cancer at least to that of the country with the smallest risk. One obvious path to a lower cancer rate is to eliminate the numerous environmental factors and life styles strongly linked to some cancers. The link between exposure to sunlight and skin cancer is unquestionable, as is the link between tobacco use and lung cancer and between tobacco use and vascular disease. Bruce Ames has argued cogently that many age-related cancers are the result of common oxidizing agents, including many such agents found in foods. Many common oxidants can also promote vascular disease. These immensely complicated biomedical puzzles will take decades to unravel, but their understanding will provide a huge opportunity for us to better our health in our later years.

Saddleback tortoises of Pinzon Island, in the Galapagos Archipelago, may achieve ages of more than a century. This extreme longevity emphasizes the variation in life spans among animals.

The phenomenon of aging is obvious to anyone over the age of 30. Personal experience alone is enough to convince most of us of its importance as a biological process and of the need for experimental research to determine how aging occurs—and how its worst effects might be prevented! What is less apparent, however, is that our understanding of the aging process has been broadened by looking at aging in different species—what we might call the natural history of life span. Such comparisons are especially helpful for developing and testing evolutionary theories of why we age. These theories attempt to explain not only why the phenomenon of aging exists, but why differences have evolved in the rate of aging among species.

Although we know a great deal about aging in humans and a few organisms raised in the laboratory, our understanding of aging in wild populations is limited. What we do know suggests a rich variation among species in the pattern of aging and allows us to make some educated guesses

4

A Natural History of Life Span

about the underlying causes of these differences. In this chapter, we show how observations of the natural history of aging reveal interesting patterns that seem to require explanation, but that also suggest some mechanisms that may lie behind senescence.

The Gompertz Pattern of Aging

As we have seen, senescence is a pervasive deterioration of the body's functioning with age. We all recognize the declining health and gradual loss of vitality that come with aging. But for the scientist wishing to compare species, these physiological signs of aging are difficult to measure in most animals and even more difficult to compare. An easier way to depict the advance of senescence within a population is to track the increase in the death rate at progressively older ages. Like the body in general, reproductive systems function less well with age, and so another way to follow the course of aging is to record the decline in the reproductive rate, or fecundity, of individuals at progressively older age. Thus, to portray senescence from a demographic point of view, the scientist tabulates birth and death rates for large samples of individuals that have been followed from birth to the maximum age observed in the population. Until recently, biologists have focused their attention mostly on mortality rate and have largely ignored fecundity. The reason is partly that it is easier to measure mortality than fecundity, especially in males, and partly that we humans are more preoccupied with our own mortality than with the number of our progeny, which nowadays is usually not limited by biological considerations.

Senescence appears as a mortality rate that increases with age. In a population whose members never aged, individuals would still die, of course, but the mortality rate would be identical for all age

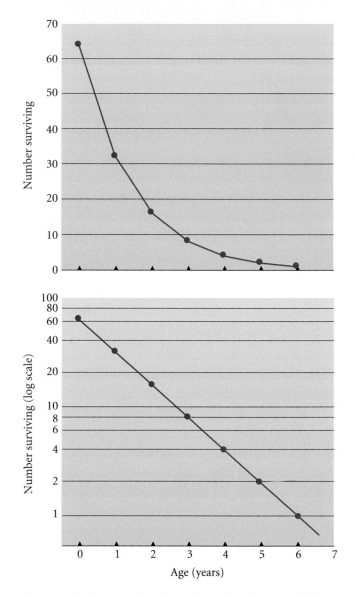

Even if aging did not exist, the number of survivors would decrease exponentially with age. Here the survival function of a cohort of 64 individuals with an annual mortality rate of 50% is plotted on a linear scale above, producing a curve, and on a logarithmic scale below, producing a straight line. In mathematical terms, for a constant mortality rate m, the fraction of individuals alive at age x decreases exponentially with age. That is, $S_x = e^{-mx}$. When this equation is log-transformed, one obtains $\log_e S_x = -mx$, which, in words, means that the natural logarithm of the fraction surviving decreases as a linear function of age with slope $= -m$.

groups. Thus, on a graph of mortality rate versus age, such a population would be represented by a straight, horizontal line, and we would find that the number of individuals surviving decreased exponentially with age. For example, if the mortality rate were 50% each year, a cohort (group of equal age) of 64 individuals would, on average, dwindle to 32, 16, 8, 4, 2, 1, and finally 0 with each advancing year. This relationship between the number of individuals surviving and age is called the survival function. When we plot the number of survivors against age, we see that the absolute rate of decrease becomes less with increasing age because, as the population dwindles, the 50% dying each year make a smaller and smaller number. The effect is the same when we plot, as is often done, the proportion of the original cohort that remains alive at each age, rather than the absolute numbers of individuals. In the analysis of senescence, it is customary to depict the number of individuals alive at each age on a logarithmically transformed scale, which makes the survival function of a nonaging population a straight line. How fast the logarithm of the survival function decreases as age increases (that is called the slope of the line) is equal to the mortality rate of the population. In the foregoing case, the slope of the line has a value of −0.5 (corresponding to 50% mortality per year), and, of course, it is negative because death always removes individuals.

The straight-line survival function is the sign of a hypothetical population that has been spared the decline brought on by aging. In contrast, in a realistic population whose members do experience aging, the mortality rate increases at older age and the line representing the (log-scale) survival function is no longer straight, but curves downward. That is, its slope becomes progressively steeper and more negative. Indeed, senescence can be quantified by how rapidly the mortality rate increases with increasing age. Suppose that individuals in a population were dying at a rate of 50% per year upon reaching adulthood, but that the mortality rate increased exponentially by a factor of 10% each year thereafter, that is, to 55% during the second year of adulthood, 60.5% (55% plus 10% of 55%) during the third year, 66.55% during the fourth year, and so on. By the end of the 5 years, a cohort that aged in this way would dwindle to about 0.8% of its original size, compared with about 3.1% in a nonaging population.

It is common for the mortality rate to increase exponentially with age in natural populations. This pattern of exponential increase is often called the Gompertz pattern of aging. The Gompertz pattern describes the effects of aging on mortality by two

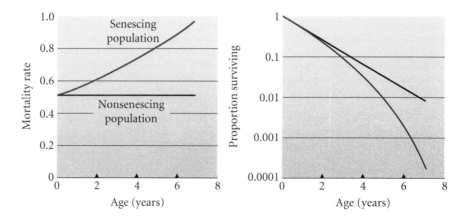

Two, related ways to characterize aging in a population are to plot the mortality rate (left) and the survival function (right). In the nonsenescing population, the mortality rate remains at the minimum, or baseline, mortality rate of 50% per year, the rate when adulthood is achieved. In the senescing population, the mortality rate increases exponentially at a rate of 10% each year. Aging causes the survival function to bend downward at higher ages, reflecting the higher mortality rate.

A Natural History of Life Span

numbers that are constant in a given population: the initial or baseline mortality rate, A, and the exponential rate of increase in the mortality rate, G. In the preceding example, the values of A and G were 0.5 and 0.1, respectively. The baseline mortality rate A, which is the mortality rate of young adults, includes death from accidents and other causes not related to aging. The Gompertz constant G measures the rate of aging and may be compared directly between different species. For example, the mortality rate in a captive population of brush turkeys, an Australasian turkeylike bird, increases exponentially at a rate of about 21% per year from a baseline of about 5% per year. The Bali myna, a bird somewhat related to the European starling, has a baseline annual mortality rate of about 9% in captivity, but this rate increases by only 9.6% per year. One can say, therefore, that the myna ages less than half as fast as the brush turkey. Because values of G are not intuitive, scientists often use an inverse measure of G, the mortality rate doubling time (MRDT). MRDT is the age by which the mortality rate has increased to twice its baseline level. For the brush turkey and myna, these values are 3.3 and 7.2 years, respectively.

Gompertz constants vary among species of mammals from as high as about 2.3 (230% per year) in laboratory rats and mice to as little as 0.09 (9% per year) in humans and elephants. These values of G correspond to mortality rate doubling times of 0.3 and 8 years, respectively. Notice that some small

---

The Gompertz Equation

$\mathcal{T}$he expression most commonly employed to compare mortality rates between populations is the Gompertz equation. According to the Gompertz pattern of aging, the mortality rate increases as an exponential function of increasing age. This course of aging is described by the equation

$$m(x) = Ae^{Gx}$$

where $m(x)$ is the mortality rate at age x, A is the initial mortality rate at age 0, and G is the exponential rate of increase in the mortality rate with increasing age. G may be regarded in the same way as the interest rate on a bank account because it governs the rate at which the initial mortality rate (investment) grows with time. The Gompertz law can also be expressed in terms of the proportion of in-

dividuals surviving to age x, $S(x)$, according to the equation

$$S(x) = e^{-\frac{G}{A}(e^{Gx} - 1)}$$

Because deaths from childhood diseases and accidents usually decline between birth and the age of sexual maturity, the mortality rate declines as well. For this reason, age 0 is often set as the age of puberty or first bearing of offspring. The initial or minimum mortality rate A is therefore the mortality rate at about the time of puberty. The Gompertz constant (G) also may be expressed as the time required for the mortality rate to double (the mortality rate doubling time, MRDT) according to the expression $\text{MRDT} = \log_e(2)/G$.

Upper left: The brush turkey *(Alectura lathami)* is one of a group of Australasian birds related to pheasants and chickens that incubates its eggs in mounds of sand warmed by the sun or by heat produced by rotting vegetation. Lower left: When the brush turkey's mortality rate is plotted on a logarithmic axis, the Gompertz parameter G (0.21 in this case) is the slope of the line relating mortality to age, and the parameter A (about 0.05) is the intersection of the line with the vertical axis at an age of 0 years. The purple line is fitted to the data for the brush turkey; the blue line represents the increase in mortality for the Bali myna inferred from the survival curve in the next graph. The dashed line represents the annual mortality rate (0.05) of a nonaging population. Upper right: Although the population of the Bali myna *(Leucopsar rothschildi)* within its native range on the island of Bali in the East Indies numbers less than 100 individuals, thousands have been raised in captive populations in zoos around the world. Lower right: The purple line has been fitted to data for individuals in zoo populations of the Bali myna to give the survival function ($A = 0.092$, $G = 0.096$). The blue line is the survival function estimated for the population of brush turkeys whose mortality rates were portrayed in the previous graph. The dashed line represents the survival function of a nonaging population with a mortality rate of 0.092 per year.

A Natural History of Life Span

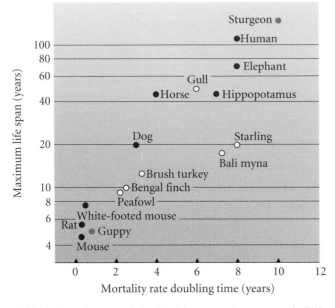

Fish, birds, and mammals having higher maximum recorded life spans also have higher mortality rate doubling times.

with a Gompertz constant of 0.2 to 0.3 per *day* during the first 3 weeks of life. Unlike the pattern that had been observed in other, smaller studies, however, mortality rate leveled off, albeit at the high rate of 12 to 15% per day, between about 3 and 8 weeks of age. Afterward it actually decreased steadily to about 4% per day at 100 days of age. Fewer than a tenth of 1% of the original population of 1.2 million was alive at the age when the mortality rate began to decrease, so few individuals survived to enjoy this relief from aging. Nonetheless, such findings have important implications for the study of aging. In particular, aging processes seem not to be uniform throughout the potential life span. Beyond a certain age, 60 days in the case of medflies, individuals may achieve a state of *potential* immortality in the sense that physiological condition apparently does not deteriorate further, at least not enough to cause a further increase in mortality rate. And what about humans? James Vaupel and his collaborators have recently

birds, like the Bali myna, age as slowly as large mammals weighing 1000 times as much, although the maximum recorded life span of the myna is, at present, less than 20 years. In general, the maximum recorded life spans of vertebrates are in the range of 5 to 10 times the mortality rate doubling time.

Although the Gompertz equation characterizes aging reasonably well, many species show deviations from the pattern, particularly at old age. Large sample sizes are needed to detect these deviations, and what better place to find large samples than in a facility for rearing Mediterranean fruit flies, or medflies, that will be sterilized and released for population control programs? In one experiment using flies supplied by such a facility in Mexico, James Carey and his coworkers began with a cohort of 1,203,646 medflies and followed their survival until the last two individuals died at an age of 171 days. As in the usual course of aging, the mortality rate increased steeply,

The Mediterranean fruit fly, or medfly *(Ceratitis capitata),* shows no aging-related increase in mortality after 3 weeks of age, and its mortality rate actually decreases after 8 weeks. The sterilized male in this photograph will be released in a program to control the population of the medfly, which is an agricultural pest.

Chapter Four

discovered a similar leveling off of mortality rate in the very oldest individuals alive in Scandinavia.

Survival data are available for so few species that we cannot dissect patterns of aging more finely at this point; even the data that are available are not strictly comparable, because the conditions experienced by the populations differed, as did the methods used to obtain the information. Therefore, although the Gompertz model of senescence illustrates the general quantitative character of aging—a more or less exponential increase in mortality rate with age through much of the adult life span—scientists wishing to make broad comparisons must at this time look to other indices of senescence. The simplest and most widely used of these is the maximum recorded life span, the oldest age attained by any member of the population. As we have seen above, the maximum life span bears a close relationship to the mortality rate doubling time, one of the parameters of a Gompertz pattern of aging.

Maximum Life Span

Determining the maximum life span is relatively straightforward for any population with birth records, such as laboratory and zoo populations, or for any population for which one can accurately estimate age. Trees can often be aged by their annual growth rings, which result from differences in the wood cells produced during different seasons of the year. Besides woody plants, some bivalve mollusks, such as clams, have annual layers of growth in their shells, as do the otoliths of fish, which are the small stones of calcium carbonate (shell material) formed in the inner ear as part of the fish's mechanism for sensing which way is up.

Regardless of how age is determined, the investigator can know only the maximum *recorded* life span, whose value depends on the particular sample of individuals examined and the veracity of the age estimate. In several human populations renowned

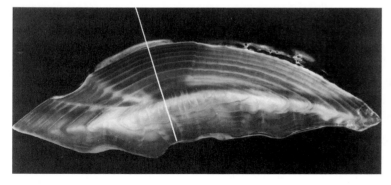

Above: Annual rings representing 9 years of growth in the otolith of the drum *Aplodinotus grunniens,* a fish captured in Lake Erie. Right: A scanning electron micrograph showing daily growth increments of the otolith of a young swordfish *(Xiphias gladius).*

for exceptional longevity (often agrarian populations in mountainous regions of, for example, Ecuador, the Central Asian nation of Georgia, or Pakistan), the birth records of claimed centenarians have been confused in many cases with the birth records of other individuals long since dead, or they have been deliberately falsified because of benefits bestowed upon elders or the whole population. In Georgia and Pakistan, dubious claims of extreme longevity were promoted because of the prestige that attended old age. In Vilcabamba, Ecuador, claims of extreme longevity had attracted so many gerontologists to the area that aging research became a major local source of revenue, which, in turn, encouraged the reporting of even more extreme longevity.

In any large population, a small number of individuals will live far beyond the average life span; detecting these individuals may require very large samples, as we have seen in the medfly study mentioned above. In a hypothetical nonaging population that experiences an exponential decrease in the proportion of individuals surviving, the maximum potential life span theoretically is infinite. The odds of finding an extremely long-lived individual are still very low, however. If the annual mortality rate in such a population were 0.5 (50%) per year, the expected maximum life span in a sample of 1000 individuals would be 10 years; to find one individual that lived to at least 20 years, one would have to determine the ages at death for about 1,000,000 individuals, on average.

In populations where aging is an inevitable part of life, aging places an upper limit on the maximum potential life span, and a larger fraction of the population approaches that age. For example, in our hypothetical population, one individual in 1000 reaches 10 years of age. If life span were truncated by an abrupt manifestation of senescence at 10 years, a sample of 1000 ages at death would likely turn up only one case of death occurring at such an old age. However, as one continued to record ages of death in

Peter Prince of the British Antarctic Survey holds a gray-headed albatross. A device for recording the amount of time the bird sits on the water has been attached to the red leg band, which has a number that uniquely identifies the individual.

the population, the larger samples still would not produce individuals dying at greater age, and soon one might be confident that the maximum recorded life span approximated the maximum potential life span. Therefore, even though aging usually produces a more gradual increase in mortality rate, and even though the maximum recorded life span depends on the sample size, the maximum recorded life span in well-sampled populations, as we have seen, is closely linked to the rate of aging (the Gompertz parameter G or its inverse, the mortality rate doubling time).

Most maximum-life-span records for animals come from zoos, partly because most zoological parks keep records of births and deaths, and partly because animals tend to live longer in the protected zoo environment than in the wild. However, some of what we know about life span has been gathered from long-term observations of marked individuals in wild populations. The animals are marked by attaching one of a variety of bands or clips, or they may even be tattooed or a toe may be clipped, depending on the type of animal. In some studies, particularly studies of fish and birds, large numbers of individuals are tagged and then recovered at a later time, either by trapping live animals or by recovering dead ones. For example, since the inception of the migratory bird banding program by the Fish and Wildlife Service of the United States, about one-half million American robins have been fitted with uniquely numbered aluminum leg bands. By the early 1990s, 13,778 of these marked birds had been retrapped or found dead. The longest interval between banding and recovery was 13 years 11 months. This does not mean that the oldest bird was only 14 years old, however, because many birds were banded as adults, when their ages could not be determined. Thus, in most populations, the longest period between banding and recovery provides a minimum estimate of the maximum potential longevity. Although 13,778 recoveries of robins may look like a pittance next to 1.2 million medflies, the 522,261 recoveries of mallard ducks should instill some confidence in us that the maximum recorded age of 23 years 5 months is close to the mallard duck's maximum potential life span.

Other studies focus more intensively on local populations, following individuals over many years. Since 1961, Charles Huntington, of Bowdoin College, Maine, has been working at a breeding colony of a small seabird, Leach's storm petrel (*Oceanodroma leucorhoa*), on Kent Island in the Bay of Fundy. During his first season there, he placed a numbered

An adult Leach's storm petrel incubating its single egg. These birds dig their nest burrows in soft earth, although in this case the roof of the nest chamber has been removed and replaced by a board to gain access for banding the adult and weighing and measuring the chick.

metal band on, among others, a breeding male known as Santiago; in the years afterward he found the bird in the same nest burrow every spring until 1992, and then again in 1994. Assuming that in 1961 Santiago was at least 4 years old, the youngest age at which storm petrels breed, Santiago is at least 37 years old. Not bad for a bird weighing only 40 grams (less than 2 ounces). A storm petrel named Ishmael was banded as a chick in 1963, and returned to breed in his natal burrow from 1969 through 1992—a life span of at least 29 years. Undoubtedly there may be a few quadragenerians in the population, and, as we have seen, such maximum ages are greatly exceeded by other kinds of bird.

Aging and Body Size

It seems intuitive that the massive lion has a larger brain than the compact house cat, while the tiny house mouse has a faster heartbeat than either. In

These elephants, gazelles, and doves gathered at a water hole in Botswana in southern Africa dramatize the wide range of body size among animals. The elephants have relatively low metabolism per unit body mass and live up to 70 years. With their higher rate of living, few gazelles live beyond 10 years. The smaller doves, however, may achieve greater longevity than the gazelles, illustrating the considerable variability in longevity–body size relationships.

making comparisons among species, we see that many biological attributes of organisms — including their metabolic rates, heartbeat frequencies, running speeds, and relative brain sizes — show a systematic correlation with the animal's body size, and life span is no exception. In general, the larger the organism, the longer its potential life span. This is most obvious when we consider the extremes. Weighing in at less than 100 grams, the chipmunk has a maximum potential life span of about 8 years. At 1000 and 5000 kilograms, long-lived hippopotamuses and elephants may achieve 45 and 70 years, respectively. When a narrower range of body sizes is considered, the relationship between size and life span is obscured by the considerable variation from the general rule. For example, at masses between 20 and 100 kilograms, we find gazelles, with life spans of 10 years, and chimpanzees, among which are individuals reaching 45 years. Thus, both the general trend and exceptions to the trend provide interesting points of comparison.

The relationship between life span and body size can be described mathematically. In fact, the way in which *any* biological attribute (Y) varies with respect to body size (M) may be characterized by the *allometric equation,* first applied to the problem of body-size relationships by Julian Huxley in 1932,

$$Y = aM^b$$

In this equation, *a* is the value of *Y* when body mass *M* is equal to 1, but the more consequential quantity is *b*. The exponent *b* is the *allometric constant* that describes the rate of increase in *Y* with respect to *M*. The diagram on this page shows the relationship between life span and body mass in mammals. Here the value of *a* is about 10 years, meaning that a 1-kilogram animal such as a guinea pig will live about 10 years, and the value of *b*, the slope of the line, is about 0.2. Thus, among mammals, life span = $10M^{0.2}$ when the age is expressed in years and mass in kilograms. In this case, where *b* is a positive value but less than 1, *Y* increases disproportionately slower than *M* and the ratio *Y/M* decreases with body size. In the hypothetical case that *b* exceeds 1, *Y* increases disproportionately faster than *M* and the ratio *Y/M* increases with body size. When *b* equals 1, *Y* increases in direct proportion to *M* and the ratio between the two is constant. In this special case, the relationship between *Y* and *M* is said to be *isometric*. The quantity *b* can also be negative, in which case *Y* decreases with increasing *M*.

The equation given above that relates maximum longevity to body mass, namely life span = $10M^{0.2}$, predicts that a 10-kilogram mammal, such as a medium-sized dog, could live 58% longer than a 1-kilogram mammal, such as a guinea pig. This increase in life span (about 1.6-fold) is thus much less than the increase in body mass (10-fold). With an exponent of 0.2, a 32-fold increase in mass is required to double the estimated life span.

Everyone has heard that 1 dog-year is equal to 7 human-years. This bit of folk wisdom comes from the observation that the average life span of a dog is about one-seventh that of a human. Thus, while 20 years is the prime of life for a human, it is old age for man's best friend (with apologies to women and cat lovers among you). This difference between dogs and humans is at least partly related to the fact that humans are larger than dogs and may be expected to have longer life spans as a consequence of their larger body size. But, does the difference in size entirely ac-

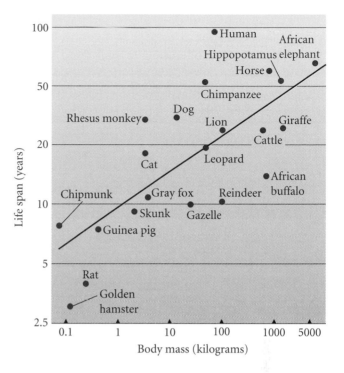

Life span and body mass are correlated in mammals. Both mass and life span are plotted on logarithmic scales, and so the allometric relationship between them appears as a straight line. The slope of this line, which is the allometric constant, is about 0.2. The amount by which a species deviates from the line is a measure of its *relative* life span, that is, that portion of the life span not accounted for by its body mass.

count for the difference in life span? The allometric equation provides an answer, since allometric relationships provide a standard of comparison for organisms of different body size. For example, even though the life span of the African elephant is about five times that of the gray fox, both species lie close to the line depicting the allometric relationship for mammals as a whole and, therefore, both species have similar life spans for their respective sizes. Because humans lie well above the line, we can tell that a second part of the difference between the life spans of humans and dogs derives from physiological factors other than those related to body size itself.

These sorts of deviations alert us to the fact that some unknown factor or factors, perhaps of physiology or ecology, are operating to pull these species away from the norm for their group. It has long been suspected that one such factor could be metabolic rate, or rate of living.

Life Span and Rate of Living

A persistent idea throughout the history of thinking about aging has been that organisms that live faster, die faster. As we have seen, smaller organisms tend to have more rapid metabolism per unit mass than larger organisms, and they have shorter life spans. Thus, mice generate more heat per unit of body mass than do elephants even though their body temperatures are about the same. Some very inactive, slow-moving species, such as tortoises, appear to have long life spans compared to more active mammals and birds of the same body mass.

There are several reasons for supposing that a higher metabolic intensity means an earlier death. Metabolism and activity presumably produce much of the wear and tear of living on the individual. In addition, free radicals and other harmful byproducts are produced in direct proportion to the rate of metabolism. Theoretically, then, rate of living should be inversely related to life span. There have been some intriguing observations made that are consistent with this idea, but in order to properly evaluate the rate-of-living hypothesis, we must place such comparisons on a firmer quantitative foundation.

There are many ways to measure rate of living, but one general yardstick is the metabolic rate of the individual. This can be portrayed as the rate of oxygen consumption under standardized conditions, which may be converted to watts of power used and Calories or kilojoules of heat produced per unit of

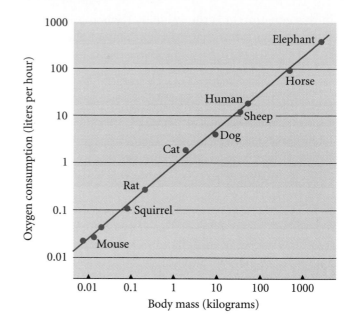

The relationship between basal metabolic rate and body mass in various species of mammals. The line represents the allometric equation $BMR = 0.7M^{0.75}$ (metabolism in liters of oxygen per hour, mass in kilograms).

time. When the subject is at rest, with an empty stomach (but not starving), and at a comfortable temperature, this measurement is known as the basal metabolic rate, or BMR. BMR has been determined for a wide variety of organisms. For mammals other than marsupials, BMR scales to body mass according to $BMR = 0.7M^{0.75}$ (metabolism in liters of oxygen per hour, mass in kilograms).

Here is where the allometric equation really proves its value, for it can be used to establish just how a measurement such as metabolic rate is related to life span. To make such comparisons, the variables must be expressed in a biologically meaningful manner. For example, the total metabolic rate of an animal from a large species is bound to exceed that of an animal from a small species. A large animal such as an elephant has got to be breathing in more

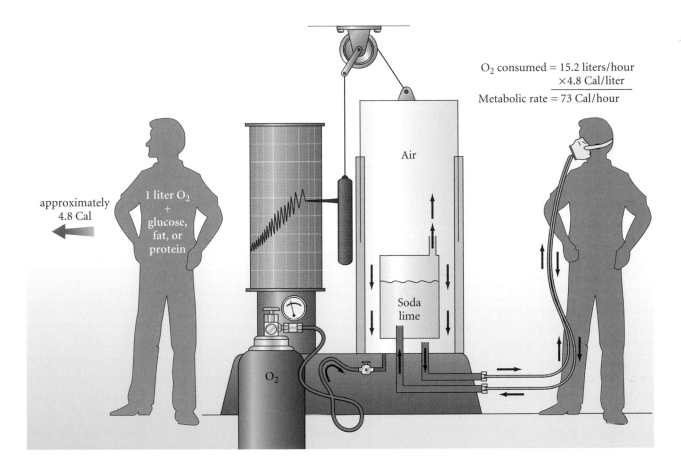

O₂ consumed = 15.2 liters/hour
×4.8 Cal/liter
Metabolic rate = 73 Cal/hour

$$O_2 \text{ consumed} = 15.2 \text{ liters/hour}$$
$$\times 4.8 \text{ Cal/liter}$$
$$\overline{\text{Metabolic rate} = 73 \text{ Cal/hour}}$$

Air

approximately
4.8 Cal

1 liter O₂
+
glucose,
fat, or
protein

Soda
lime

O₂

An example of an apparatus used for the measurement of energy metabolism in large animals. The system is closed, meaning that the air inhaled by the subject is returned to the chamber at the center. Exhaled carbon dioxide is removed by the soda lime, and the rate at which the subject consumes oxygen is measured by the change in the volume of air in the chamber, which is recorded on the drum. From time to time, pure oxygen is admitted from the gas cylinder to replace that consumed by the subject and to permit the measurement to continue for a long period. Modern technology has largely replaced such apparati with open-flow systems that measure the concentration of oxygen in the air after it is exhaled.

oxygen and generating more energy per hour than a small animal such as a mouse. But small animals are the short-lived ones that we expect to have higher metabolic rates. We need a different measure of metabolic rate, one that is independent of body mass.

Such a measure is the metabolic rate per unit of mass, which measures the metabolic intensity of the individual's cells, tissues, and organs, independently of its overall size. Because total metabolism increases less rapidly than body size ($b < 1$), when we divide by body mass to obtain basal metabolic intensity

(BMI), we find that the intensity drops as animals become larger. That is, basal metabolic intensity scales to body mass with an exponent less than 0, specifically BMI $= 0.7M^{-0.25}$ (metabolism in liters of oxygen per kilogram of body mass per hour). Thus, smaller organisms tend to have a greater metabolic intensity than larger organisms.

Are metabolism and life span related? Metabolic intensity has an allometric slope of -0.25, which is a very different number from the value of 0.20 observed for maximum recorded life span. However, the comparison is not yet really valid because of a discrepancy in the unit of measurement: the units of metabolic intensity—metabolism per unit time—are *inverse* to the units of life span, which are time. To obtain the inverse of an allometric slope, one merely changes the sign of the exponent. Thus, time per unit of metabolic intensity—that is, the period required to accomplish a given amount of metabolic work—has a slope of 0.25. This slope is statistically indistinguishable from the allometric slope for maximum recorded lifetime (0.20), suggesting a reasonable correspondence between the two. Thus, it does seem as if organisms that live faster, die faster.

This parallelism between metabolism and life span has an interesting consequence. Suppose we know the basal metabolic rate per unit mass of a squirrel to be about 1 liter of oxygen per kilogram per hour. We can multiply that rate by the number of time units (hours) in a life span to obtain the metabolism per unit of tissue mass during the life of the organism—the total liters of oxygen consumed or Calories produced per unit mass over the animal's entire course of life. For a maximum life span of about 7 years (61,368 hours), a long-lived squirrel would consume a bit more than 60,000 liters of oxygen per kilogram. A 500-kilogram horse has a basal metabolic intensity of about 0.2 liters of oxygen per kilogram per hour, one-fifth that of the squirrel. However, because a horse might live to 35 years (five times the life span of a squirrel), it might consume the same amount of oxygen per kilogram over its lifetime. Have we stumbled across a sort of universal law? Could it be that all animals have the same lifetime metabolism per unit mass?

The metabolic intensity (metabolism per unit time) summed over the maximum potential life span (time) yields the maximum potential lifetime metabolic intensity, what the Dutch biologist A. A. Goede has called the life-span energy potential, or LEP. Because the allometric constants for life span and metabolic intensity are of approximately equal value but opposite sign, they add to zero when life span and BMI are multiplied together (since when two quantities are multiplied, their exponents are added). As a result, LEP is independent of body mass (b is equal to 0); that is, on average, it is the *same* among organisms of different body mass.

Many measures of metabolic intensity have allometric slopes similar to that of basal metabolism. The time required to circulate the total blood volume has an allometric exponent of 0.21 in mammals, indicating that mammals of any body size circulate, on average, the same total volume of blood during their lifetimes. Similarly, the length of the period between heartbeats ($b = 0.25$), the time required to metabolize half the glucose in the blood (0.25), and the time required to synthesize a given amount of protein (0.25) all have allometric constants similar to that of life span. Thus, regardless of their body mass, all mammals have, on average, the same number of heartbeats, metabolize the same amount of glucose per unit mass, and synthesize the same amount of protein per unit mass during the course of their lives. Many other biological processes have similar scaling with body mass, all of which reinforce the general idea that the short life spans of small animals and the long life spans of large animals result in the same total lifetime metabolic activity.

This idea in turn raises the possibility that the organism can survive only a set amount of metabolic activity before the wear and tear on irreplaceable molecules, cells, and tissues has made the organism inviable. Thus, empirical observation seems to agree with the rate-of-living hypothesis—that metabolic activity itself is a cause of aging.

If rate of living alone determined aging, then the life-span energy potential should be approximately the same for all organisms. In one study, it was found that 108 nonpasserine species of bird had an average LEP of 2200 kilojoules (kJ, a measure of energy equal to about a quarter of a Calorie and about 20 liters of oxygen consumed) per gram of body mass. In fact, LEP in this sample was not perfectly uniform: about a third of the species had values either above about 3300 kJ or below 1100 kJ. Yet considering that the body masses of these species varied about 1000-fold between the largest and the smallest species, there is a certain degree of consistency here.

There is yet another way to find support for the rate-of-living hypothesis. The idea is to see whether the proposed relationship between metabolism and life span continues to hold among different types of organisms when body mass is held constant. Basal metabolic rate provides the most widely available index to rate of living, and this measurement varies widely among species. Among terrestrial vertebrates, the most conspicuous differences in BMR are between warm-blooded classes (birds and mammals) and cold-blooded classes (reptiles and amphibians). At a body mass of 1 kilogram, basal metabolic rates average 3.8 watts (W) for mammals (about the wattage of a flashlight; watts are directly proportional to oxygen consumed per unit time, 0.18 liters of oxygen per hour for each watt). At the same body mass, the BMR is 4.5 W for nonpasserine birds, 6.8 W for passerine (perching) birds, 2.3 W for marsupial mammals, and 0.33 W for reptiles. Thus, reptiles have metabolic rates only one-tenth those of mammals and birds. How do their life spans compare?

Perhaps it is not surprising, and it seems consistent with the rate-of-living hypothesis, that many amphibians and reptiles have long life spans. Recorded maximum life spans in captivity are 55 years for the giant salamander (*Megalobatrachus maculata*), 36 years for a toad (*Bufo*), and 30 years for the axolotl (*Ambystoma maculata*), 70 or more years for various turtles and tortoises, 20 years for the king snake (*Lampropeltis*) and water snake (*Natrix*), and 50 to 60 years for alligators. However, while these life spans are long, most are within the range for birds and mammals of similar size in spite of the 10-fold difference in rate of living. Thus, the comparison between warm-blooded and cold-blooded vertebrates does not support the rate-of-living hypothesis. However, because these groups differ so much in other physiological and ecological traits it is difficult to consider this comparison a definitive test.

Birds and mammals resemble each other physiologically in their high body temperatures and high rates of living. However, birds generally have even higher metabolic rates than mammals. We have seen that their BMRs are measured to be 4.5 W for nonpasserines or 6.8 W for passerines at 1-kilogram body mass compared to 3.8 W for mammals. The higher metabolic rates of birds go along with their somewhat (approximately 3°C) higher body temperatures. Thus, birds should have shorter life spans than mammals, but instead their maximum recorded life spans tend to be longer. We saw above that, for animals of 1-kilogram body mass, a bird's life span of 16 years surpasses a mammal's life span of 7.5 years in natural populations, and the difference is 28 years versus 12 years in captivity. The lifetime energy potential of birds is higher as well. Considering both the higher metabolism and the longer life spans of birds, their life-span energy potential (2200 kJ per gram) is, on average, almost four times that of non-primate mammals (640 kJ per gram). Thus, the comparison between birds and mammals also fails to support the rate-of-living hypothesis. This is not to say that the wear and tear of life does not cause aging. Rather, other factors must also influence the rate at which aging occurs. The search for clues to these factors often has started with investigators making further comparisons of aging among different types of organisms.

Flight and Aging

It has often been remarked that bats tend to live longer than mammals of similar body size that don't fly. The approximately 12-gram little brown bat *(Myotis lucifugis)* may live to more than 30 years, which is six times the value of 5 years predicted for mammals from the allometric relationship of life span to body mass, and places the bat well among the longest-lived birds, like the little storm petrel. Other species of bats may have similarly prolonged lives. Could flying somehow lead to longer life?

There are many possible reasons that aging could be delayed in bats, however, and the longevity of flying animals may be a fortuitous consequence of some other cause-effect relationship. We will nevertheless offer a speculation here. Flight is so demanding physiologically that a flying mammal or bird can-

not function properly unless its physiology is maintained at close to the optimal condition. Thus, flying animals experience strong selection for maintenance and repair mechanisms that not only maintain cells and tissues in excellent working order, but put off the manifestations of wear and tear. Just think about the higher quality of maintenance given to passenger aircraft than to buses, and how much longer the average airplane remains in use.

Still another approach has been tried in the attempt to identify factors that could explain why rates of aging vary so, and that is to look for statistical correlations between life span and various physiological or other attributes, under the assumption that factors showing the strongest correlation with life span are most likely to contribute directly to variation in the rate of aging. The task is, however, almost hopeless, for two reasons. First, life span is so poorly esti-

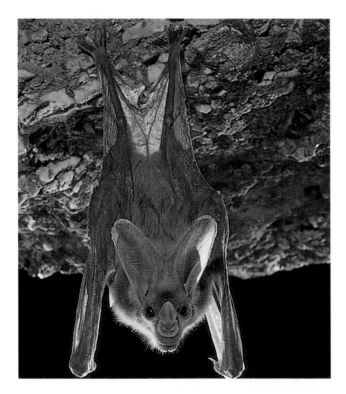

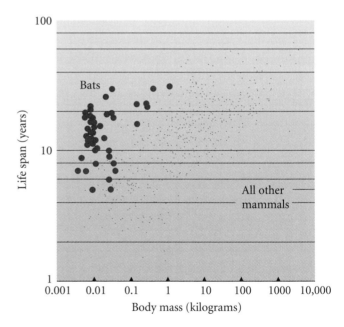

Most bats, such as the ghost bat *(Macroderma gigas)* of Northern Australia (left), enjoy relatively long life spans compared to nonflying mammals of similar size.

mated in most animals that uncertainties in measurement obscure the details of its correlation with other factors. Second, so many aspects of an animal's anatomy and physiology vary in concert that singling out one or a few of these as more "important" than the others makes little sense. Life span has been related to every imaginable aspect of anatomy and physiology, from spleen weight and cholesterol level to enzyme activities and sleep time. Furthermore, for all the relationships between life span and either physiological or anatomical measurements, there are counterexamples such as the differences between birds and mammals that cause us to doubt the generality of any mechanism of aging based on such a relationship.

Development and Life Span

The deterioration that our bodies experience with age can be measured as a rate of change in mortality rate or reproduction rate. Because aging can be characterized as a rate, such as the Gompertz parameter, it has a corresponding time duration, such as the maximum potential life span. It seems reasonable to ask, therefore, whether the duration of the adult life span is correlated with the duration of other life stages. The most obvious of these is development.

Many regard development as the antithesis of aging, but its beginning may also set in motion the physiological processes that ultimately lead to death. What happens during development may even determine the characteristic rates of these processes. When we broadly compare organisms of vastly different size, we find that the duration of development and length of life are related because both also depend on body size. As size increases, all of life's processes are slowed down and stretched out. Elephants are among the longest lived of mammals and have among the longest gestations; mice grow up and reproduce within a single season. For our size, we humans have

both long potential life spans and long development periods.

Development and aging may be related in fundamentally different ways. In the first scenario, there may be no direct causal connection between the two. Most cell types are formed by differentiation early in the embryo's development, long before aging begins. Moreover, the changes that come with aging in most species differ in essence from the changes taking place in the developing body. Nonetheless, the physiological "clocks" regulating development and aging could share some of the same "gears and ratchets." For example, they could use the same proteins to instruct genes to turn off or on in response to hormones.

In the second scenario, the adult body plan, which is clearly an outcome of development, influences aging in fundamental ways by determining which types of molecules and cells can be replaced. Those that are irreplaceable, like the proteins (crystalins) in our eye lenses and the neurons in our brains, are at risk for accumulating damage during aging. The ovary provides another striking example. Because the numbers of egg cells and hormone-producing follicles are fixed by birth, the onset of menopause, when the last of these cells disappear, is a direct outcome of cell proliferation during embryonic development.

A third possibility is that the construction of bodies that last a long time during aging requires a long phase of development. We realize intuitively that high-quality goods take longer to produce: a Mercedes-Benz spends more time on the assembly line than a less carefully engineered automobile. Perhaps the long times that most vertebrates take to develop, by comparison with flies or worms, make possible their long adult lives: their bodies have extra time to detect and correct errors in construction and to build in redundancy that provides extra safety factors.

Little is known about how aging is affected by such means of quality control, but one hint comes

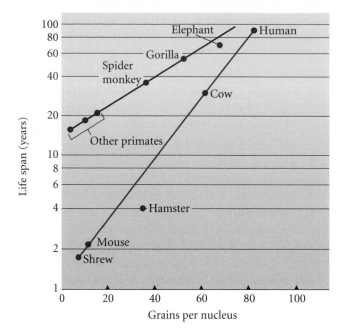

Longer-lived species seem more able to repair damaged DNA, suggest the results of an experiment that measured the number of silver grains exposed in an emulsion sensitive to the presence of radioactively labeled thymidine, a nucleotide base used in the repair of broken DNA. The position of primates above the line for most mammals tells us that other factors must also be at work to give them longer life.

emulsion sensitive to the radiation given off by the label, so the investigators can tell where DNA is being repaired by noting where the radioactively labeled thymidine is being incorporated into the DNA. The amount of repair is quantified by the number of silver grains exposed in the developed emulsion—that is, the number of grains per cell nucleus. Scientists have applied this ingenious test to a number of mammals and have found that longer-lived species are indeed more likely to repair damaged DNA. Here seems to be a way in which our bodies can overcome the unfortunate consequences of wear and tear.

Variation in Life Span within Species

As we search for clues to the causes of aging and its variation throughout the animal and plant kingdoms, it is only natural to consider variation in life span within populations in addition to differences between populations. Exploring such differences could point us toward "aging" genes inherited in some families and not in others or toward types of activities or environmental hazards that could contribute to wear and tear. One way to examine variation within a population is to compare life spans among easily distinguishable subsets of the population.

There is no question that certain styles of living predispose one to an early death. Nowhere is this more striking than in the contrast between queens and workers in a honey bee hive, described in Chapter 1. Even though both are female, and they have similar genetic makeups, a queen may live a decade or more whereas the life span of a worker is only on the order of a few months. This difference may be explained in part by wear and tear on the workers, who spend most of the day gathering nectar and pollen,

from studies on the rates of DNA repair. Scientists have actually been able to evaluate the capacity of cells to repair damage to their DNA. The procedure calls for laboratory cultures of fibroblasts (dermal skin cells) to be allowed to settle on glass slides, where they are exposed to ultraviolet radiation that will cause breaks in the DNA strands. The cultures are then provided, for a period of 12 hours, with the radioactively labeled nucleotide base thymidine, which the cell uses in the repair of the broken strands. The culture medium also contains hydroxyurea, a chemical that inhibits normal DNA replication but allows the broken DNA strands to be repaired. The slides are coated with a photographic

abrading and tearing their wings in the process, while the queen is confined to the hive where she is lovingly cared for by workers and does little more than produce eggs. Indeed, the deaths of honey bee workers might be programmed to coincide with the end of their "useful" life as provisioners to the hive. Because they do not contribute genetically to the progeny of the hive, these deaths could be viewed as physiological suicides that benefit the colony overall.

The males and females of some species have different life spans, and these tend to be species in which males play different roles in reproduction or other aspects of the life history. Our own point of view on this matter is strongly colored by the nearly universal observation in human populations that women outlive men, by as many as 5 to 10 years on average. In part, men tend to have earlier deaths because they lead more dangerous lives and are more likely to die from accidents or violence. It is also clear, however, that men succumb to all sorts of diseases at a much higher rate than do women. For example, while deaths from stomach cancer among women aged 55 to 64 years varied over a nearly 10-fold range of values among 26 developed countries of the world (from about 1 to 10 deaths per 10,000 women annually), the mortality rates for men in the same age range in each of these countries were about twice those of women. The large variation among countries strongly implies an environmental cause for the male bias in the impact of this disease, but the differences between the sexes suggest that men have greater exposure to, or are more vulnerable to, the factors that cause stomach cancer.

One simple, but undoubtedly incorrect, explanation for this sexual difference, popular since the early part of this century, is that males have only one X chromosome (one of the so-called sex chromosomes) and so any genetic defects on this chromosome are fully expressed. In females, most such genetic defects on one X chromosome would be masked by the expression of normal genes on the

A mating pair of *Heliconius* butterflies. Whereas in mammals, including humans, the female is XX and the male is XY, in butterflies the female (right) is the heterogametic sex (XY chromosome pair). *Heliconius* can live as adults for up to 6 months, which is long for insects.

other X-chromosome. The problem with this explanation is that only one of the two X chromosomes is actively expressed in any particular cell of a woman, who therefore finds herself in much the same genetic predicament as a man. Furthermore, in many animals—butterflies and birds, for example—females have a single X chromosome and males possess a pair, but males do not live longer, in contradiction to the X-chromosome hypothesis.

Alternatively, the reproductive activities of males and females probably have different physiological consequences, and these may in turn explain why one sex outlives the other. Different hormones regulate the reproductive cycle in the two sexes, and their different effects on aging may be pronounced. For example, high levels of the hormone testosterone are necessary to the development and maintenance of male sexual activity. But aggressive behavior is often increased by high testosterone, and when males fight

A copulating male and female of the brown antechinus (*Antechinus stuartii*), a common marsupial mammal of eastern Australian woodlands. Males usually die after a single breeding season from the physiological consequences of the stress of intense fighting.

than females because they don't have to endure the stresses of producing eggs or caring for offspring. However, where there is severe competition among males for opportunities to mate with females, it may be the males that bear the greatest stress, as happens in the marsupial mouse *Antechinus*. As male mice battle one another, their adrenal glands release high levels of the stress hormone corticosterone, which damages tissues and eventually leads to death. Thus, the marked differences between men and women in human life span may be explained by circumstances of environment or physiology peculiar to us.

Even in the case of the sexual difference in life span in our own species, it would seem that the difference is more closely related to the baseline mortality rate than to the rate of aging itself. Gompertz equations have been fit to mortality data for males and females in various European countries, which keep excellent population records, and the equations show that the baseline mortality rate A may be much higher in men than in women, and is highly variable among populations. On the other hand, the Gompertz parameter (G), which measures the rate of change in mortality with age, varies little between sexes or countries and may even be somewhat lower for men than for women. The higher mortality of men results from the greater susceptibility and exposure of men to such mortality factors as accidents and violence that may strike regardless of age.

In summary, studies comparing different species emphasize the near universality of aging. The seeming inevitability of aging in our bodies' somatic tissues contrasts conspicuously with the apparent absence of aging in the germ line. Aging may result from some general mechanical and biochemical "wearing out" of the body—parts may wear, as when overuse damages the ankles of ballet dancers or the hands of typists, or maintenance and repair mechanisms may fail, thereby intensifying the body's natural wearing out (the janitor ages along with the building he maintains). Nonetheless, although aging may be nearly universal, there is tremendous varia-

over females they may receive serious wounds. As levels of hormones, particularly estrogens, decrease following menopause, women become more likely to experience the loss of mineral from bones and other manifestations of aging.

Although human males suffer somewhat higher adult mortality, and have shorter life spans than human females, such gender differences appear to be more the exception than the rule in the rest of the animal kingdom. Whether male or female, laboratory mice and fruit flies have similar life spans; male hamsters tend to outlive females. In many natural populations of mammals and birds, males live longer

tion in rates of aging among animals with otherwise similar body size and physiology. That variation suggests that the rate of aging may be considerably modified and raises the question, Can aging be put off indefinitely in a large, complex organism, or are there bounds to this flexibility? If such bounds exist, are humans close to the limit, or is there reason to believe that life may be substantially prolonged in the future? We will be able to answer these questions only after we achieve a better understanding of the reasons for variability among species and the mechanisms by which it is achieved.

In this chapter we have seen that the rate of aging—or the rate of physiological deterioration—may be influenced by the activity of hormones and other physiological processes associated with reproduction. That is, in some respects aging may be an unavoidable consequence of reproduction, although for human females some aspects of aging accelerate *after* reproduction ceases. In the Darwinian sense, the whole purpose of the individual is to reproduce itself, and so it is both ironic that aging might be accelerated by reproduction and logical that this most demanding and important physiological activity might exacerbate aging. In the next chapter, we will look more closely at the relationship between aging and reproduction, as we consider animals and plants that time episodes of reproduction very differently during the course of their lives. In addition, because asexual organisms maintain a potentially immortal germ line without benefit of sexual reproduction, we shall look closely at the few groups of organisms that reproduce strictly by asexual means, to determine whether, in most organisms, there is a relationship between sex and the absence of aging in the germ line.

A spawning male sockeye salmon in a small stream in Alaska. Like most members of its species, this fish will die soon after its single episode of reproduction. The bright color and hooked jaw are special traits that develop at the time of breeding for the purpose of attracting mates and fighting with other males over the best spawning sites.

For us humans, it is hard to think about reproduction without thinking about sex. The two naturally go together and, as we shall see, are intimately involved in the concepts of aging. Certainly, we humans cannot reproduce without sexual intercourse. Indeed, throughout the animal and plant kingdoms sex is the rule. But there are exceptions. Some types of organisms do reproduce themselves without resorting to sexual union. So much do we take sexual reproduction for granted, however, that these exceptions provoke curiosity and seem to beg for explanation. In fact, it should be the other way around. Evolutionary biologists have wondered for decades why animals and plants bother with sex at all. Sex and aging are connected in the minds of many scientists because the secret of how the germ line manages to avoid aging may lie in sexual reproduction.

5

Aging
and
Reproduction

Sexual Reproduction

Each individual produced by a sexual union inherits two sets of nearly identical genetic material, one from each parent. These two sets of genes carry somewhat differing traits for appearance, physiology, and behavior; the differences in these genes are examples of the variation that occurs in every population. The most distinctive feature of sexual reproduction is the formation of gametes, or germ cells (eggs in the case of the female and sperm in the case of the male) by two special cell divisions, which together are called meiosis. Meiosis begins in each parent with a single cell containing complete copies of both the grandparents' sets of chromosomes—that is, a diploid set of chromosomes. During meiosis, that single cell replicates its DNA once, but divides twice, to produce four gametes or gamete precursors, each containing only a single (haploid) set of the genetic material. This set is neither maternal nor paternal, but is usually a more or less random combination of chromosomes from both parents. In addition, near the beginning of meiosis, the matching chromosomes inherited from each parent may exchange parts by a process called crossing over—which further mixes, or recombines, the genetic factors received by each gamete. Thus, the gamete contains a random half of the genes of its diploid progenitor; the genes included in each gamete produced by an individual are a mixture of the genetic material of the individual's mother and father.

During fertilization, an egg and a sperm unite to form a single cell, called the zygote, which contains sets of genes from both its mother and its father. Fertilization thus restores the diploid chromosome number. A zygote's particular set of genes—or genotype—is a random and unique mixture of the genetic material of its four grandparents. Following fertilization, the zygote undergoes a series of cell divisions to form the embryo. Unlike meiosis, however, these cell divisions are not sexual in nature and are called mitoses (singular, mitosis) to distinguish them from meioses. Each cell division results in the production of two "daughter" cells (in fact, the use of a gender label is inappropriate), each of which has a genetic makeup identical to that of its cell parent. Thus, the genes in all the cells within the individual produced by mitotic cell divisions are basically identical, whereas between the generations there is a mixing of the ancestral genotypes that produces new combinations of genetic factors.

Now the paradox of sex is this. As a result of the mixing of parental genotypes in the offspring, each son or daughter has only half the genetic material of its mother (and father). Thus, with each subsequent generation, half of the unique combination of genetic factors in the mother (and father) is lost. Now consider the alternative of asexual reproduction: the mother produces a diploid egg by mitosis and this egg begins to develop into an embryo without being fertilized. Each daughter produced by such asexual reproduction contains genetic material identical to that of the mother, not just half. Thus, from the standpoint of the evolutionary fitness of each female in the population, her genes would be passed on to future generations twice as frequently through asexual reproduction as through sexual reproduction. This penalty of half one's genes exacted by sexual reproduction is referred to as the *cost of meiosis*. Given this high cost, why should sexual reproduction be so common, indeed prevalent? The egg contains all the nutrients necessary to form the embryo; the sperm's only contribution is its genetic material. Why not dispense with males altogether, produce a diploid egg by mitosis or some modification of meiosis, and start the new generation with a full complement of the mother's genes?

The answer to these questions seems to be that enough advantages are gained by producing new combinations of genotypes in the offspring. Over

The fates of the maternal and paternal chromosome sets of the mother, in both mitosis and meiosis. During mitosis, the chromosomes of the parental cell are passed intact to the daughter cells. During meiosis, the maternal and paternal chromosomes pair, replicate, and then exchange pieces during the process called crossing over. Each gamete receives a random member of the original pair, including recombined segments from the opposite member of the pair that were exchanged during crossing over.

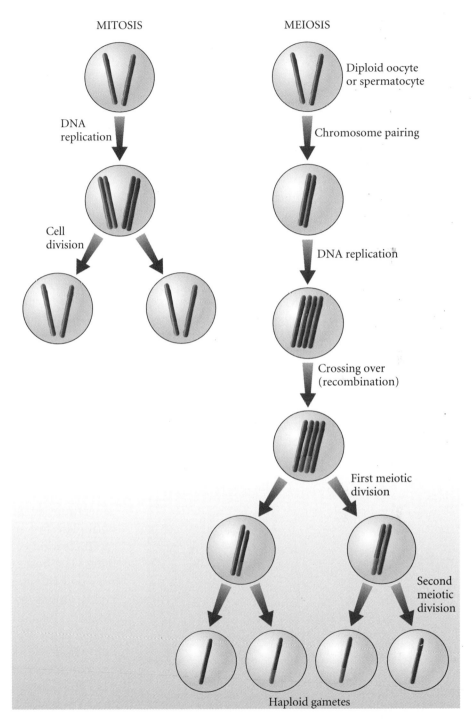

MITOSIS

DNA replication

Cell division

MEIOSIS

Diploid oocyte or spermatocyte

Chromosome pairing

DNA replication

Crossing over (recombination)

First meiotic division

Second meiotic division

Haploid gametes

time, the value of particular genetic material deteriorates, for two reasons. First, the DNA molecules that make up the genetic material and encode the instructions of life suffer various kinds of damage. They are injured by radiation, free radicals, chemical transformations, mechanical abuse, errors in replication during mitosis, and so on—what we can consider wear and tear. Any particular lineage of genes passed from mother cell to daughter cell during mitosis accumulates certain of these flaws, and those flaws eventually impair cell function. Second, because the environment continually changes and because it varies from place to place, genetic factors that are well suited to present conditions at one place may serve an organism's progeny less well in the future or in another locality.

Under pressure from deterioration and change, an organism's best strategy may be to mix its genetic factors with those of another individual. In that way,

This fossil of a horseshoe crab (*Europroops danae*) from the Late Carboniferous Period, 275 million years ago, reveals an animal very similar in form to its modern descendants.

the two parents produce new combinations of genotypes in their offspring, and at least some of these new combinations might by chance be superior to those of the parents. These superior genotypes would arise at random from the union of gametes that had received chromosomes lacking genetic mistakes that had accumulated in the germ lines of their parents. Possibly, these "superzygotes" might have new combinations of genes that would be particularly advantageous under new environmental conditions. Thus, sexual reproduction is thought to keep a lineage's head above the rising waters of mutational and environmental change.

Are these advantages of sex enough to offset the twofold disadvantage of meiosis? Certainly over the long run, scientists agree, sex helps to create the genetic novelty necessary for evolutionary change. Not everything changes, however. Horseshoe crabs and oysters today look much the same as the fossilized remains of their ancestors, which lived hundreds of millions of years ago. Paradoxically, they have not abandoned sex.

William D. Hamilton III, a zoologist at Oxford University, has suggested that the variety produced by sexual reproduction is crucially important to keep evolutionary pace with rapidly evolving parasitic and disease populations. These organisms are small compared to their hosts, and they may undergo many generations of prolific reproduction within a host's body. The fast turnover of generations leads to the rapid creation of new genotypes with superior attributes. The host can counter these pathogenic organisms only by generating a high degree of genetic variability among its offspring (by sexual reproduction, that is). Hopefully, a few of the offspring might receive a particular set of genetic factors that can provide resistance to new strains of pathogens. When one considers that the flies that infest crops, the bacteria that cause staph infections, and the protozoa that are responsible for malaria, along with many other pests and disease organisms, have evolved resistance to most of the common pesticides and antibiotics within a single human generation, the pressing need to protect one's lineage against this kind of "environmental" deterioration becomes evident.

Once we realize that sexual lineages are far better at avoiding genetic deterioration than are asexual lineages, one connection between sex and aging becomes obvious. The germ line periodically undergoes sexual reproduction and thereby "rejuvenates" itself genetically. The soma, in contrast, is produced from the zygote entirely by mitosis—that is, without sex—and is bound to accumulate genetic defects and thus deteriorate physiologically, or "age."

Of course, the germ line also undergoes asexual reproduction within the soma of the individual, and is liable to gather genetic defects. For example, as we have seen, human females produce their full complement of nearly 1 million oocytes before their birth. This proliferation of cells represents on the order of 20 cycles of mitotic cell division. After birth, the number of these potential egg-producing cells decreases rapidly until fewer than a quarter are left at age 20 and only a few tens of thousands remain by age 40. It is tempting to speculate that the lost oocytes are cells that have sustained some sort of genetic damage, and whose removal (death?) prevents the formation of defective gametes. Such genetic damage may also be the reason that thousands of times more oocytes are produced than will ever mature into gametes: it is a long time from conception to the peak child-producing period of 15 to 30 years of age, plenty of time for wear and tear to do harm to the genetic material of any given cell. However, the large increase of birth defects as menopause approaches is due to abnormal movements of chromosomes, rather than mutations.

An intriguing observation made by Austin Burt and Graham Bell bears out the view that sex keeps the germ line young. In mammals that delay the age of sexual maturity, the oocytes are exposed to agents of genetic damage for a longer time. Burt and Bell

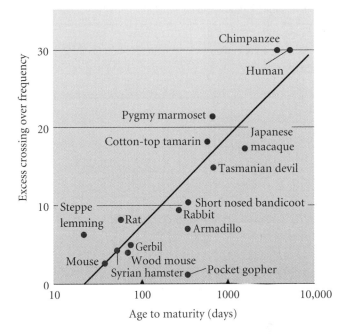

The frequency of crossing over during meiosis is higher in mammals that take longer to reach the age of maturity. The excess crossing over frequency is the number of crossing over events in excess of one for each chromosome, summed over all the chromosomes in the cell. This index takes into account the fact that a single crossing over event appears to be necessary for chromosomes to segregate properly during the first meiotic division.

have noted that the chromosomes in such mammals undergo a higher frequency of crossing over and recombination at meiosis, as if to compensate for the greater exposure to damage. This observation is consistent with the idea that sex acts to purge the germ line of mutations by forming new combinations of genes in offspring, some of which just by chance might include no mutations.

Genetic damage may be the primary reason that the germ line periodically undertakes sexual reproduction, but the soma suffers from other kinds of biochemical change and wear and tear as well. At least part of this may result from the stress of repro-

Aging and Reproduction

101

Reproduction is stressful for most animals. Here, two young male warthogs *(Phaeochoerus aethiopicus)*, relatives of the pigs that are widespread throughout Africa, engage in a physical contest of the sort that will eventually determine their social status and mating access to females.

duction itself, or else from physiological changes in the reproducing organism. Every activity entails risks, and reproduction is no exception. The potentially lethal consequences of complicated pregnancies and births are enough to drive the point home. If the long life of the soma were the only consideration, evolution would probably have dispensed with reproduction a long time ago as hazardous to health. Of course, it is indispensable for self-perpetuation and thus stays with us.

The clone of cells that makes up the soma of the organism proliferates and leaves descendants without the genetic advantages of sexual reproduction. DNA is extremely vulnerable to damage while it is actively being translated into cellular proteins, and also while it is being replicated during cell division (mitosis). Even when inactive, it may be harmed by ultraviolet light and other forms of intense radiation and by some of the highly reactive byproducts of cellular metabolism. Thus, the rate of damage to the soma ought to be proportional to the rates of cell prolifera-

tion and metabolic activity. All these "risk factors" are increased by sex and reproduction: the organism is taxed by the added activity involved in the search for mates, defense of territory, and courtship; by the production of new tissues in support of these activities; and by the increased energy requirements of producing eggs or seeds and sperm, supporting the growth of embryos in mammals, and feeding dependent offspring in mammals and most birds. The damage may be repaired as long as the body has well-functioning repair enzymes and a healthy immune system. But to the degree that the stress of reproduction reduces the effectiveness of repair and immune responses, aging will be accelerated all the more.

Given that reproduction should increase wear and tear on the soma, evolutionary biologists predict that the course of aging may be tied closely to the pattern and intensity of reproduction—that is, to the age at which reproduction begins, the number of offspring raised at different ages throughout the life span, and the termination of reproduction.

Age at Maturity

The number of descendants left by an organism is a yardstick of its Darwinian fitness. Thus, delaying reproduction is costly to fitness because potential offspring are not produced. Yet many organisms, including humans, put off their first attempts to breed until quite late. In general, the age at maturity is closely related to the maximum potential longevity and average life span of the species, so that species that forego early reproduction can generally count on reproducing at older ages. Still, when reproduction is delayed, the loss of offspring must presumably be balanced by some advantage gained by maturing sexually later in life. For the most part, such advantages are thought to come from growing large or from accumulating experience or knowledge before beginning to breed. However, these benefits are hard to pin down.

Populations of scrub jays in central Florida are thought to be limited by their food resources. There isn't enough suitable habitat to go around, and many individuals are unable to secure territories for breeding. A long-term study by Glen Woolfenden and John Fitzpatrick at the Archbold Biological Station has shown that young birds will often forego breeding at the age of 1 year, when they are physiologically capable of reproduction, and remain instead as nonbreeders in their parents' territory. The parents tolerate these young because, although they may consume valuable food resources, they also help to feed the parents' offspring, which, of course, are their younger brothers and sisters. In addition, some of the young birds benefit from staying at home instead of setting out on their own because they stand a good chance of inheriting the home territory should one of their parents die. About 30% of adults die each year from various causes, and so the young often don't have to wait long. And because they have the advantage of familiarity and prior ownership, unsettled birds from outside rarely can evict them.

In birds, the rather close relationship between life span and age at maturity may have a simple explanation: when adults have low mortality rates, space for new breeders opens up infrequently. When breeders are removed from their territories in experiments, their places are often quickly claimed by young birds that had been previously excluded from suitable breeding habitat. Individuals that normally would delay breeding can come into reproductive condition at an earlier age. No physiological inability to breed early appears to be somehow associated with a longer life. It is just that many birds have to postpone breeding when many older, socially domi-

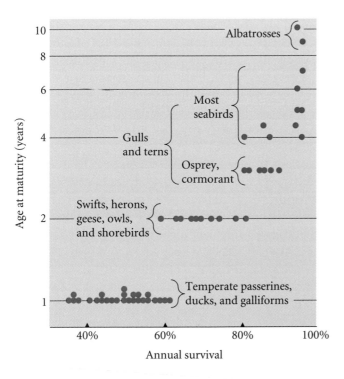

The higher the age at sexual maturity the greater the maximum potential life span, as shown here for birds. Although the graph plots the annual survival rate rather than the maximum potential life span, in birds the annual survival rate is highly predictive of maximum potential life span.

A Florida scrub jay and researcher Glen Woolfenden. The extreme tameness of these birds and their fondness for peanuts have made it relatively easy to mark them with leg bands and conduct population studies on birds of known age and relationship.

nant birds are surviving to old age. When young individuals are forced to postpone reproduction in order to wait for space to open up, one may hardly apply the idea that aging removes old individuals from the population to make way for the young, as August Weismann had suggested over a century ago. Indeed, breeders don't give up their territories or social positions until they are too old and decrepit to keep them, which is rarely observed. After all, because an individual is more closely related to its own children than it is to its grandchildren, there is no

reason evolutionarily speaking, why it should water down its own genetic contribution to future populations by withdrawing in favor of its offspring. Tolerating their presence so that they might inherit the family home is going far enough.

The males of many kinds of fish defend reproductive territories to which they attract females to lay their eggs. Because fish continue to grow in size throughout their lives, older males are also larger males and hence more successful territory holders than their younger counterparts. Thus, the males of such fish species delay reproduction until they achieve a suitable size for social dominance. In fact, abstaining from reproduction may allow these fish to allocate more resources to growth and hence reach breeding size sooner. Females mature and breed at a younger age and smaller size.

In the bluegill sunfish, a proportion of the males adopt an alternative, nonterritorial reproductive tactic: they attempt to breed at an early age (2 years) and small size by "stealing" copulations with females attracted to a larger male's territory. The larger males put great effort into caring for eggs and do not breed until they are at least 7 years of age. The cuckolding males are true reproductive parasites because fertilized eggs do not survive without the constant attention and protection of a territorial male. The decision to become a territorial male or a "sneaker male" is made early in development and may have a genetic basis. After sneaker males begin to reproduce, they grow slowly and die at high rates, often from attacks by larger, territorial males.

In the coho salmon, males assume different reproductive tactics depending on the size they attain during their first year. Larger juveniles tend to mature into reproductive "jacks" at about 18 months of age. At that time they return from the ocean to their natal streams, where they attempt to sneak copulations from females. Smaller juveniles remain at sea for an additional year, during which time they grow and mature into "hooknose" males, which upon returning to their natal streams fight one another to es-

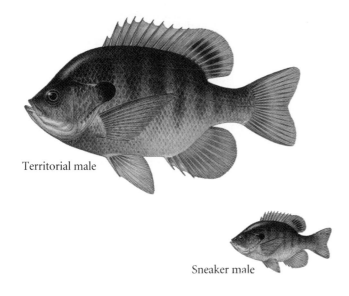
Territorial male

Sneaker male

In the bluegill sunfish, genetic factors determine whether males will develop into territory holders at a relatively advanced age, or into sneaker males at a younger age and smaller size.

tablish spawning territories. Unlike most coho, the jacks live to spawn for more than one season.

An interesting twist on the delayed breeding in male bluegill sunfish and coho salmon is seen in several species of territorial wrasses that inhabit coral reefs. These fish start out by being females early in life and then turn into males when they are large enough to defend territories. When males are removed from a patch of reef, the largest females begin to change into males and take up territories. In contrast, many plants and invertebrates are first male and then switch to being female as they become larger. The apparent rationale for the male-first pattern is that it is more costly to be a female than a male because a female must produce expensive eggs or seeds. Thus, when territorial defense or other form of social position is not an issue, an individual may exist as a male when small with little cost in growth rate, and become female when it (she? he?) is large and can produce a large brood of eggs or set of

seeds. Both the female-first and the male-first scenarios are referred to as sequential hermaphroditism, and these unusual arrangements carry the message that mating systems and gender are very flexible.

How does all this relate to aging? We do not suggest that any of you forego reproduction in the hope of living longer. To be sure, reproduction increases wear and tear on the individual, and studies with many animals have shown that when individuals can be prevented experimentally from breeding, they are liable to live longer. There is little evidence in human societies, however, that reproduction accelerates aging or shortens life span, as long as food supplies are adequate. Indeed, human females, who bear the brunt of the physiological stresses of reproduction, as a rule live longer than do males. As we saw in the previous chapter, there is little evidence to suggest that the sexes differ consistently in life span in most other groups of animals.

An animal's investment in reproduction one year may have striking consequences for its future reproduction and life expectancy. When female beetles and flies are prevented from mating, they often live longer. Linda Partridge of the University of Edinburgh found that both male and female fruit flies lived longer when kept apart. The presence of females seems particularly deadly to the male: males raised with females were dead before 40 days had passed, whereas almost 80% of those raised without females were still alive after 60 days. Their wings were especially likely to be damaged during courtship and mating and in fighting between males.

Similar effects are found in mammals. For example, female red deer (hinds) that rear calves to the point of weaning (milk hinds) may be left with insufficient fat reserves to survive the winter or else to breed the following year. Females that have either failed to conceive or lost a calf shortly after birth, called yelds, are more likely to survive and breed again. Moreover, the older the parent the more parental investment threatens future reproductive success. Whereas the annual mortality rates of milk hinds stay below 10% through 10 years of age, the death rate increases rapidly thereafter, to more than 40% by age 14.

Age and Fecundity

After an individual matures, its reproductive rate may increase for several years as the individual continues to grow and acquires experience or wisdom. The most straightforward cause of the rise in fecundity is the female parent's increasing body size. Generally, the larger the mother the more eggs she produces. Such effects are particularly pronounced in fish and plants, which grow more or less indefinitely throughout their lives. More difficult to explain is why the reproductive rate often increases with age in animals, such as birds, that reach adult size before breeding and do not grow further. Presumably an increase in skill or experience is an important factor here. For example, older pelicans come up with a fish after a dive more frequently than do younger birds. Many such skills and other adult attributes must be learned through experience, and are not specifically encoded in the genetic material.

The reasons why some behaviors are learned rather than instinctive are varied. It might be advantageous to learn the appropriate behavior when it needs to be adjusted to a varying environment, or when important information is too complex to be encoded genetically. Modern computers provide something of an analogy. The microprocessors in digital watches and small calculators are hard-wired to perform certain kinds of simple tasks, like multiplying numbers or advancing the time. Larger computers are fed additional instructions in the form of software, which may be tailored to the individual user's needs and changed over time. In this case, the computer does not actively learn as do animals, although some specialized computers are now being programmed to do just that.

Among mammals of similar body size, humans take an inordinately long time to mature and then to become proficient breeders. Deer, bears, porpoises, and others of similar size start to breed when they are only 1, 2, or 3 years old. Why do we humans put things off so long? Presumably the delay is connected with the immense amount we have to learn about our surroundings and social interactions before becoming fully "adult." Almost certainly we grow slowly and retain a juvenile appearance and demeanor because precocious breeding would distract us from our important learning tasks. Developing organisms also may learn more readily than, or differently from, fully matured adults.

Certain oceanic seabirds approach humans in the length of time they put off maturity. Fulmars and albatrosses, for example, may not begin to breed until they are 10 years old (and do not reach their peak of success as breeders for another 10 years). What are they doing all this time? Young wandering albatrosses spend most of their first few years wholly at sea, then make progressively more frequent appearances in the breeding colony during the breeding season, when they go through the motions of courtship as if practicing for the big day. What experience albatrosses need to acquire is unclear. On the one hand, their courtship and breeding rituals appear no more complex than those of species that begin to breed at 1 year. On the other hand, they may have to master considerable skills in oceanography, meteorology, and navigation in order to exploit efficiently the million or more square kilometers over which they range in search of food. Possibly, an albatross may require 10 years of accumulated experience before it can predict where the best feeding conditions are at any one time, or will be in the future.

It makes sense to delay reproduction only when the average life span is long. Thus, long life would seem to be a prerequisite for any species to develop an extensive capacity to learn and the ability to use large amounts of highly specific information. In ad-

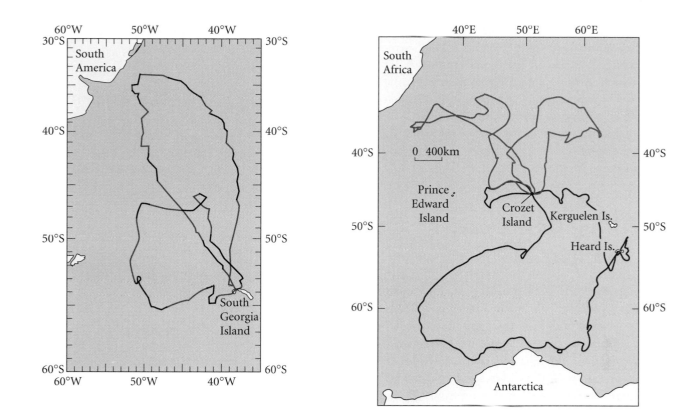

These tracks trace the foraging trips of wandering albatrosses during the incubation and chick-rearing periods from colonies on South Georgia Island (left) and Crozet Island (right). The positions of the birds were calculated from signals sent by radios fitted to each bird and received by satellites. The trips ranged up to 15,000 kilometers in length, and as much as 900 kilometers were covered in a single day. The two examples from South Georgia Island are consecutive trips taken by a single female between spells incubating her egg.

dition, once a species has developed such a capacity, its members may be able to prolong life by avoiding risks and finding food more readily, and so it is possible that learning, delayed reproduction, and long life are mutually promoting.

At the other end of the life span, reproduction tends to decline and may cease altogether, as in human women and the roundworm *Caenorhabdites elegans.* In many species, however, the data on reproductive decline in old age are quite mixed. Although mortality rates appear to increase with age in these organisms, reproductive rates often show no evidence of dropping. Perhaps the physiological degeneration of older individuals is balanced by their increasing body size, reproductive efficiency, or parental investment. Older parents may be willing to work harder because they can expect to have fewer offspring in the future. Hence they risk less when they take on the increased stresses of breeding.

In humans, female menopause may anticipate normal life expectancy, or the loss and aging of oocytes may simply make attempts to reproduce later in life of less value. Alternatively, menopause may have developed so that women could avoid the increasing chances of dying in childbirth later in life, which would jeopardize dependent offspring. Whether menopause is the result of physiological decline or a response to the loss of oocytes is difficult to determine; in evolution, a mechanism, such as loss of oocytes, does not always elucidate ultimate causation.

Breeding Only Once, or Semelparity

Many animals and plants undergo a single episode of breeding and then die, in the pattern called semelparity. Most commonly, this pattern is seen in so-called annual species that grow up and breed within a single season and exist through the winter (or dry season in the tropics) as eggs, seeds, pupae, or various other arrested stages of development. The advantage for the individual is that it need not pay the cost to survive as an adult through the unfavorable season and may put the resources it saves into reproduction during the current breeding period. In some such cases, aging is built into the life history so that the individual dies spontaneously when breeding is through. In others, the individual continues breeding until it is killed by cold or drought.

Many insects, including mayflies and many moths, do not feed as adults and therefore must die soon after they emerge as adults from the pupa. Indeed, some species behave in ways that speed their deaths, and some of these behaviors have been interpreted as leading to a programmed death evolved to benefit offspring. Silk moths do not feed as adults, and some species mate and lay their eggs over a period of a few days, then become highly active. Their activity depletes energy reserves, thereby speeding death, and wears the scales off the wings. These species have soft scales that rub off easily, and the

A tropical io moth of the genus *Automeris* from Costa Rica, flashing its "eye-spots" on the hind wings as a startle response to predators. This is one of the family of silk moths (Saturniidae) that do not feed after emerging as adults and therefore die soon after mating and laying their eggs.

adults soon lose their characteristic appearance. This transformation has been construed as an adaptation to make it more difficult for predators to learn how to recognize the adult moth as prey, and thus more difficult for predators to find the offspring when they emerge as adults. The best support for this idea comes from observing the very different life histories of some close relatives of these moths. The related moths are distasteful to predators and survive much longer after reproduction. Far from trying to disguise their appearance, they are strikingly colored or patterned to warn predators of their unpleasant taste. Their wing and body scales are much more durable, and they do not become hyperactive, as palatable species do, to promote scale wear.

Interesting cases of semelparity have been found in long-lived species as well. Some of these species may grow for years or even decades without maturing sexually and then enter into a single all-consuming reproductive episode that is soon followed by death. While uncommon, this reproductive pattern is widely scattered throughout the animal and plant kingdoms, and has been adopted by organisms as

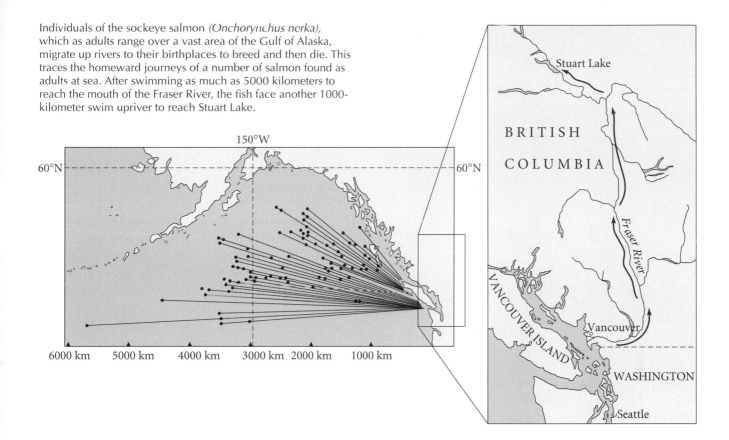

Individuals of the sockeye salmon *(Onchorynchus norka)*, which as adults range over a vast area of the Gulf of Alaska, migrate up rivers to their birthplaces to breed and then die. This traces the homeward journeys of a number of salmon found as adults at sea. After swimming as much as 5000 kilometers to reach the mouth of the Fraser River, the fish face another 1000-kilometer swim upriver to reach Stuart Lake.

varied as agaves, bamboos, periodical cicadas, and octopuses. Although many species of salmon have also evolved a semelparous life history, the trait is very rare in vertebrates as a whole, and is unknown in birds and placental mammals. Vertebrates may benefit so much from the accumulated experience of breeding that they may need to undergo several breeding episodes to realize their full reproductive potential. Semelparity also precludes parents from caring for and teaching their offspring, both activities that may contribute to the development of long-lived vertebrates.

To breed once and die is thought to be the choice of species that must pay a high cost to initiate reproduction. When an organism must totally reorganize its life plan or drastically reallocate resources or body tissues to make just a single egg or sperm, then it may be advantageous to throw everything into reproduction rather than setting aside reserves and carrying on afterward. The migration of salmon to their spawning grounds, the metamorphosis and emergence of periodical cicadas, and the growth of an immense flowering stalk by agave plants all represent immense commitments to breeding before even a single egg is laid or flower produced.

In the case of the Pacific salmon, females migrating upriver to spawning grounds arc so single-minded that they dispense with feeding altogether. Instead, they convert the energy and nutrients in their digestive tissues and muscles to eggs in order to produce as many as possible in the single breeding effort. Males also do not feed, and they exhaust

The Kaibab agave *(Agave kaibabensis)* flowering in the Grand Canyon of Arizona. The plant grows as a rosette of thick, fleshy leaves for up to 15 years, then sends up a huge flowering stalk, sets seed, and dies.

breeding, these plants send up an immense flowering stalk, built from nutrients taken from other parts of the plant. Thus the plant as a whole dies a programmed death, after perhaps as much as a century of growth, for the sake of a single, immense reproductive episode. Why have a few plants adopted this strategy, while most others have not? Agaves live side by side in North American deserts and shrublands with their close relatives, the yucca plant, yet yucca plants reproduce repeatedly year after year. Why the difference? It is true that yuccas produce a more modest flowering stalk, and thus the investment in a particular breeding episode is not so great as in agaves. Yuccas also have deeper root systems and may be able to take advantage of more perennial sources of water. For the shallow-rooted agave, it may be advantageous to wait for the one exceptionally good year and then give everything to the effort.

Bamboos do not seem to be so opportunistic, but rather an entire population flowers in remarkable synchrony at a precise age, and afterward the adult plants die off. Individual plants that originally came from the same population apparently flower in synchrony even after being separated from one another and transplanted to botanical gardens around the world. The reasons why bamboos flower together and then die are not entirely clear, but the strategy may be a way to reduce the number of seeds and young plants that fall victim to predators and disease. When breeding occurs regularly each year, seed eaters and pathogens proliferate and keep reproductive success low. By synchronizing reproduction at long intervals, bamboos can keep pest populations low during nonbreeding years and then overwhelm the capacities of the now scarce pests to attack seeds and seedlings during these explosive breeding episodes.

Semelparity almost certainly preceded synchrony in the bamboo. Imagine a population of yearly blooming bamboos in which a single plant adopted the semelparous strategy. The plant would leave fewer progeny by putting off breeding, and, more-

themselves defending spawning sites and enticing females to lay their eggs there. For the salmon, the alternative to semelparity would be to reduce the season's reproductive investment, maintain body condition, and return to the ocean to make the trip to the spawning grounds again. And this is precisely the tactic adopted by its close relations the steelhead trout and Atlantic salmon.

Semelparity in the agave may be similar to that of the Pacific salmon in the tremendous investment required to initiate reproduction. To prepare for

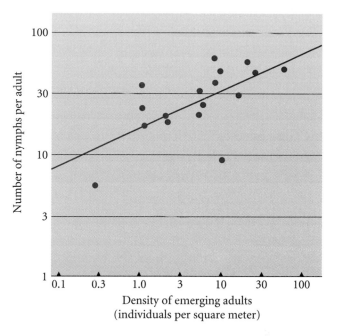

Left: An emergence of the 17-year cicada *(Magicicada)*. These adults will mate and lay eggs within a few weeks, and the developing nymphs have remained underground, feeding on root sap, for 17 years. Right: When Rick Karban, of the University of California at Davis, compared different areas within the same emerging brood of periodical cicadas, he found that the most successful breeders were in the areas of densest population. This "safety in numbers" may explain why the adults of the periodical species emerge from their underground homes in synchrony.

over, its progeny's chances of surviving would not have improved because it alone could not overwhelm pest populations. It would seem that semelparity can evolve only when the number of surviving offspring is actually increased by delaying reproduction to make a single, immense effort later in life. Having evolved semelparity, bamboo might further improve its chances of reproductive success by evolving synchronization.

Periodical cicadas provide a good example of this strategy. In the periodical species of cicada, the larvae—or nymphs, as they are called—live underground, where they feed on the roots of trees. After 7, 11, 13, or 17 years, depending on the species, individuals stop feeding, transform themselves into adults, and emerge synchronously over a large area to take part in a brief but intense episode of reproduction. The root sap on which the cicada nymphs feed is the fluid that rises from the roots of trees to the leaves. Because this sap has so few organic nutrients—carbohydrates and proteins—cicada nymphs grow very slowly. And because they are relatively safe in their underground homes, it is to their advantage to put off breeding until they are large and can produce many eggs. When they emerge above ground to breed, they can no longer feed on tree roots and are committed to reproduction and death. Once this life style has been settled upon, synchrony is strongly favored as a means of avoiding heavy losses to predators.

The only semelparous mammal is a marsupial, the mouse-sized *Antechinus*. In these species, reproducing males have greatly enlarged adrenal glands, which send elevated levels of corticosteroids into the bloodstream. These are symptoms of extreme stress, caused by the males battling one another for the opportunity to mate. Most male marsupial mice die at the end of their first breeding season from the ravages of too much stress, including the suppression of the immune system. It is noteworthy that females live longer and that males deprived of opportunities to breed may survive to an age of 2 or 3 years.

In the final analysis, the special relationship between breeding and death in semelparous organisms is unlikely to shed light on aging more generally. The immense commitment to a single breeding episode simply leaves the adult without the resources to survive. This strategy is adopted primarily for ecological reasons, and deaths do not appear to result from aging processes intrinsic to the physiology of the organism. Thus, we should probably regard semelparity in long-lived organisms as an evolutionary curiosity in that the causes of death are much more focused than in the other long-lived species.

How Do Asexual Clones Avoid Aging?

An article with the somewhat unsettling title "Aging without Sex" caught our attention recently. In it, the authors R. K. Butlin and H. I. Griffiths of the University of Leeds went on to describe a curious group of freshwater ostracods (crustaceans) that are known not to reproduce sexually, but that nonetheless have a fossil record going back several hundred million years. Such asexual reproduction presents us with an enigma concerning aging, but it also offers considerable insight into the process of aging and into the difficulty of limiting its effects.

We have discussed the role of sexual reproduction in maintaining the potential immortality of the germ line. Indeed, the sexual union is in part the ba-

sis of the distinction between soma and germ-line, along with the unique ability of germ-line cells to produce entire organisms as their offspring. When somatic cells divide, they produce other cells in a series of asexual divisions. The germ line, too, relies on asexual cell replication to produce a supply of eggs and sperm, but a sexual link is interposed in the chain of asexual cell replications at the time of fertilization. Perhaps the potential immortality of the germ line derives from the acts of meiosis and fertilization, which together allow the creation of new genetic combinations. Sexual reproduction clearly is an important way for the population to purge itself of mutations accumulated in the somatic phase of the germ line's existence and, more important, for a parent to produce at least some highly fit offspring.

The idea that sex serves to cleanse the germ line runs into serious trouble when confronted by the existence of species that reproduce without relying on any form of sex at all. Some kinds of salamander and various microscopic crustaceans of lakes and oceans have propagated for thousands or millions of generations without sex. These animals have apparently not accumulated the kind of genetic damage that one might think inevitable in a germ line not purged frequently by sexual recombination. How do these asexual populations manage, and can they shed any light on the mechanisms of aging? In particular, it would be interesting to know whether the soma also does not age in these species. Whether the soma ages or not, whatever conveys to the germ line its potential immortality cannot be sex.

Biologists have for many decades worked with clones of cells produced asexually in the laboratory. The clones are formed by mitotic cell divisions from one or a small number of cells removed from a particular tissue of the body. The observation that clones show a form of aging, the Hayflick limit, has strongly influenced thinking about aging in individuals, whose somas are, after all, merely giant, walking clones of cells originating from a single fertilized egg.

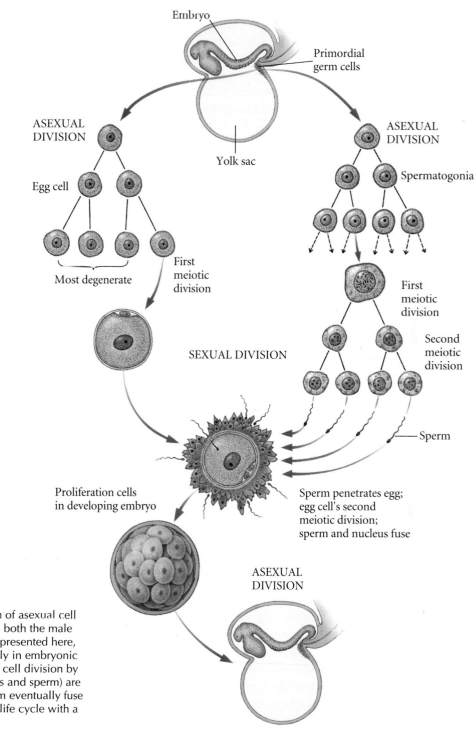

Embryo

Primordial
germ cells

Yolk sac

ASEXUAL
DIVISION

ASEXUAL
DIVISION

Egg cell

Spermatogonia

Most degenerate

First
meiotic
division

First
meiotic
division

SEXUAL DIVISION

Second
meiotic
division

Sperm

Proliferation cells
in developing embryo

Sperm penetrates egg;
egg cell's second
meiotic division;
sperm and nucleus fuse

ASEXUAL
DIVISION

A sexual link is interposed in the chain of asexual cell replications that form the germ line. In both the male and female of a typical mammal, as represented here, the germ lines, which are set aside early in embryonic development, undergo many cycles of cell division by mitosis before the sexual gametes (eggs and sperm) are formed by meiosis. The eggs and sperm eventually fuse to form the zygote and perpetuate the life cycle with a new generation.

Why shouldn't the aging of an individual organism resemble the aging of a laboratory cell culture?

Perhaps it is presumptuous of scientists to think that they can care for cells in a test tube as well as the body can care for its own cells. For example, even the most nutritious medium does not deliver the daily rhythm of hormones and nutrients experienced by all cells of the body. So it is not yet even fully agreed whether the aging observed in cell cultures is an intrinsic feature of asexual cell proliferation or an artifact of the problems we have maintaining cell cultures adequately in the laboratory. Furthermore, when cells in fibroblast cultures are prevented from changing into functioning cell types by the addition of various growth factors, cells may go on to proliferate for up to three times as many generations. This result seems to link aging in some way to the differentiation of cells into skin cells, in the case of fibroblast cultures, and agrees with the observation that cells in differentiated tissues and organs, such as the heart and nervous system, do not readily proliferate to replace damaged neighbors.

Plants and animals have many mechanisms of reproducing asexually. Many of these mechanisms create offspring with the same genotype as the parent, and variation among offspring is produced entirely by mutation. Because most mutations are deleterious, one would expect clonal lineages eventually to die out as the organisms became dysfunctional or failed to evolve rapidly in times of great change. Biologists frequently point to the fact that most asexual species are evolutionarily very young—only hundreds or thousands of generations, at most—and suggest that clonal lineages necessarily have abbreviated existences. Yet a few large, asexually reproducing groups, such as the tiny, aquatic bdelloid rotifers and chaetonotoid gastrotrichs, apparently have had long evolutionary histories going back millions of years. Some individual asexual species, which are within groups that normally reproduce sexually, evidently have also been around a long time.

The age of a lineage can be estimated from the amount of genetic difference between it and its nearest relative. Lineages that no longer interbreed diverge from each other as each accumulates different mutations. In European rock lizards of the genus *Lacerta,* many all-female, asexual species have been formed from the hybridization of two sexual species. These hybrid asexual species seen to be of recent origin, since genetically they differ very little from the parent species. The hybrid species are also nearly uniform genetically, suggesting that they are the descendants of a single offspring of the sexual union of a male and female of different species. In contrast, several hybrid, asexual lineages of the mole salamander *Ambystoma* have accumulated so many differences in their gene sequences that investigators have estimated their ages to be as great as 5 million years.

A common form of asexual reproduction in plants is the sprouting of new shoots from vegetative parts, such as roots, rhizomes, or modified stems and

Groups of these aspens (*Populus tremuloides*) have slightly different colors, defining the edges of clones of individuals. All the individuals in a clone are derived from the same ancestor by sprouting from the spreading underground roots.

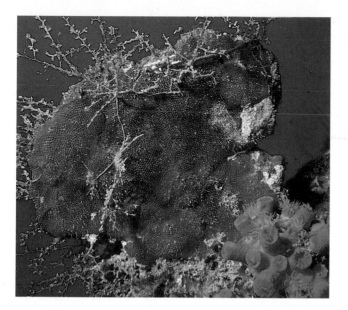

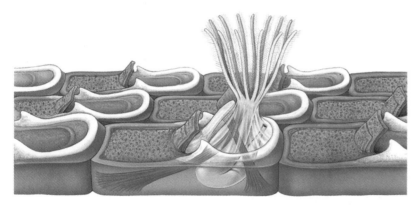

A red-tinted colony of the bryozoan *Steginoporella* (top left) has spread over rocks in the warm tropical waters of the Caribbean Sea. A close-up of a 4-millimeter hole drilled in a *Steginoporella* colony (top right) that has been filled in by the production and growth of new zooids. The capacity to repair this kind of damage decreases with the age of the zooids. A *Steginoporella* colony is made up of thousands of individual zooids, each formed by asexual reproduction (cloning) and arranged like the several drawn here. Inside the hard, boxlike exoskeleton is found the fleshy part of the animal, which can extend itself outside the exoskeleton to capture food or retract and disappear inside.

leaves. Many cultivated plants, such as bananas, are propagated exclusively by planting cuttings that take root or by grafting cuttings onto other root stocks. The ovule (egg) and embryo stages, which are part of the normal life cycle of most plants, are bypassed. Thus, the products of vegetative "reproduction" should together be considered a single organism. An aspen clone, in which new "trees" grow by sprouting from the spreading root system of the original "parent tree," makes up a single individual in the same way that the branches that "sprout" from a trunk belong to a single tree. Some clones of aspens, or of creosote bushes in the deserts of western North America, may be thousands of years old and contain thousands of aboveground stems. Although both these plant species produce seeds by sexual reproduction as well, it is clear that individual cell lines persist for very long periods in clones without showing signs of aging. Certainly the cell lines at the growing tips of giant sequoia and bristlecone pine trees may be several thousand years old and yet continue to produce viable seed.

Many animals that form colonies, such as corals, reproduce vegetatively when the colony is growing. Such animals are referred to as modular organisms because each individual in the colony repeats the body plan of the parent module from which it arose, just as each growing shoot of a plant is a modular part of the whole. The entire coral colony is an individual genetically, but each module has all the working parts necessary for independent existence. In fact, a module may be capable of producing eggs and sperm for sexual episodes of reproduction, which are required to form new colonies. Bryozoans are small marine invertebrates that form colonies on hard substrates, such as rocks or shells. Colonies of the bryozoan *Steginoporella* grow outward from a central point of establishment, so that individual zooids in the middle of the colony are older than those at the margin. With advancing age, zooids decline in their ability to feed and regenerate, become more fouled (overgrown) by other organisms, and accumulate ever larger amounts of stored metabolic waste products. To test the regenerative abilities of zooids, biologists Stephen Palumbi and Jeremy Jackson drilled 4-millimeter-diameter holes in the center and

Signs of Senescence in the Bryozoan *Steginoporella*

Character	Young Zooids	Old Zooids
Location in colony	Distal	Central
Fouling by other animals	Slight	Heavy
Color	Salmon red	Dark brown (from waste products in gut lining)
Percentage of damaged zooids	3.6	5.9
Brown bodies per zooid	1.5	6.3
Percentage of zooids feeding	90	75
Regeneration rate (mm^2/day)	0.27	0.06
Percentage of holes fully regenerated	60	9
Percentage of holes without regeneration	5	72
Percentage of zooids that overgrow adjacent colonies on contact	87	9

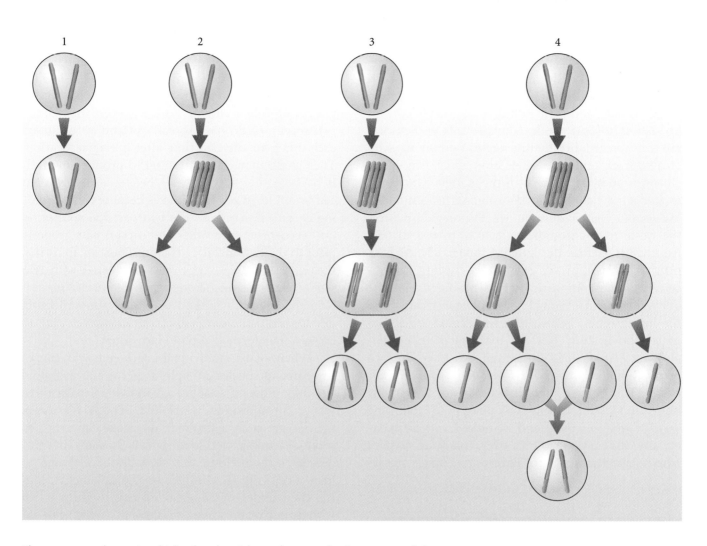

There are several ways in which a female might produce eggs having two sets of chromosomes rather than the usual one: (1) the direct transformation of diploid germ-line cells into egg cells, (2) the suppression of the second meiotic division, (3) the modification of meiosis to produce diploid cells, or (4) the fusion of two haploid cells produced by a normal meiosis.

peripheral parts of colonies and observed the spaces as they were filled in by new zooids. The older portions of colonies were regenerated at less than a quarter the rate that new portions were.

Many kinds of plants and animals reproduce asexually, but in doing so produce zygotes that pass through the normal stages of embryonic development. Individuals in such populations, although ge-netically identical or nearly identical to their parents and siblings, do have a distinctly individual existence and they age like any other soma does. The germ line, however, persists without any sexual mixing of the genetic material and without aging. Plants and animals that reproduce asexually, as opposed to vegetatively, form seeds and eggs by a variety of mechanisms. The trick, of course, is to make a seed or egg with the entire chromosome complement of the mother. Because an embryo can develop only inside an egg furnished with the proper nutrients, all such asexually reproducing plants and animals are by definition female, and their populations usually contain no males. In some species, diploid cells in the ovary are transformed directly into eggs; in others, eggs are created from a modified meiosis in which two sets of chromosomes are retained in the gamete. One route to achieving a double chromosome set is to suppress the second meiotic division, which normally reduces the number of chromosome sets from two to one. Another is to fuse the haploid nuclei formed by a normal meiosis; in this case each offspring may receive a unique complement of her mother's genes.

Many asexual animal species were created from the interbreeding of two distinct sexual species. Genetic studies show that the mole salamander *Ambystoma platineum* is an asexual hybrid of the two normal, diploid species *A. jeffersonianum* and *A. laterale.* The origin of these hybrids is not thoroughly understood, but probably took place in the following way. *A. jeffersonianum* and *A. laterale,* which today occupy the same habitats over much of eastern North America, may once have been a single species

The silvery mole salamander *Ambystoma platineum,* which is a triploid, asexually reproducing hybrid between two other species, *A. jeffersonianum* and *A. laterale.* The axolotl *(A. maculata)* can live at least 30 years.

that became separated into two groups, and prevented from interbreeding, by geographical barriers. One possibility is that sometime during the last ice age they were forced by ice sheets into isolated refuges of milder climate. As the glaciers melted, the two species could have spread out and encountered each other for the first time after a long separation. They could then have interbred to produce hybrids. It happens that such hybrids between species often cannot undergo normal meiosis because corresponding chromosomes from the two parental species do not "recognize" each other and cannot pair properly prior to the first meiotic division. Thus, an abnormal meiosis ensues, and eggs may be created with two sets of chromosomes rather than the usual one set. Nonetheless, such diploid eggs may spontaneously develop into an embryo and continue developing to create a fully formed, diploid individual.

When such an individual interbreeds with one of the parental species, a haploid sperm and a diploid egg may unite to produce an individual with three sets of chromosomes, a "triploid." The *A. platineum* hybrids are such a triploid, all-female "species." To produce triploid eggs, the egg cell (oocyte) first undergoes a premeiotic mitosis without cleavage to form a cell with six chromosome complements. This cell then undergoes normal meiosis to form a cell with three chromosome complements, which can develop into a normal embryo. The hybrids still depend on the parent species because the triploid egg will not begin to develop unless it has been penetrated by a sperm from a male *A. jeffersonianum.* The sperm does not, however, contribute to the genotype of the developing embryo.

It's not uncommon for asexual hybrid species to require some system of sexual interaction. One of the most unusual of such systems belongs to the small cyprinodontid fish *Poeciliopsis,* a molly that inhabits streams in the Caribbean drainage of Mexico. There are several hybrid, asexual, all-female clones in the genus *Poeciliopsis;* all were produced by the union of the normal diploid species *P. lucida* and one of sev-

Offspring of the molly *Poeciliopsis* inherit genes from both the mother and father, but females only pass on the chromosomes inherited from the mother. The male genes are discarded when eggs are formed for the next generation.

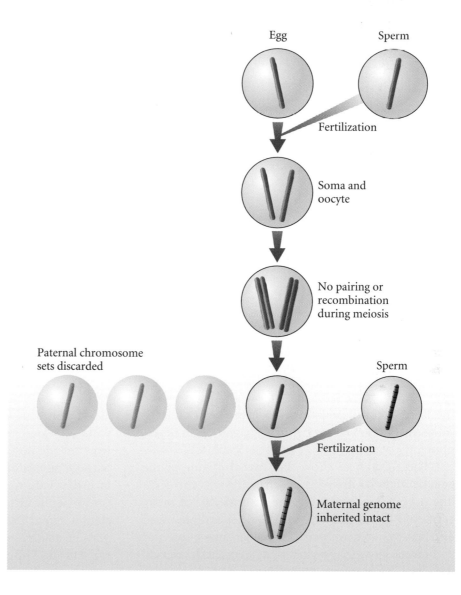

Egg   Sperm

Fertilization

Soma and oocyte

No pairing or recombination during meiosis

Paternal chromosome sets discarded

Sperm

Fertilization

Maternal genome inherited intact

eral other species of the same genus that also inhabit the streams of the Caribbean drainage. The fish in two of the clones seem at first glance to reproduce by normal sexual means: they are diploid, produce haploid eggs, and mate with *P. lucida* males. The catch is that although the male genes are expressed in the offspring, they are then discarded when eggs are formed for the next generation. Thus, gene complements from the mother and father never mix, and the maternal genes are transmitted from generation to generation as a pure clone. The third hybrid is a triploid, evidently formed in the same manner as the *Ambystoma* hybrids. And like the *Ambystoma* hybrids, this population of fish produce triploid eggs by a

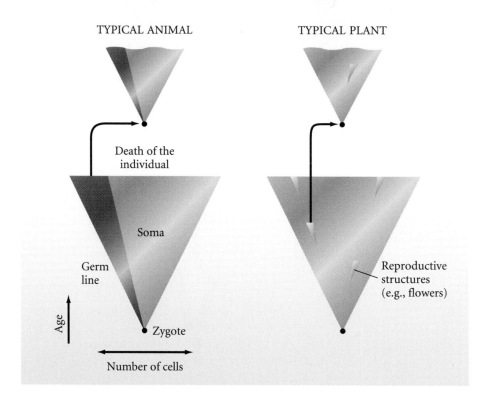

TYPICAL ANIMAL

TYPICAL PLANT

Death of the
individual

Soma

Germ
line

Age

Zygote

Number of cells

Reproductive
structures
(e.g., flowers)

A major difference between plants and
most groups of animals is the stage of
development at which the germ line is
set apart from the rest of the soma. The
germ line is set apart very late in plants
and in some primitive animals.

modified meiosis, and the eggs must be stimulated by sperm from *P. lucida* before they will begin development.

These examples show that sexual mixing of the genetic material itself is not what prevents the germ line from aging. Moreover, the extreme age of many vegetative clones tells us that the generations need not be separated by periods of egg formation and embryonic growth. Species that are strictly asexual may not have much evolutionary future, because they lack the ability of sexual species to produce a wide variety of new sexual combinations. Indeed, as we have seen, many of these clones have appeared only recently. Moreover, they do not exhibit signs of evolutionary persistence; in particular, few have themselves produced descendant species. Here again, however, the conspicuous exceptions of bdelloid rotifers and *Ambystoma* salamanders lead us to question whether sexual reproduction is necessary for the longevity of either species or germ lines.

If clones are able to survive for a long time, even without sexual reproduction, then it is hard to see why the tissues of the body couldn't also survive without aging, since they too are clones of a sort. In fact, there are many such clones in the body. These comprise the cells of the soma, which in most forms exhibit aging. They also include the germ line, which may be partitioned off from the rest of the soma early in development—as early as the first week of embryonic development in mammals—and which undergoes sexual reproduction each generation. Plants differ from most animals in that the soma and germ lines are not separated. Plants grow by means of cells proliferating at the tips of shoots and roots, in specialized tissue called meristem. These meristems produce branching buds that may develop into new shoots or leaves, or into the flowers that eventually produce gametes. Thus the cells that give rise to the flowers of an oak tree have shared most of their ancestry with the cells that produce new leaves or branches. To be sure, there is a germ line in plants, indeed perhaps thousands of them, each leading to a single flower. But these germ lines differ from the single germ line of an animal in that they are not separated at a stage early in development, and in fact, are formed just before reproduction.

There is another type of clone within each cell of the body that reproduces asexually, even between generations. Examples include the mitochondria of animals and plants and the chloroplasts of plants. Mitochondria and chloroplasts are two of the many distinct structures called cell organelles that perform the cell's vital functions: photosynthesis in the case of choroplasts and the oxidation of small organic molecules to retrieve energy in the case of mitochondria. Mitochondria and chloroplasts probably originated as symbiotic bacteria that invaded cell lines of higher organisms over a billion years ago. They contain DNA and have genes that encode a number of proteins essential to the functioning cell. The mitochondria and chloroplasts, whether in cells of the soma or the germ line, reproduce themselves by a simple mitosislike replication of the DNA and fission, such that each organelle produces two identical daughters. The mitochondrial and chloroplast DNA that is inherited between generations is strictly maternal, so there is no sexual mixing of genomes. Pollen grains and sperm cells contain mitochondria, as they must to metabolize sources of energy, but their mitochondria normally do not enter the egg or ovule upon fertilization. Thus, these cell organelles in all living creatures can trace their history back through maternal lineages over a billion years to a common ancestor. This is certainly potential immortality without sex!

There is evidence that some clones of mitochondria in the soma do age. In some parts of the brain, small sections of the mitochondrial DNA seem to be spontaneously deleted, and the frequency of these deletions is multiplied manyfold with age. Of course, these defective clones are shed with the soma, and so the defects do not perpetuate themselves through the germ line. Such defects presumably do not arise in the germ line or else they are in some way elimi-

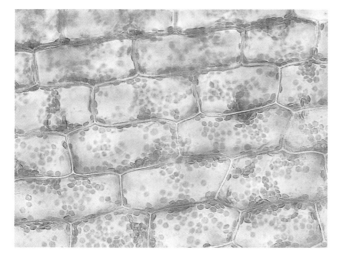

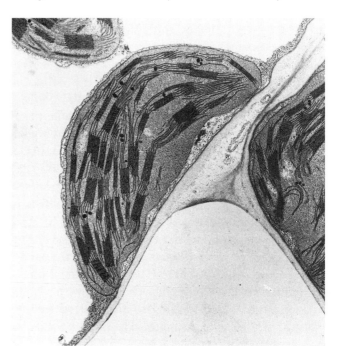

Above: Chloroplasts in the cells of the aquatic plant *Elodea*. These organelles contain DNA and reproduce within cell lineages by asexual fission. Right: An electron micrograph of the chloroplast in a leaf cell of a corn plant shows the complex structure of the organelle; the membrane layers contain the molecules responsible for photosynthesis.

nated, perhaps when defective cells or organelles die and are replaced by others lacking the defects. Without this capacity for regeneration, dead cells could not be replaced and the clone would dwindle to extinction.

Lineage Selection and Potential Immortality

The germ line persists in asexually reproducing species and cell organelles far beyond the life span of the soma. Its persistence tells us that sexual reproduction per se is not critical to achieving immortality, but rather that something connected with the production of new generations of individuals is necessary.

For clones to maintain high fitness, they must somehow save themselves from the damage wreaked by mutations. An individual organelle, cell, or organism would seem to have three possible ways of protecting itself: it could avoid mutation in its DNA altogether, produce back mutations that restore the DNA to normal, or produce new mutations that somehow cancel out the old bad ones. Because forward and back mutations at a particular point in the DNA molecule are equally rare, the probability that a mutation causing a dysfunctional gene will occur *somewhere* in the DNA molecule is far greater than the probability that a back mutation will occur at that same position and restore the gene to normal. Similarly, it is also unlikely that a new mutation at a different position will counteract the bad effects of the first mutation: the probability that a mutation will be beneficial is low to begin with, and the probability is even lower that a mutation will be the particular one needed to counteract an earlier mutation.

This line of reasoning leaves a clone with a single way of avoiding genetic deterioration: selective elimination of defective lineages. The susceptibility of DNA to mutation appears to be an unavoidable weakness inherent to the molecule and its mechanisms of replication. Errors and damage seem inevitable. Perhaps these can be managed by preventative or repair mechanisms at some cost, but they can never be completely eliminated. Thus, the absence of mutations from the DNA of a clonal lineage can never be ensured other than as a statistical probability. Mutations can happen at any time, but just by chance some lines will have avoided them during a finite period.

A simple model shows how the play of chance can maintain a healthy clone. Suppose that the cells of a clone have a 20% chance of suffering a lethal mutation between the time they are formed by mitosis as daughter cells and the time they themselves undergo mitosis. If these genetic defects were the only cause of death, the population would increase by a factor of 1.6 per generation (2 daughters per cell minus 0.4 deaths, on average), and the lethal mutations would purge themselves from the population. Even sublethal mutations, those that reduce the chance of survival (but not to 0) or prolong the length of the cell generation, could not increase in frequency in the population because the afflicted lineages would not keep up in number with the unafflicted lineages. Thus, clones of cells may be maintained relatively free of genetic defects, because defective cell lineages cannot produce progeny as rapidly as those that, by chance, have escaped mutation.

This model can explain the absence of aging in a clone as a whole even though individual lineages may accumulate defects and fall by the wayside, that is to say, age. Could the germ line during its sojourn within the soma be such a case? The human female begins life with about a million oocytes, whose steady decline in number from birth through adulthood eventually leads to menopause. Less than 1 percent of the original eggs mature, while the rest are lost, possibly due to genetic damage of some type—that is, to selective elimination. So far, maternal aging

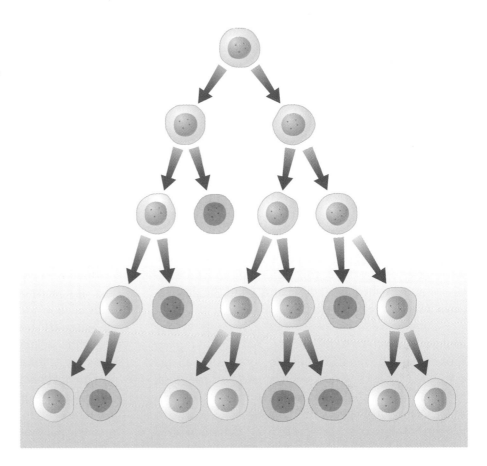

Lineage selection in a clone of cells. Individual cells that are damaged fail to reproduce or die, and they are replaced by the progeny of healthy cells. In this way, the clone as a whole avoids dying out from accumulated mutations or other damage.

is best proved to produce imbalanced numbers of chromosomes in eggs rather than DNA mutations. Witness the fact that as a woman ages from 20 to 50 years, her chances of giving birth to a child with Down syndrome or another chromosonal imbalance increase a hundredfold. It is intriguing that aging men are not more likely to have offspring with chromosome imbalances. Cells with such imbalances seem to be selected against and removed as sperm are produced in adult men.

The strategy, then, is to produce many more oocytes than are needed and then to winnow the bad ones. The oocyte, though, is not the only stage of development at which genetic defects are weeded from clonal populations. Selection also may work during and after fertilization, when the complete genotype of the zygote is determined. At these later stages clones are kept genetically uncontaminated in several ways: through the rejection of defective male gametes, the abortion of flawed embryos, and the death of imperfect larvae. For example, sperm and pollen grains must actively compete to fertilize eggs and ovules. This competition usually includes a long journey—as when a human sperm swims through the uterus and fallopian tube of the female reproductive tract or a pollen grain grows a long tube through the flower's style to the ovary containing the ovules. Winning this competition requires speed, which cannot be achieved without well-functioning genes. In this case, the female's reproductive system sets up a competition so that only genetically normal gametes can fertilize her eggs.

Even in sexually reproducing organisms, lineage selection must be an important way of preventing genetic defects that might cause aging. This is so because each tissue is essentially a clone of cells in which newly formed cells may replace those that die. For selective elimination to work within a clone, daughter cells must be produced at a rate that is high compared to the probability of serious genetic defect. So long as that is true, the clone may remain relatively unblemished as a whole and avoid the deterioration that comes with aging.

Lineage selection can stave off aging only so long as new cells are constantly being produced to replace those that suffer genetic defects. Otherwise, all the cells in a system would accumulate damage until eventually they could no longer function properly. This is where the soma runs into trouble. Most organisms grow to a particular size and then stop growing. To be sure, cells continue to proliferate and die in many tissues, particularly in the inner lining of the intestine and in the bone marrow where red blood cells are produced, but the rate of cell proliferation slows with age in soma tissues and nearly ceases in the brain and heart soon after birth. Some fully matured and functional cells, such as neurons and the muscle cells of the heart, are incapable of cell division. Indeed, further replication is incompatible with the functions of many types of cells. Thus, when the accumulation of genetic defects, or other kinds of damage, in somatic cell lineages is the underlying cause of aging, and when damaged cells are not replaced by continuous cell replication, then aging and eventually somatic death become inevitable.

The germ line is only a small portion of the body, and the individual can afford to produce thousands or millions of oocytes or spermatocytes that will die before they are ever used, because so few are needed. This strategy is simply not practical for other parts of the body, because most cells in other tissues must function and those that are slightly impaired cannot be discarded and replaced. The brain, particularly in mammals, has very little in the way of neuron proliferation and replacement once fully formed, because each cell has highly specific connections with others, often over long distances. Cells that die generally are not replaced, so the number of cells in the brain decreases with age, to the point that memory, concentration, and reasoning are impaired, along with more primitive brain functions such as hormone control. Furthermore, it is expensive to continually replace cells and molecules within cells, since the body must devote energy, nutrients, and cell machinery to the process. These costs of potential longevity must be balanced by the benefits of longer life or paying those costs will not make economic sense for the organism.

In conclusion, the potential immortality of the germ line does not seem to be tied up with sexual reproduction after all. Rather, it appears to be achieved by cells proliferating rapidly enough to replace those that have by chance deteriorated genetically. The soma itself cannot employ this strategy to any great extent because it either cannot afford or cannot manage the degree of cell turnover needed to continually rejuvenate the clone.

This model of potential immortality shows how asexual clones can avoid clonal senescence. Plants need not age if, as some meristems die out, they are replaced through the new growth of others, or if enough undamaged cells proliferate within an individual meristem. Organisms such as sea anemones, jellyfish, and flatworms, in which gametes are formed from somatic cells (the germ line does not have a separate existence), need not age because the simply organized soma experiences considerable cell turnover. The cells that eventually produce eggs or sperm are selected from among many available cell lineages within the soma. Then there are the myriad single-celled organisms—the bacteria, protozoa, and yeast, for example—that can repeatedly divide to produce a million genetically identical individuals in less than a day. Lineage selection also explains why clones of these single-celled organisms have little difficulty in maintaining themselves—no stagnant somas are involved. To be sure, cells may accumulate damage (that is, they may age), but these fail to propagate themselves.

The idea that the maintenance of clonal purity imposes a cost means that organisms, not just germ lines, might delay aging indefinitely if they are able or "willing" (in an evolutionary sense) to pay the price. This price may come in the form of higher mortality earlier in life or a lower reproductive rate. That is, an organism may have to compromise between reproductive success in early life and at later ages. How these conflicting costs and benefits have been resolved within different species is the central issue in explaining the evolution of diverse patterns of senescence, as we shall see in the next two chapters.

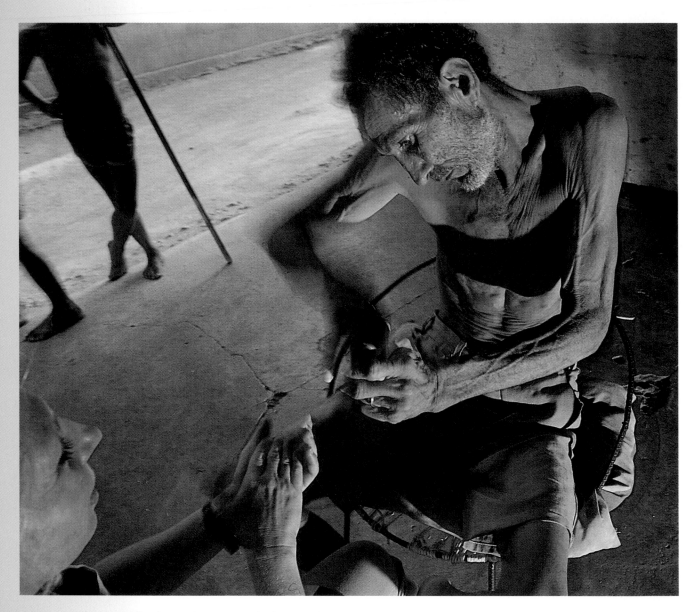

A Venezuelan man with advanced Huntington's disease. This genetically determined affliction, which often causes the limbs to shake violently, is an extreme example of the action of genetic factors whose effects do not become apparent until adulthood.

How can a feature of life like aging that is so debilitating be so pervasive? To answer this question, we must move beyond the "how theories" discussed in the last four chapters, to "why theories" that seek to provide evolutionary explanations of why aging exists. The "how" perspective addresses the physiological and biochemical causes of the deterioration that we experience with aging, often in the hope of forestalling it. "How" theories look at the activities of free radicals, at wear and tear on the blood vessels, at the mutagens that cause cancer. The "why" perspective sees aging as an expression of our genetic makeup, and it sees variations in how species age as the result of the genetic differences that have evolved between them. These perspectives are, of course, entirely compatible, and the contemplation of each has enlightened the other. Like every aspect of our body's structure and function, the chance of a heart attack, the dementia of Alzheimer disease, and the spread of cancer are influenced by our genes. But if aging is caused by bad

6

Genes
and
Aging

genes, why haven't these genes been eliminated by natural selection, along with the threat they pose to survival and reproductive success? Answering this question has posed a major challenge to evolutionary biologists.

Genetics and Evolution

Most of us think of evolution as changes in animal or plant lineages over long periods of time—that is, we view evolution from a paleontological perspective. Indeed, the transitions between fish, amphibian, reptile, mammal-like reptile, mammal, and finally mankind embody a lot of evolution! Our ancestral lineage's slow and fitful course is easily perceived in the long geological history of the fossil record, which provides us a sort of diary of our journey along the way. When we view the history of life up close, however, we enter a new and much narrower time perspective: we can perceive evolution as small changes in the genetic makeup of populations. Although much of the germ line has survived its immense journey intact—we have most of the same genes as frogs, for example—the divergence of humans from their long-extinct amphibian ancestors represents the accumulation of many small modifications of the genetic material. Biologists refer to the study of such small incremental changes as microevolution, or population genetics. Evolutionary theories of aging, which address the "why" perspective, are microevolutionary theories firmly rooted in the principles of population genetics.

Each genetic factor, or gene, is represented by a small section of one of the DNA molecules that make up the individual's genome. Typically, each gene comprises several thousand of the millions of chemical subunits known as nucleotides, or bases, in our DNA. In humans, the haploid genome of the egg or sperm contains almost 3 billion of these subunits, making DNA molecules that total nearly a meter in length and contain perhaps 100,000 genes. Of course,

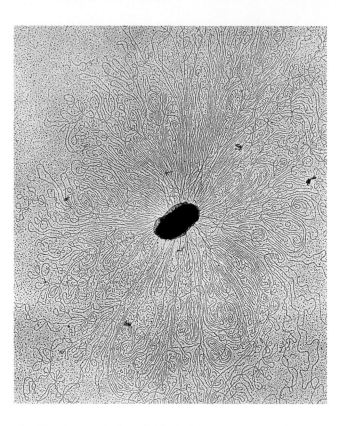

The DNA from a single individual of the gut bacterium *Escherichia coli,* which has been lysed to allow the contents of the cell to spread out on a surface.

the DNA must be twisted and folded very compactly to fit into the cell's nucleus. The particular sequence of nucleotides in a gene may vary slightly from individual to individual because of the accumulation of changes, which we call mutations. These different versions of the same gene are known as alleles. Thus, the gene that controls eye color in humans has one form in those of us with brown eyes and a different form in those of us with blue eyes.

Evolutionary biologists are interested in the frequency with which each allele of a particular gene appears within a population. That frequency is simply the proportion of the copies of the gene that are of that allele. What proportion of the genes in a population is the allele for blue eyes and what proportion the allele for brown eyes, for example? Because each individual has two copies of each gene, one inherited from the mother and one from the father, the total number of copies of a gene is twice the number of individuals in a population. A person may have two copies of a particular allele, in which case that person is said to be homozygous for that gene, or a person may have individual copies of two different alleles, in which case he or she is heterozygous.

The study of population genetics and evolution seeks to understand changes in the frequencies of alleles from generation to generation. Do more people in this generation have the genes for Alzheimer disease or hyperlipidemia than their parents did? Many processes can alter the frequencies of alleles, among them mutation, natural selection, and the unpredictable nature of birth and death in populations. Biologists would like to understand the evolution of aging by understanding the circumstances under which a genetic factor that promotes aging can increase in frequency within a population.

A close look at the structure of the DNA molecule shows that each strand of its double helix comprises a chain of nucleotide bases, of which there are four chemically distinct types—adenine, cytosine, guanine, and thymine. The bases are attached in linear fashion along a backbone of sugars, which are themselves joined together by phosphate bonds. The single, complete link of the DNA chain, consisting of a base, a sugar molecule, and a phosphate group, is called a nucleotide. The nitrogen bases may occupy any position in the DNA sequence. The opposing bases on each of the two strands of the double helix are always paired as adenine-thymine and cytosine-guanine. A weak attraction between the hydrogen atoms of opposing bases keeps the two strands of the helix zipped up. Because of the complementarity between the strands, each strand can act as a template for fabricating a new strand during DNA replication.

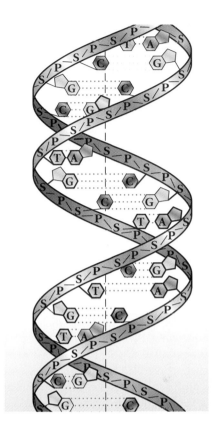

The DNA molecule consists of a backbone composed of units of the sugar deoxyribose (S) joined together by phosphate groups (P) to which the four types of nucleotide—the purines adenine (A) and guanine (G) and the pyrimidines thymine (T) and cytosine (C)—are attached, one to each sugar. The two complementary strands of DNA are wound in a double helix held together by hydrogen bonds (dotted lines) between the bases. Each opposing base pair in this structure consists of one purine (A or G) and one pyrimidine (C or T).

The order of the bases in a DNA molecule determines the order of the amino acids in the proteins produced from the molecule; thus, DNA is the ultimate blueprint for building our bodies and maintaining their good functioning. Each amino acid is encoded by a set of three nucleotides called a codon. Although some amino acids may be encoded by any

Evolution in the Peppered Moth

One of the most striking examples of a change in allele frequency in response to natural selection was observed in the peppered moth (*Biston betularia*) in England. The peppered moth is a species of medium size that by night flies in search of mates or suitable plants on which to lay its eggs and by day rests on the bark of trees. Its usual coloration is a salt-and-pepper mottling that closely matches the background upon which it rests. Thus, it is difficult for predators, such as birds, to spot the moths, and they often escape predation because of their cryptic coloration. During the last half of the nineteenth century, moth collectors noticed occasional moths of this species that were uniformly sooty black in color. These moths had become melanistic—the black pigment in their scales had increased dramatically. By crossbreeding black and mottled moths, investigators were able to show that this melanistic appearance was controlled by a dominant allele of a single gene. Thus, moths that inherited only one melanistic allele (called *carbonaria*) still expressed the dark coloration.

During the first half of the twentieth century, the frequency of *carbonaria* alleles increased dramatically, to nearly 100% in some places, particularly in areas of heavy industrial pollution. Experiments conducted during the 1950s by a physician and amateur butterfly collector, H. B. D. Kettlewell, demonstrated that melanistic moths survived longer than the typical forms where soot pollution had darkened the trunks of trees. For example, in a wood near Birmingham, in the industrial heartland of England, melanistic individuals had almost twice the survival rate of mottled individuals. Further observations showed the obvious. On polluted tree trunks, the light-colored typical moths stuck out like beacons and were readily discovered by birds. In unpolluted areas away from industry, the opposite was true.

Kettlewell's study was one of the first to demonstrate that the action of natural selection could result in a change in allele frequency in a natural population. One of the most gratifying aspects of the peppered-moth story is that, with the advent of smoke control programs and the return

Typical and melanistic forms of the peppered moth (*Biston betularia*) resting on a lichen-covered tree trunk in an unpolluted countryside in England. On this background, the melanistic form stands out; its frequency in the population is kept low by predation. The typical form (just below the right wing of the melanistic individual) is well camouflaged.

of forests to a cleaner state, the frequencies of melanistic moths have also decreased—in the region around Kirby, from more than 90% to about 30% in a period of 30 years. This rapid change in allele frequency is consistent with the survival disadvantage of about 12% experienced by the melanistic form.

one of several DNA triplets, no one DNA triplet encodes more than one amino acid. Hence the genetic code has redundancy, but not ambiguity. For example, the amino acid phenylalanine is specified by the codons AAA and AAT; proline is specified by the four triplets that begin with TT, thus TTA, TTT, TTC, or TTG. Four letters taken three at a time provides 64 different combinations, but, because only 20 amino acids are incorporated into proteins, there is bound to be some redundancy in the genetic code. A consequence of this redundancy is that some mutations, particularly those causing a change in the third nucleotide of a codon, may not cause a change in the protein that is produced by a gene. Thus, such mutations do not affect an organism's structure or functioning and are neither helpful nor harmful.

Not all nucleotide sequences encode proteins used in cell structure and functioning. Many sequences specify promotor or enhancer sites where various small molecules bind to the DNA and initiate or otherwise regulate protein synthesis. In addition, much of our DNA is unused; it is neither transcribed to produce proteins nor to regulate gene expression. Apparently, some of this "silent" DNA represents junked genes from earlier times in our lineage. No longer used, and therefore no longer exposed to natural selection, many of these junk genes have by now mutated beyond recognition.

DNA can be altered in a number of ways. Ionizing radiation may create breaks in the nucleotide chain, and free radicals or other substances may react with nucleotides and alter their chemical composition. DNA that has been so damaged no longer functions as well. This type of damage usually is not inherited because breaks and altered nucleotides can be repaired during the cell divisions that take place before the formation of eggs and sperm. And even if a defective gamete should form, it rarely succeeds in producing a viable zygote. Thus these changes primarily affect somatic tissue and, as such, may contribute to aging by inhibiting the formation of essential proteins.

A study of the fruit fly *Drosophila melanogaster*, by J. E. Fleming and his colleagues at the Linus Pauling Institute of Science and Medicine in California, has provided some indications that just such a decline in protein production may take place as we age. Three groups of male flies, aged 10, 28, and 44 days, were provided a supplement in their diet of the amino acid methionine, which was labeled with the radioactive isotope sulfur-35. Any proteins produced at these three ages would thus be labeled, whereas protein produced earlier in life would not. In this way, the methionine labeling allowed Fleming to examine how protein production changes at specific ages.

After the flies had fed on the radioactive diet for a brief period, they were ground up and their proteins were extracted. The different kinds of proteins were placed on a gel and subjected to two-way electrophoresis, a technique that separates proteins according to their size, electrical charge, and acidity. To make the proteins visible, the gel is coated with a photographic emulsion that is sensitive to the radioactivity in the methionine. The radioactivity exposes the emulsion, which is developed like any photographic film to reveal the locations of the proteins in the gel.

The procedure uncovered hundreds of different proteins from the flies, each recognized by its position in the gel. Fleming and his colleagues found that 28-day-old flies had 7 proteins not found in younger and older flies, implying that new genes were being expressed. More germane to the issue of aging, 100 other proteins were carefully measured on the gels, and 2 of those were found to be significantly less common (by more than one-half) in middle-aged flies, and 10 of them were less common in old flies, compared to the youthful 10-day-olds. Most of the proteins were not identified, and their function is not known, but these results nonetheless suggest that some change has taken place during the life of the fly in the genes that either encode these proteins or regulate their expression.

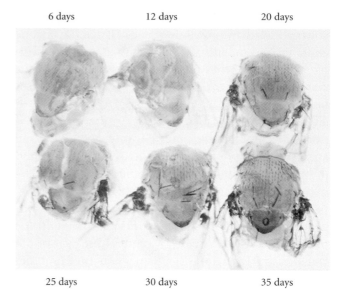

6 days   12 days   20 days

25 days   30 days   35 days

The fruit fly (left) is a common subject of genetic experiments. One such experiment (right) found a gene of unknown function, called *deathknell,* that shows progressive increases in expression during aging. A so-called reporter gene was inserted into copies of the *death-knell* gene in live flies; it produces a blue protein whenever *deathknell* is active. At 6 days of age, there is no sign of the gene's activity in a fruit fly thorax, but by 35 days much of the thorax is stained blue.

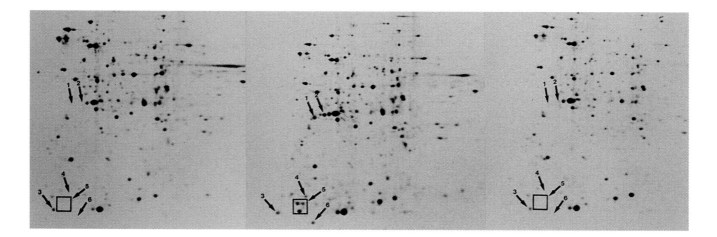

Two-directional separation of proteins, on the basis of their size and electrical charge, extracted from young (10 days), middle-aged (28 days), and old (44 days) fruit flies (*Drosophila melanogaster*). The small box and the arrows indicate several proteins that are expressed in middle-aged flies but are absent from younger and older individuals.

The DNA also can be changed when one nucleotide is substituted for another in the nucleotide sequence. Such a change (mutation) causes a different amino acid to be inserted into the gene's protein product, which in turn may function less efficiently or even perform a totally different activity than expected. Such changes generally are passed on to the next generation if they occur in the germ line, because repair enzymes recognize nothing unusual in the structure of the mutated DNA strand. For example, the sickle-cell trait of human hemoglobin is caused by a substitution of an adenine base for a thymine base in the 17th position of the DNA sequence. The DNA is perfectly normal, but the change in the sequence of bases causes valine to be inserted in place of glutamic acid in the amino acid sequence, with profound consequences for the hemoglobin molecule.

The sickle-cell mutation makes the amino acid chain fold in such a way that the resulting hemoglobin molecules stack together in compact groups, giving the red blood cells their characteristic sickle shape. Blood cells of this shape are unavailable for binding oxygen, which of course is the primary function of hemoglobin in the bloodstream. A person who inherits the sickle-cell allele from both parents develops a severe form of anemia. Interestingly, when the gene is inherited from only a single parent and is

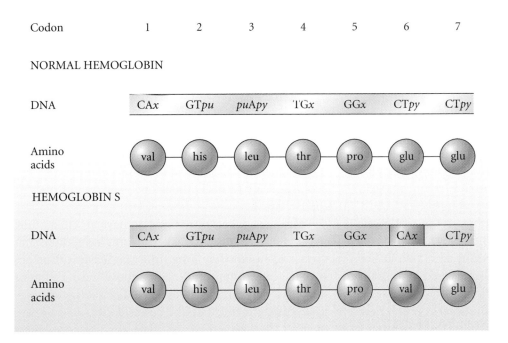

The mutation that produces the sickle-cell trait is a change from T to A in the 17th position (sixth codon triplet) of the hemoglobin DNA sequence; it results in the amino acid valine being substituted for glutamic acid in the sixth position of the protein chain. In the third position of the codon triplet, *pu* indicates either purine base (C or T), *py* either pyrimidine base (A or G), and *x* any of the four bases. The amino acids are: val = valine, his = histidine, leu = leucine, thr = threonine, pro = proline, glu = glutamic acid.

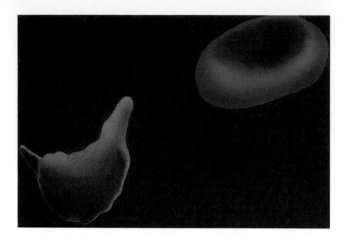

Scanning electron micrographs of normal (left) and sickled (right) red blood cells.

paired with a normal copy of the gene, then the resulting sickle-cell "trait" causes a milder level of anemia but also confers resistance to malaria. The parasite that causes malaria is a protozoan that feeds off hemoglobin in the red blood cells. Because malaria parasites do not grow well in cells containing sickle-cell hemoglobin, the disease is limited. This advantage conferred by the sickle-cell trait explains why sickle-cell anemia is most common among populations from tropical regions of Africa, where malaria is endemic.

Mutations like those that result in the sickle-cell trait may be inherited by offspring and change the genetic character of the generations to come. Other types of mutation can also be transferred from parent to child; they include the deletion of a nucleotide position in the DNA sequence, the insertion of a new position between two existing ones, the rearrangement of large blocks of genetic material, and changes in the regions of the DNA molecule that control the reading of a gene's protein-coding sequence. When such mutations occur in cell lineages of the soma, they are not passed from one generation to the next and they do not contribute to evolution itself. But

when they occur in the germ line and are neither repaired nor removed, they do contribute to the genes of future generations. Very occasionally, mutations are beneficial and generate the kinds of change that eventually led frogs and humans to evolve from the same common ancestor.

Certain nucleotide substitutions do not change the amino acid composition of proteins. Such genetic changes in no way interfere with the body's normal functioning and are regarded as being neutral with respect to natural selection. That is, natural selection will not eliminate the change from following generations, but neither will it favor it. Even when a mutation does alter the structure of a protein, it may still escape the eye of natural selection if the altered protein can still function normally. Yet even though a particular allele is neutral with regard to natural selection, its frequency may increase in a population because new copies of the allele are continually added by mutation. Its numbers may also fluctuate randomly up or down due to chance, in a process called genetic drift. Consider that the genetic makeup of each generation is a sample of the genetic makeup of the previous generation. Which genes are passed on and which are not is to some degree a matter of chance because random accidents may kill even superbly fit individuals or lower the number of their offspring.

However, when mutations do have an effect, they may, in turn, influence whether an individual survives a comparatively long time and leaves offspring. In this case, when two individuals have different forms of the same gene, they will, not by chance, leave different numbers of descendants. As a consequence, the frequencies of alleles in the population change from generation to generation, as we have seen in the example of the peppered moth. In that case, the allele for melanistic coloration became more common in populations that lived in polluted woodlands. Over longer periods, one allele may replace the ancestral form of the gene altogether—that is, the mutation may become fixed in the population. Over time, new mutations appear, some of which themselves may become fixed.

A good way to measure an individual's evolutionary fitness is by the number of descendants that he or she leaves. That number in turn depends on how long the individual survives and how fast it produces offspring. All other factors being equal, forms of a gene that convey a high fitness to their bearers will become more common and eventually replace alleles with less salubrious effect, just as happened in the case of the peppered moth. This inevitable consequence of the differential fitness of individuals is referred to as natural selection, in the sense that the most fit individuals are "selected" to be the progenitors of future generations.

Within a population, alleles rise and fall in frequency as they respond to mutation, drift, and selection. Which of these evolutionary forces is the most powerful influence is not preordained, however, for their relative strengths vary considerably. The strength with which mutation can change the frequency of a particular allele is approximately the same as the mutation rate; in such organisms as fruit flies, corn, mice, and humans, generally about one in ten thousand to one in a million gametes carries a mutation with visible effects on any particular gene. The relative strength of the forces causing genetic drift is approximately the inverse of the population size, which may be in the thousands or millions. The strength of selection depends on the number of descendants produced: selection is strong for a particular allele when individuals with that allele leave many more offspring than individuals with the most common allele in the population. When selection is strong, it is thought to play the predominant role in evolution. For example, early in this century, the melanistic form of the peppered moth survived twice as well in polluted woodlands as the typical form. Such extremely strong selection is likely to be caused by drastic and rapid changes in the environment,

which these days are often the result of human activities. Under more ordinary circumstances, individuals bearing different alleles of a gene may vary in fitness by an amount more on the order of 1% or less, but such values are still large compared to the effects of mutation and drift.

Not all selection causes evolution, however, and not all evolution is caused by natural selection. Evolution is a change in the genetic composition of a population, and hence it follows upon selection only when the fitness differences between individuals have a genetic basis. Some individuals may be more fit than others because they grew up in a particularly favorable environment or simply because of accidents or sheer luck (the chance escape from a predator, for example, or the discovery of a particularly rewarding food item). In such cases, differences in fitness cannot be inherited and do not result in evolutionary change.

Most genetic mutations reduce fitness, just as almost any random change in the notes of a Mozart sonata would grate on the ears, and natural selection tends to weed such genetic disharmony out of the gene pool of a population. This removal of deleterious mutations is evolutionary in that genetic change occurs in the population, but the overall effect is to preserve the status quo. Thus, natural selection acts both as innovator and conservator in evolution, depending on the genetic variation available to it.

As we have seen, forces other than selection can cause gene frequencies to change. One of the most important of these in thinking about aging is mutation itself. The chance of a mutation occurring at a particular point in a DNA sequence is very low. A good estimate is that the average rate of mutation is about one change per 10 billion nucleotides per generation in most DNA, and perhaps about one change per 100 million nucleotides per generation in mitochondrial DNA. Low, yes, but when one considers that each gene may comprise hundreds or thousands of DNA nucleotides, that each individual has thou-

Spontaneous Mutation Rates for Some Genes

Organism	Trait	Mutation Rate (per million gametes)
E. coli bacteria	To streptomycin resistance	0.0004
	To virus T1 resistance	0.003
	To arabinose dependence	2
Salmonella bacteria	To threonine resistance	4.1
	To tryptophan independence	0.05
Drosophila flies	To yellow eye color	120
	To eyeless	60
Corn	To shrunken kernels	1.2
	To purple kernels	11
Mouse	To albino	10
	To nonagouti coat color (not grayish)	30
Human	To achondroplasia	6–13
	To aniridia	3–5
	To myotonic muscular dystrophy	8–11
	To Huntington's disease	5
	To neurofibromatosis	50–100
	To retinoblastoma	5–12

Note: arabinose is a simple sugar; threonine and tryptophan, amino acids; achondroplasia, failure of cartilage to develop normally resulting in dwarfism; aniridia, failure of the iris of the eye to develop; neurofibromatosis, numerous tumors and other growths of the skin and nerves; retinoblastoma, a cancer of the retina of the eye.

sands or hundreds of thousands of genes, and that each population has thousands or millions of individuals, some kind of gene mutation becomes a frequent event. Thus, while mutation may not be the creative evolutionary force that selection can be, it nonetheless provides a continual supply of genetic variation on which selection can work. Equally important for evolutionary theories of aging, because most genetic changes are harmful, mutation tends to reduce the fitness of individuals below the maximum fitness possible. The difference between perfection and our actual genetic makeup is our genetic burden, or mutation load.

Why Do We Think Aging Is an Evolved Phenomenon?

Evolution builds upon genetic variation within populations. Once, for example, there lived the common ancestor of humans and frogs; the individuals of this species would have displayed the expected range of differences, many of them genetically inherited. For example, certain individuals could have had better eyesight, while others might have had faster reflexes. At some point, two populations of the ancestor species would have become separated and formed two distinct lineages. Over time, the independent lineages gradually would have come to differ genetically one from the other as, to pick a purely hypothetical example, strong eyesight was selected for in one population and not in the other, and as different new mutations arose in each independent line. The frog and the human are the present-day manifestations of separate evolutionary pathways that diverged over 200 million years ago. The differences between the two species represent the accumulation of thousands upon thousands of independent genetic changes in each lineage. Regardless of the particulars, genetic variation within populations and genetic differentiation between populations are signposts telling us that evolution is at work.

Both of the above signposts are clearly present to tell us that aging is influenced by evolutionary change. Fairly good predictors of the length of a person's life, barring accidental death, are the life spans of his or her grandparents, meaning the genetic constitutions that each has been endowed with. In numerous populations of plants and animals, individuals have been observed to vary from one another in the pattern of aging; we can tell which variations are rooted in the genes rather than the environment by looking for resemblances among relatives (that is, among siblings or between parents and their offspring). For example, one study of humans showed that longer-lived parents had longer-lived offspring: the children of parents who lived beyond 80 themselves lived on average 6 years longer than the children of parents who died before 60. Additional studies show that when parents are longer lived, the offspring have lower rates of degenerative disease, particularly coronary heart disease.

Many studies of inheritance are complicated by the fact that parents and offspring experience similar environmental factors that may bear on health and longevity. More direct evidence comes from studies of twins, particularly those raised apart. Such twins share all their genes if the twins are identical, or monozygotic, and half their genes if they are fraternal, or dizygotic, but in either case the twins are subjected to different environmental influences. Even when raised together, monozygotic twins should be more similar than dizygotic twins and share more attributes under genetic influence. The similarities in the course of aging are striking. In one study, monozygotic twins died, on average, within 3 years of each other, whereas dizygotic twins of the same sex died within 6 years. The difference between the ages at death of any two individuals chosen at random would on average, of course, be greater yet.

Finally, to clinch the issue of whether aging is an evolutionary phenomenon, scientists have simulated the action of natural selection in the laboratory and watched the life spans of fruit flies and flour beetles grow or shrink in response. We'll have more to say about these experiments in the next chapter.

Differences between species in the course of aging are striking, as we have already seen. We presume, because of the long history of evolutionary independence between species, that these differences have a genetic basis. Pacific salmon, for example, are genetically programmed to exhaust themselves in a single episode of reproduction, whereas the genetic programming of their Atlantic cousins allows them a somewhat longer life span with more chances to breed. However, because it is not generally possible to interbreed individuals of different species, we cannot estimate the genetic contribution to these varying patterns directly. Instead, we turn to another approach: the so-called common-garden experiment. The idea is to maintain separate populations under identical environmental conditions, often for several generations. Because environmental differences are

Twin Studies

*I*t is natural to measure a trait such as height or blood pressure using numbers, but scientists, in their ingenuity, have been able to give numerical ratings to even seemingly nonnumerical traits. The most obvious example is the use of I.Q. points to rate intelligence, but scientists have also developed numerical rating systems for personality traits like extroversion and for health problems like heart disease. They find, of course, that different people have different scores, within some overall range. The question is, why do these traits vary from person to person? Do they vary because people have different genes or because they live and grow in different environments?

Once a trait can be analyzed numerically, twin studies can be used to ascertain to what extent the trait is influenced by genes. Identical twins have identical genes, and so when they are reared apart as are, for example, adopted twins, similarities are considered to be only genetic; and the correlation between twins is a measure of the genetic influence on variation in the sample as a whole. Geneticists also estimate the influence of genes from studies of twins raised in the same environment, that is, with their birth families. In this case, their method is to compare monozygotic (MZ) twins and dizygotic (DZ) twins. In contrast to genetically identical monozygotic twins, dizygotic twins share only half their genes on average. Thus,

the total variation (V_P) among pairs of identical twins is the variation owed to genes plus the variation owed to the environment ($V_G + V_E$), and the total variation among pairs of dizygotic twins is half the genetic variation plus all the environmental variation ($0.5V_G + V_E$). Thus we may estimate the genetic contribution to variation as twice the difference between the variation we observe in monozygotic and dizygotic twins, that is,

$$2[V_P(MZ) - V_P(DZ)] = 2[V_G + V_E - 0.5V_G - V_E] = V_G$$

The variation among monozygotic and dizygotic pairs of twins has been estimated for different measures of personality, behavioral disorders, and medical disorders. Some of these estimates are shown in the accompanying graph. To see the relative genetic influence on each trait, you look at the difference between the amounts of variation associated with monozygotic and dizygotic pairs of twins. This value is low for alcoholism in women, breast cancer, and ischemic heart disease (that caused by blockage of coronary arteries), but relatively high for schizophrenia, Alzheimer disease, autism, hypertension, and rheumatoid arthritis.

eliminated, it is safe to attribute persistent differences between the populations to genetic factors. This technique is valid only when the populations are sufficiently similar that one can be certain to create identical environments for them.

In a sense, the common-garden experiment has been performed repeatedly as people have emigrated from their homelands to different parts of the world.

A prominent example of this phenomenon, illustrating the influence of environmental rather than genetic factors, concerns human breast cancer. As we saw earlier, the incidence of this disease is about 10 times higher among women in North America than in Japan. However, Japanese women living in Los Angeles are as likely to develop breast cancer as Caucasians living in the same area. Thus, because the

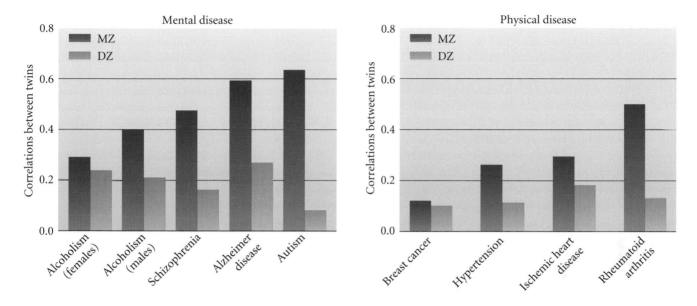

One way to estimate the genetic influence on a trait such as arthritis is to compare studies of monozygotic (MZ) and dizygotic (DZ) pairs of twins. Are twins in a monozygotic pair much likelier to match in arthritis than twins in a dizygotic pair? Then the trait has a strong genetic component.

differences between Japanese and Caucasian women disappear in the common garden of Los Angeles, genetic factors cannot be responsible for the variation in the incidence of breast cancer. In this particular example, nutrition, especially the fat content of the diet, has been implicated as the environmental factor at fault. As noted in the graph on this page, twin studies have revealed that genetic factors are respon-

sible for a very small proportion of the incidence of breast cancer.

We can clearly perceive the influence of genes on patterns of aging by looking at different strains of animals reared under the same laboratory conditions. Each strain is genetically uniform and is produced by close inbreeding, often brother-sister mating, of small numbers of individuals to form the next generation. After each generation of inbreeding, the progeny possess a smaller sample of the genetic variation of the original source population because so few individuals are bred as parents. As alleles are lost, an inbred line that once could have, say, fur in one of five colors may now have fur in only one color.

Although many generations of close inbreeding produce genetically uniform populations, each of these populations has, just by chance, a different genetic composition. Therefore, when such populations are kept under the same conditions, any differences in their survival rates must be rooted in their genes. In fact, the average life span often differs dramatically between inbred lines. Unfortunately, many deleterious recessive alleles are expressed in inbred lines, and they can lead to disabilities and disease. Thus, only a rather small number of inbred lineages can be maintained, and the average life spans in these lineages are usually less than the average in the parental population from which they were derived.

A major problem has hindered scientists from using inbred lines to study the influence of genes on aging: the breeder has no control over which genes are made homozygous in such inbreeding programs and so no control over which genes can be studied. Ideally, we would like a technique for examining the independent effects of a particular gene. One method is to introduce different alleles of the gene into identical genetic backgrounds. The breeding program required to accomplish this is complicated, but the result is a variety of populations that differ at only a small part of the genome. For example, strains of mice have been produced that differ only with respect to the H-2 region of the main histocompatibility complex, a cluster of genes that regulates many aspects of the immune response. Those mice whose immune function declined more slowly with age had a longer life span and reproduced to later ages.

When we put together the evidence that has been accumulating from a variety of sources, we see that differences in the patterns of aging within populations have a genetic basis and that differences between populations are the result of evolutionary change. That aging is an evolved phenomenon, or at least that its course can be modified by evolution, raises fundamental questions about why we age and why some of us creatures age faster or slower than others.

The Evolutionary Dilemma of Aging

How can a phenomenon—aging—that reduces survival and fecundity, and hence reduces evolutionary fitness, result from evolution? Why have the bad genes that cause aging not been weeded out of populations by natural selection? This paradox has intrigued biologists for over a century and has led to a number of creative attempts at its resolution. One has been to declare aging beneficial, if not to the individual at least to its descendants or to the population as a whole. Older individuals use resources but are less productive than younger ones. Perhaps, it was thought, senescence removes the burden of the old from family lineages and populations, leaving the more fit behind. As Alfred Russel Wallace, codiscoverer with Charles Darwin of the theory of evolution by natural selection, put it, "and thus we have the origin of *old age, decay, and death;* for it is evident that when one or more individuals have provided a sufficient number of successors they themselves, as consumers of nourishment in a constantly increasing degree, are an injury to those successors. Natural selection therefore weeds them out, and in many cases favours such races as die almost immediately after they have left successors." This idea is still with us. In his book *How We Die: Reflections on Life's Final Chapter*, the surgeon Sherwin B. Nuland says, concerning aspirations for longer life and better health, "Too bad. Medicine has a job to do, but nature does too, and will do it, medicine be damned. Nature's job is to send us packing so that subsequent generations can flourish." Nuland goes on to say that "medicine that does not respect limits set by nature can make death unnecessarily unpleasant, and can distort life too."

The idea that the deaths of old individuals can make room for young ones is not, at first glance, so farfetched. Seedlings of the tropical tree *Tachigalia* grow up in the clearing left when their parent dies after its single episode of reproduction. Young scrub jays often inherit the territories of their parents. However, the idea that such effects could fashion a general evolutionary foundation for aging has three serious flaws. The first is that it presupposes that aging already exists. In the absence of aging, there would be no reason for the old to make way for the young because the old would continue to have as many offspring as ever. Thus, the old making way for the young as an evolutionary rationale for aging could only modify a process that had previously existed and not itself be an original cause.

The second flaw is that evolution would favor genes that terminate life only when resources made available by the death of a parent are passed to its offspring. If these resources are divided among the population as a whole, then the connection between the genetic makeup of the parent and the fitness of the offspring (which inherit this genetic makeup) breaks down. Third, while the accelerated death of aging individuals might benefit the family lineage, putting off the physiological effects of aging would certainly benefit the individual. Because individuals are replaced more rapidly than are family lineages within populations, selection can act more frequently on individual traits than on the attributes of family groups. Thus, when the fitness consequences of genes for individuals and lineages conflict, individual selection is generally thought to have the upper hand — in this case, tending to put off rather than accelerate death from aging.

If aging is not actually beneficial, perhaps it is neutral under most circumstances. When an individual does not begin to age until after it has produced all its offspring, aging cannot affect its evolutionary fitness. Thus, genetic mutations expressed only late in life might accumulate in populations because they are beyond the reach of natural selection. This could occur in two ways. First, reproductive life might be shorter than the maximum potential life span, in which case many individuals would stop reproducing before they died. In our species, for example, women stop bearing children at menopause although they may have decades of life left. If parents did not care for their offspring beyond birth, then their bodies could begin a physical decline after the end of the fertile period without affecting fitness. Of course, its loss of fertility implies that the reproductive system ages, and thus this argument for the evolution of senescence also requires the prior existence of senescence.

Second, even in the absence of aging, individuals die of accidents that strike without regard to age. Thus, no matter the size of the population, there exists an age beyond which no individual has lived. A harmful gene expressed after this age would, of course, be selectively neutral because its damaging effects would never appear in a natural population. However, when such a population is protected from its usual causes of death, many individuals would live beyond the normal maximum life span. Thus, animals raised in a laboratory, in a zoo, or on a farm might regularly outlive their ancestors and show all the signs of old age. Almost certainly this is true of human populations, since technology and medicine have made it possible for many more of us to achieve old age.

The idea that aging only takes place in individuals that survive beyond the normal life span of their species would gain support if aging were absent or rare in natural populations. However, this plainly is not the case. Long-term studies of populations of mammals, for example, show that both reproductive rates and the annual probability of survival clearly decrease as the animals grow old. Female lions bear fewer cubs each year after about 10 years of age, and males show a precipitous decline in the number of cubs they sire beginning at 8 years. In the red deer, the patterns are similar, except that females (hinds) maintain a high reproductive rate through age 13. Survival rates of both stags and hinds begin to drop off rapidly after age 10. Such studies suggest that the effects of aging are indeed felt by animals in natural populations. Any successful theory of aging must explain why aging persists in the face of natural selection as well as how species come to vary so much in their patterns of aging.

More theories have indeed been offered. Scientists have made various further attempts to resolve the evolutionary dilemma of aging, and their proposed solutions rely on several categories of evolu-

tionary mechanism: (1) wear and tear, (2) mutation accumulation, (3) a process called antagonistic pleiotropy, and (4) wear and repair. None of these mechanisms are mutually incompatible, and all may make some contribution to aging.

Aging may be an inevitable consequence of life itself, reflecting wear and tear on the organism, the accumulation of toxic metabolic byproducts, damage to proteins and DNA from ultraviolet radiation and toxins in food or air, and so on. In this case, the causes of aging lie outside the genetic blueprint, even outside the body itself, and are beyond the reach of evolution. Two lines of evidence suggest that wear and tear cannot, however, be the whole story. First, the germ line itself does not age. Seemingly, the germ line is somehow rid of the accumulated defects from wear and tear, perhaps through a mechanism for repairing them. Second, species with similar physiology may have strikingly different life spans. We have

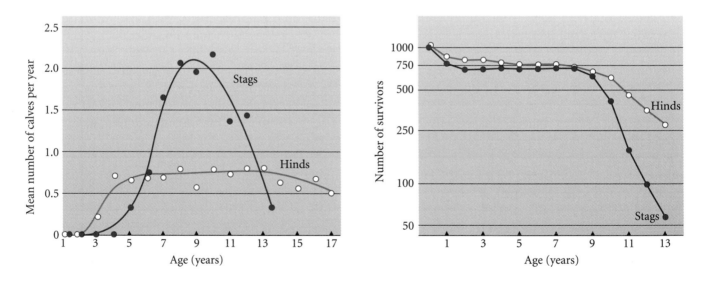

The number of surviving male red deer, along with the number of calves they sire, begins to decline very rapidly at an age of about 10 years. The number of surviving hinds (does) begins to decrease at about the same age, although more gradually, and their reproductive rates are relatively little affected.

Aging and Selenium

An especially striking example of how an environmental factor can influence aging comes from Finland. Men living in eastern Finland have the highest rates of vascular aging among the human populations of Europe. Their singularly rapid aging may be in part the result of their high blood cholesterol levels, but a more unusual factor seems also to be at play. The soils and waters of eastern Finland contain unusually low amounts of selenium, a trace element (that is, one present in the body normally only in minute quantities). Men have levels of selenium in the blood averaging 0.081 micrograms per liter (μg/L) in Helsinki and 0.056 μg/L in eastern Finland, compared to 0.21 μg/L in the United States and 0.36 μg/L in Venezuela. Comparisons among states in the United States, and among countries throughout the world, have suggested that circulatory disease is common where selenium blood levels are low, and vice versa, especially among men.

Selenium is a component of the enzyme glutathione peroxidase, which converts hydrogen peroxide (an active oxidizer) to water. Selenium deficiency causes a reduction in the activity of this enzyme, so that more hydrogen peroxide is presumably present to oxidize and damage tissues. Dr. A. A. Goede, a scientist at the Reactor Institute of Delft University, The Netherlands, has recently suggested that the long life spans of birds, especially seabirds, may be related to the high levels of selenium observed in their tissues.

seen, for example, that many birds are long lived compared to mammals, yet birds and mammals do not differ significantly in their physiology and should undergo similar wear and tear. We might argue that these variations in patterns of aging are themselves the result of environmental factors, but these are unlikely to explain the range of variation that we see in rates of aging because animals living in the same environments and eating the same foods may be either long lived or short lived. The aging of the body would itself appear to be modified by genetic factors: genes can influence the rates at which harmful chemical reactions proceed, the rates at which DNA and large molecules are repaired, and the responsiveness of the immune system. Thus, while aging might be inevitable, its course is subject to evolutionary modification.

According to a second theory, our aging bodies are feeling the effects of deleterious mutations that have accumulated in the population and are passed from generation to generation through the germ line. Such mutations could be responsible for aging if their harmful effects did not appear until later in life. This mutation accumulation theory, being an evolutionary theory, is wholly distinct from the physiological mechanism of mutation accumulation proposed in Chapter 2. The mutations of Chapter 2 accumulated in the somatic tissues of a single individual, not in the germ lines of a population, and their harmful effects were not necessarily delayed. The question is, Why would some inherited mutations do no obvious harm until later in a person's life?

Mutations, like wear and tear, seem to be inevitable. Even when mutations are damaging, however, other genetic factors may be able to suppress their expression entirely or at least delay their expression until late in life. As a result, the organism's capacity to reproduce itself will continue undiminished for at least some period. The individual is consequently more fit in the evolutionary sense, and the genetic factors able to put off the damaging mutations will be passed on to an ever expanding proportion of the population. This idea still places aging in the category of the inevitable, but the damaging consequences of mutations may be more or less offset, at least for a time, by any genetic factors that can stall their expression. The pattern of aging displayed by a particular population represents a compromise between the creation of deleterious mutations, their removal by selection, and the delay of their expression by modifying genetic factors, which are themselves subject to mutation and selection.

A third idea is the proposal of George C. Williams of the State University of New York at Stony Brook. To explain aging, Williams points to genes that do good for the organism early in life but do harm later. A gene that expresses itself in more than one attribute of the individual is called a pleiotropic gene. An example of a pleiotropic gene is the gene for myotonic dystrophy (MyD). MyD is the most common form of muscular dystrophy to strike adults, affecting between 30 and 50 of every million individuals. The gene responsible for MyD has a dominant expression; that is, only one copy of the gene need be inherited to develop the disease. However, the effects of the gene are far-ranging. Most significantly, skeletal muscles can no longer relax and eventually degenerate, but MyD also causes cataracts, diabetes, malfunctioning of the testes and ovaries, irregular heartbeats, and mental retardation. The MyD gene is considered pleiotropic because it produces a variety of effects in a wide range of organs.

Sometimes several of the attributes influenced by a pleiotropic gene have opposite effects on evolutionary fitness, a situation Williams called antagonistic pleiotropy. We know of many genetic factors that produce antagonistic pleiotropy, in many different organisms. For example, the same genes that give a chicken a heightened immune response also impose costs by requiring the chicken to expend more energy. When a chicken uses its available food energy to the maximum, as it often does during breeding, the energy it allocates to immune function may take away from the energy it can spend on growth or reproduction. Thus, genes influencing the immune response may help the chicken survive, but hinder it from reaching adult size and leaving offspring. We can imagine an optimum balance between the antagonistically pleiotropic expressions of such genetic factors. Whether an allele becomes fixed in a population depends on whether its positive effects on fitness outweigh its negative ones. In the case of the chicken, that balance depends on the threat of disease, which places a premium on good immune response.

Another example of antagonistic pleiotropy is the so-called human *thrifty* genotype. People with this trait convert food to fat very efficiently. Under conditions of fluctuating food supply, as perhaps experienced by our pre-supermarket ancestors, fat deposits provided some insurance against periods when food was scarce. Now we are paying the price for this onetime advantage as older individuals accumulate fat and develop cardiovascular disease and diabetes. These consequences have been brought home forcefully in many populations that have recently made the transition from traditional diets to western-style eating habits, so-called coca-colonization. On Nauru Island in the western Pacific Ocean, the natives have become well-to-do since the recent exploitation of phosphate mineral wealth. Now they have abandoned traditional fishing and agriculture and rely more and more on imported food. The change in diet has made obesity rampant among Nauruans, many of whom also develop diabetes during the peak of their reproductive years, when it threatens their fertility and even their survival. This highly unnatural situation emphasizes the fact that the *thrifty* genotype has both good and bad consequences for fitness. Because diabetes does its damage only later in life, *thrifty* is an example of an antagonistically pleiotropic genetic factor that could contribute to senescence.

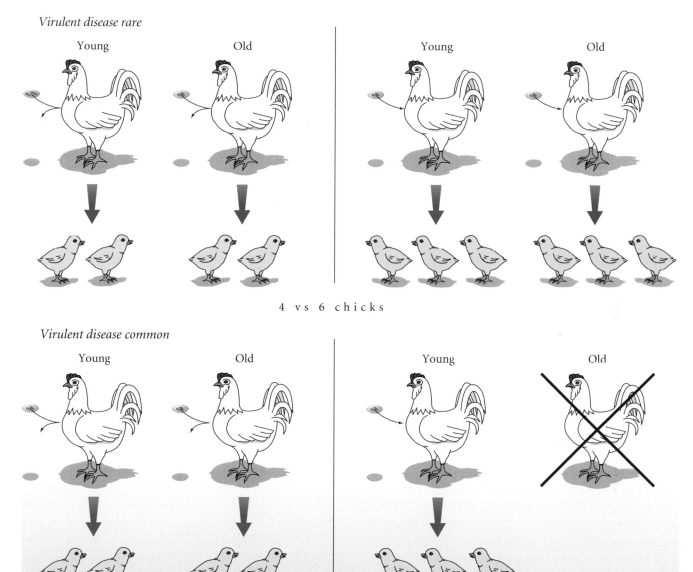

STRONG IMMUNE RESPONSE, REDUCED FECUNDITY

WEAK IMMUNE RESPONSE, HIGHER FECUNDITY

Virulent disease rare

Young   Old   Young   Old

4 vs 6 chicks

Virulent disease common

Young   Old   Young   Old

4 vs 3 chicks

When virulent disease is common, it is better to sacrifice fecundity for a better immune response.

How could antagonistic pleiotropy lead to aging? The reasoning is uncomplicated. Every population has a higher proportion of young than old individuals if only because accidental deaths from such causes as predation and adverse weather, not to mention war and automobile accidents, continually pare down the size of older and older age groups. As a result, genetic effects expressed later in life will always appear in fewer individuals than genetic effects expressed earlier in life. Because selection can act only on expressed genetic variation, it puts more weight on the fitness consequences of genes expressed earlier in life than on those of genes expressed later. In other words, genes expressed late in life are "hidden" from selection when the individuals bearing them die before the genes are expressed. As the prominent British biologist Peter Medawar put it, "A relatively small advantage conferred early in the life of an individual may outweigh a catastrophic disadvantage withheld until later."

Finally, we come to the fourth theory of aging. It suggests that patterns of senescence may represent a balance between the two opposing mechanisms of wear and repair. On the one hand, daily activity and contact with the environment continually create wear and tear on the body. On the other hand, the body has genetically programmed mechanisms to prevent or repair damage, or otherwise restore itself to proper functioning. Presumably, repair mechanisms are not cost free: they use time and resources that could otherwise be used for growth and reproduction. This explains why our genes haven't made our bodies capable of repairing all of the damage they experience. The wear and repair hypothesis is in some sense opposite to the antagonistic pleiotropy hypothesis. In the latter hypothesis, genetic factors cause aging while enhancing early reproduction; in the "wear and repair" hypothesis, genetic factors counter aging but reduce fitness at early ages as repair mechanisms accrue costs.

To see how genes can control a maintenance mechanism that counters aging, we look at an example recently reported by W. C. Orr and R. S. Sohal of Southern Methodist University in Dallas. In a study of fruit flies of the species *Drosophila melanogaster*, Orr and Sohal showed that fruit flies carrying extra copies of the genes for the enzymes superoxide dismutase and catalase lived as much as one-third longer, did not begin "slowing down" until later, and experienced less oxidative damage to their proteins. These enzymes convert the highly reactive superoxide anion (O_2^-) to the relatively benign hydrogen peroxide (H_2O_2), which is converted by another enzyme to water (H_2O) and oxygen (O_2). Clearly the enzymes were removing a damaging oxidant, but at a price, because flies with the added genes consumed oxygen at a higher rate and hence paid higher metabolic costs.

Evolutionary theories of aging have two essential components: factors that accelerate aging and factors that delay aging. Aging may be accelerated by wear and tear, something that evolution cannot influence directly, and by genes that express their damaging effects to an increasing degree as organisms age (as demanded by the hypotheses of mutation accumulation and antagonistic pleiotropy). Aging may be delayed by genetic factors that postpone the age at which deleterious mutations are expressed, by mechanisms that prevent errors in DNA and proteins, and by mechanisms that repair errors in, and damage to, molecules, tissues, and organs. Theories differ on whether genes control the acceleration or the delaying of aging, and on the costs and benefits of these genes.

Evolutionary theories of aging that depend on genes being expressed late in life also presuppose that the individual ages. How else could, or why else would, the expression of a genetic factor be withheld until late in life if old individuals did not differ physiologically from young ones? Of course, once senescence has become established, changes in the body brought by aging could provide a physiological clock able to cue a gene to begin to act. Genes can influence how we age, of course, and they can even make

Four Theories of the Evolution of Aging

Theory	Cause of Aging	Inherited?	Source of Variation among Species
Wear and tear	Extrinsic damage caused by ionizing radiation, free radicals, and mechanical damage; somatic mutation.	No	Variation in metabolic rate and environment, although neither is adequate to explain the observed range of variation.
Mutation accumulation	Mutations with deleterious effects expressed late in life.	Yes	Differences in the strength of selection with progressing age to remove such alleles, related to the baseline mortality rate.
Antagonistic pleiotropy	Genes with beneficial effects early in life and detrimental effects later.	Yes	Differences in the strength of selection early and late in life affect the balance of beneficial and deleterious effects.
Wear and repair	Extrinsic damage caused by ionizing radiation, free radicals, and mechanical damage; somatic mutation.	No (cause), yes (variation)	Variation in maintenance and repair mechanisms (inherited).

us age in new ways, but only after some form of aging already exists. Yet, if genes can't be the first cause of aging, how did it come into existence? Even in the absence of genetically based senescence, physiological age might be established by (1) wear and tear, (2) physiological changes brought about by growth and maturation, or (3) the exhaustion of a substance of limited quantity provided prior to maturity, such as the total number of oocytes available for the formation of eggs.

One way of distinguishing among the various evolutionary theories of aging would be to examine specific genes that we know play a role in the variation we observe in rates of aging. How do these genes act? Are they in fact not expressed until late in life, as required by some theories? Or, are they expressed early in life to the benefit of the organism, only becoming harmful later? Do they accelerate aging or delay it? We shall now look at a number of studies that have attempted to address just these questions.

The Genetics of Aging: Single Gene Effects

We don't actually see genes, but we do see their effects. Until recently, scientists had to infer the presence of genes, and the rules for their inheritance, by observing the wrinkled skin of a pea, the patterns formed by variously hued kernels of corn, the color of a pair of eyes. That is, scientists work out an organism's inner blueprint by studying its outward appearance. The appearance of an organism, including its physiology and behavior, is referred to as its phenotype to distinguish outward demeanor from genetic constitution, or genotype. Thus, the analysis of genes is ultimately the analysis of phenotypes as well.

Genetic analysis makes use of two important tools to understand how genes contribute to our outward appearance. One of these is Mendelian genetic analysis, which focuses on individual genes that have clearly visible effects, such as eye color or blood type in humans or flower color in plants. The other, often called quantitative genetic analysis, is interested in the summed contributions of many genes, the effect of each alone being too small or indistinct to identify independently. Both kinds of genetic factors may contribute to aging. The mutation accumulation theory predicts the existence of large numbers of genes, expressed relatively late in life, having both small and large effects. The antagonistic pleiotropy hypothesis predicts the existence of genes expressed both early and late in life with opposing effects, but makes no distinction with respect to the magnitude of those effects. Let's see what genetic analysis has discovered.

Mendelian analysis is named after Gregor Mendel, the Austrian monk who worked out the basic rules for the inheritance of flower color and certain attributes of pea seeds in the middle of the nineteenth century. Mendel crossbred individuals with different phenotypes to determine the manner in which genes are transmitted from parent to offspring. Because such phenotypes as the wrinkled seed coat of a pea have a simple genetic basis, they serve as markers for the genes themselves. Human eye color, for example, is largely controlled by a single gene, which may take the form of one of two alleles: one that produces brown eyes and another that produces various shades of blue, gray, and green (that is, not brown). We learn in high school biology that children inheriting a brown allele from one parent and a nonbrown allele from the other have brown eyes, but that their own children may have blue eyes if they pass on the nonbrown allele and their mate passes on another nonbrown allele. The nonbrown allele is not lost in the hybrid offspring but merely masked, because it can reappear unaltered in subsequent generations. The discipline of experimental genetics has since discovered immense complexity in gene expression superimposed on this basic mechanism of inheritance. This complexity includes epistasis, where two or more genes interact to control a phenotypic trait, and modification, where one gene modulates the expression of another.

Human populations contain large numbers of known mutant genes whose inheritance is guided by simple Mendelian rules. Some of these produce serious disease, such as sickle-cell anemia or juvenile-onset diabetes. Curiously, relatively few of these mutations express themselves at advanced age. Examples of genes that do, however, include the gene for Huntington's disease and the genetic factors responsible for some kinds of familial Alzheimer disease. The dominant mutant gene at the root of Huntington's disease causes neurons in parts of the brain to deteriorate. Symptoms of the disease most frequently appear during a person's 30s or 40s and lead to death within 15 years. The symptoms appear before the age of 10 in some individuals, however, suggesting that the gene may be expressed throughout life, but that its effects must reach a certain threshold before symptoms appear.

Of the thousands of inherited human diseases, only about 7%—the so-called progeroid diseases—produce symptoms in children and young adults

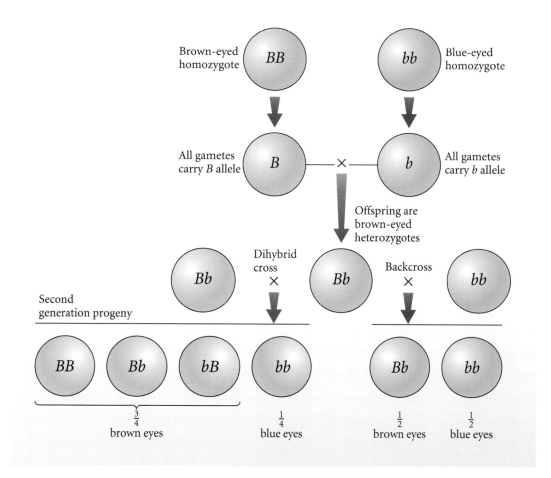

When someone who is homozygous for blue eye color (*bb*) mates with someone who is homozygous for brown eye color (*BB*), all their children are heterozygous for eye color (*Bb*) and the brown allele, being dominant, is expressed to the exclusion of the blue allele. When one of these heterozygote individuals mates with another heterozygote (*Bb* × *Bb*), we expect one quarter of the offspring to be homozygous for the allele for blue eye color (*bb*) and to have blue eyes. Half the offspring are heterozygotes, on average, and the remaining quarter are homozygous for brown eye color (*BB*). When a heterozygote mates with an individual homozygous for blue eye color, half of the progeny should carry the *Bb* genotype and have brown eyes, and half should carry the *bb* genotype and have blue eyes.

that resemble one or more of the pathological conditions normally produced by age. Examples of such genetic conditions are the extremely rare Hutchinson-Gilford and Werner progerias. In the Hutchinson-Gilford syndrome, of which only about 20 cases have been recognized worldwide, the symptoms of severely retarded growth, abnormal skeletal development, atherosclerosis, and absence of sexual maturation usually cause death by the age of 12 years. Sufferers of the slightly less rare Werner's syn-

Some Human Genes of Clearly Visible Effect, Inherited by Mendelian Rules

Trait	Mode of Inheritance	Effect on Fitness
Adherent ear lobe	Autosomal recessive	None apparent
Sickle-cell anemia	Autosomal recessive	Fatal
Galactosemia	Autosomal recessive	Fatal
Phenylketonuria	Autosomal recessive	Mental retardation, reduced life span
Tay-Sachs disease	Autosomal recessive	Motor neuron impairment, death
Red-green color-blindness	Sex-linked recessive	None apparent
Duchenne muscular dystrophy	Sex-linked recessive	Fatal
Hemophilia	Sex-linked recessive	Uncontrollable bleeding, often fatal
Facial freckles	Autosomal dominant	None apparent
Huntington's disease	Autosomal dominant	Usually appears after reproductive age
Retinoblastoma	Autosomal dominant	Cancer of the eye, usually fatal

Autosomal genes are those found on any chromosome except for the sex chromosomes, X and Y. Sex-linked genes reside on the X chromosome and are expressed in males (XY individuals) even though they are recessive because the exceptionally small Y chromosome has few genes. Galactosemia is the inability to metabolize the simple sugar galactose.

drome, which makes its appearance during adolescence, stop growing, develop atherosclerosis and skin pathologies, and often die in their 30s. Both progerias, however, spare the brain. However, because no single one, or even a few, of the progeroid genetic mutations causes all the traits that we see in the elderly, it is likely that normal aging in our species is influenced by many genetic factors similar in action to the progeroid genes.

Nonetheless, a single mutation can have a profound effect on aging, either good or bad. One spectacular case of such a mutation has been discovered in the soil nematode, or roundworm, *Caenorhabditis elegans*. This species is becoming increasingly popular for genetics research because of its small size, ease of culture, and short life span (about 20 days). Moreover, individuals of *C. elegans* can actually fertilize themselves, allowing scientists to create the ultimate

A child with progeria (Hutchinson-Gilford syndrome). Such children typically grow to 40 inches in height and 25 to 30 pounds. Although they have normal intelligence, they show many symptoms associated with aging, including balding and atherosclerosis. These children have frequent heart attacks and strokes, and few survive beyond 15 years.

in inbred lines. And, because these nematodes have proved so useful, scientists have developed an abundance of available genetic mutants to experiment with.

Mutants of a gene called *daf-2* are able to greatly prolong adult life span in *C. elegans*. *Daf-2* is one of the genes in the developmental pathway that leads to formation of a special larval stage, called the dauer. A nematode in the dauer stage exists in a state of arrested development for up to 3 months. Such resting stages normally are formed only in response to such unfavorable environmental conditions as high temperature. However, nematodes with the mutants of *daf-2* form dauers even when these environmental cues are absent. The adults emerging from these mutant dauers have unusually long life spans (for *C. elegans*, that is), averaging about 40 to 60 days.

A very useful property of these *daf-2* mutants is that the developmental switch is pressed only at temperatures of 20°C or higher; thus only at these temperatures will the dauer stage form. Scientists have used this property to investigate whether it is the dauer stage itself that prolongs life, or whether the *daf-2* mutant has some other life-prolonging effect. Their strategy is to raise the larvae at low temperature (15°C) and then switch them to a higher temperature (20°C) after the age at which the dauer stage is initiated. The *daf-2* mutant is activated, but the dauer stage never appears. In such experiments, which produce normal adults fully able to reproduce, life span is still prolonged dramatically by a factor of about 2. Thus, when the expression of the *daf-2* mutants is triggered by heat, the genes prolong life span without promoting dauer formation. The exact mechanism is unknown, but the *daf-2* locus is known to influence the expression of a number of genes with later onset, and many physiological pathways for its expression are possible.

Scientists have found life-prolonging mutants of yet another gene in *C. elegans*. This gene, called *age-1*, is of particular interest because it illustrates some attributes of antagonistic pleiotropy: although we don't know why, worms with certain alleles of this gene live greatly prolonged lives, but leave far fewer offspring. For example, one of the alleles—*age-1(hx546)*—increases the mean adult life span at 25°C from 15.0 to 25.5 days, and the maximum life

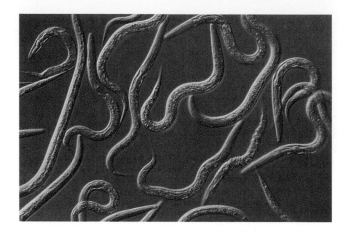

The roundworm *Caenorhabdites elegans* has become a popular subject of research on the genetics of development and aging because of its simple body plan, consisting of only 959 cells, and short generation time with life spans less than one month. Adults are less than 1 millimeter in length.

span from 22.0 to 46.2 days. In one comparison with "wild type" individuals lacking the mutation, worms with *hx546* produced more than 75% fewer eggs (72 eggs versus 317). Although the action of the allele remains a mystery, we can ask whether any one stage in the life span is its target. Does one particular stage of life last longer than normal? Certainly the worm's early development is not affected, and even the length of the adult's egg-laying period remains the same. Thus, only the final period of life, after egg laying, is prolonged, and the allele apparently does nothing to improve reproductive success late in life.

Suppose we compile all the evidence from *C. elegans*, human populations, and other organisms, particularly the fruit fly *Drosophila*: What do we learn about "aging" genes? On balance, the paucity of genes whose major expression comes late in life is disappointing compared to the abundance of genes expressed during development. That result is not promising for the mutation accumulation and antagonistic pleiotropy theories of senescence, which both require the presence of genes that are first expressed at older age. Among the few genes expressed late in life that are conspicuously damaging, even fewer have been shown to have the earlier beneficial effects required by the antagonistic pleiotropy model. A possible exception is Huntington's disease, which considerably shortens life but has also been shown to increase fertility about 9% above normal levels. Alleles that we know to prolong life while reducing fecundity are the *abnormal abdomen* allele in the fruit fly *Drosophila mercatorum* and, as we have seen, the *age-1* allele in *C. elegans*. In addition, individuals with the life-span-prolonging *e1370* allele of the *daf-2* gene of *C. elegans* left on average only 212 offspring instead of the usual 278. The brevity of this list, however, emphasizes how few examples of antagonistic pleiotropy have been discovered. It is also unclear whether we can trust what mutants found in laboratory organisms tell us about the genetic basis of aging.

The Quantitative Genetics of Aging

Because scientists have found so few manifestations of specific "aging" genes, we may hypothesize that aging is influenced by a large number of genes that individually make small, unnoticeable contributions. The effects of so many genes, of such small weight individually, cannot be treated by Mendelian analysis, and we must instead resort to the techniques of quantitative genetics.

Any trait, whether it be height, number of offspring produced per year, or age at death, will vary among individuals in a population. Some individuals are short, some tall; some die young and some old. For example, in a sample of 174 college men studying general genetics at the University of California, Berkeley, height varied from 60 inches (5 feet) to 76 inches (6′4″) and had an average just over 70 inches (5′10″). Men of different heights either differed in their genetic makeup or were reared in different conditions, the taller ones perhaps having had the advantage of better diets. The amount of variation among individuals in a trait such as height may be quantified by assigning to it a number called the variance (V) of that trait. This number is a statistical measure of the deviations of individuals from the average of the population. In computational terms, the variance is the average of the squared deviations of individuals from the mean of the population.

Genetic and environmental factors contribute independently to variation in a trait such as height. A convenient property of the variance is that the different components of the variance simply add together to obtain the total. That is, $V_{phenotypic} = V_{environmental} + V_{genotypic}$. The genetic component can be estimated by observing the resemblances between parents and offspring or among siblings. Thus, while we cannot determine the effects of particular genes, we can perceive the overall genetic contribution to variation in height, intelligence, and many other traits. The partitioning of phenotypic variance into its genetic and environmental components is the heart and soul of quantitative genetics.

How can quantitative genetics be used to evaluate theories of aging? Both the mutation accumulation and antagonistic pleiotropy theories of aging, for example, require that harmful genes be expressed with greater frequency later in life. These deleterious genes are distributed unevenly among individuals in the population, creating variance in, say, heart disease or bone strength. Both theories predict that this variance should increase with age. As more of these harmful genes are expressed late in life, more genes will act on a single attribute such as heart disease and the variance in the appearance of that attribute among individuals will increase. To estimate genetic

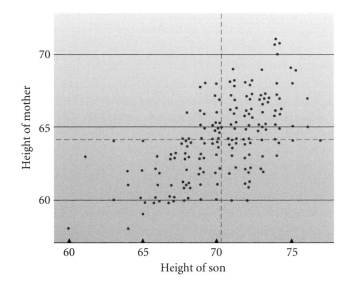

The relationship between the heights of 174 college men and the heights of their mothers. The positive correlation between the two suggests that height is inherited, even though the mean values for the sons (70.2 inches) and their mothers (64.2 inches) differ, since each individual's genes influence its height relative to the mean value for females in the case of mothers and that of males in the case of sons. This particular illustration is complicated by the fact that mothers and their sons tend to have similar nutrition and health care, which might influence height in the same direction independently of any genetic connection. Furthermore, tall mothers tend to mate with tall fathers, which would strengthen the appearance of a correlation between the heights of mothers and their sons.

variance requires a large sample size, and so our estimates come mainly from experiments on fruit flies. The results of these experiments are ambiguous: one study gives no indication that variance in fecundity, for example, increases with age, while another shows that there is a marked increase.

The antagonistic pleiotropy theory makes an additional prediction: individuals that are more successful breeders early in life should be less successful, on average, later. Here the evidence from quantitative genetics is more compelling, at least for fruit flies. In a large breeding program with *Drosophila*

Calculating the Phenotypic Variance of a Trait

To calculate the variance within a sample, one must (1) add the individual values to obtain the total, (2) divide by the number of individuals to determine the average, or mean, value for the population, (3) calculate the differences between each individual and the average, (4) square these deviations, (5) find the total of the squared deviations, and (6) divide the total by the size of the sample to obtain the average of the squared deviations from the population average—in other words, the variance. These steps are shown below for a small sample of heights of college students.

Notice that the units of the variance are the square of the units used to measure the trait, in this case square inches. To put things on a more familiar scale, one may calculate the standard deviation, which is the square root of the variance, or $\sqrt{9} = 3$ inches in this case.

In a large sample, the distribution of measurements will often approximate a bell-shaped, or normal, curve. In the figure below, a normal curve is superimposed on the distribution of heights of college men in a genetics class at Berkeley. About two-thirds of the individuals fall within one standard deviation of the mean value, and about 95% fall within two standard deviations of the mean.

Hundreds of genes may influence height, each one giving growth a small boost or a small check. The only way to look at their total effect, whether adding to height

Calculating the Variance in Height of a Sample of Students

Individual	Height (inches)	(3) Deviation from Mean (inches)	(4) Squared Deviation (inches^2)
1	75	5	25
2	73	3	9
3	72	2	4
4	72	2	4
5	71	1	1
6	70	0	0
7	68	−2	4
8	67	−3	9
9	67	−3	9
10	65	−5	25

(1) Total = 700 inches   (5) Sum of squared deviations = 90 square inches
(2) Mean = 70 inches   (6) Variance = 9 square inches

or subtracting from it, is to compare a person's actual height to the mean height of the population. The genetic pluses and minuses exactly balance for someone whose height is identical to the mean—that is, if there has been no distorting environmental influence. In fact, someone whose genes alone would give him a height of, say, 74 inches may have his height pushed up or down by environmental factors.

Since the average height represents the genetic "midpoint" where opposing genes are in balance, genotypic variation in a population will center around the mean as well. The second figure shows how the total variance is partitioned into its genetic component, centered around the mean, and its environmental component, which here

is shown only for individuals with a genotypic value of 74 inches. In fact, you can imagine that every possible genotypic height value would have such a curve centered on it, to illustrate that when the genotypes of two individuals are identical, differences between them may be caused by differences in their environments. The curves for genotypic and environmental variation are narrower than the curve for phenotypic variation because the first two types of variation have a smaller range, as they must if they are to add to produce phenotypic variation. In this hypothetical example, the genetic variance (5 square inches) and the environmental variance (4 square inches) add to produce the total phenotypic variance (9 square inches).

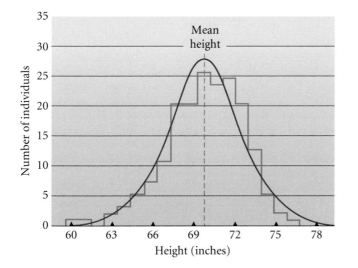

A normal curve is superimposed on the distribution of height of 174 college men.

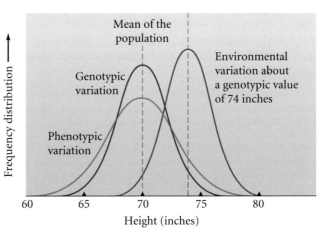

Total phenotypical variation can be partitioned into its genotypic and environmental components.

melanogaster, females that produced more eggs than average during the first 5 days of adult life were found to produce fewer eggs than average during the following 10 days, and they died sooner as well.

Another kind of genetic analysis is to compare traits among inbred lines. Because, after several generations, inbred lines lose most of their genetic variation, deleterious genes whose expressions usually are masked by "typical" or "normal" alleles (the way that the blue-eye gene is masked by the dominant allele producing brown eyes) become visible as a flaw or weakness in the individual. In one experiment with *Drosophila melanogaster*, investigators made 1083 individuals homozygous for the second chromosome through a complicated breeding scheme. Of these chromosomes, 14.7% contained recessive genes that were detrimental and fully 26.2% had recessive genes that were actually lethal.

Which alleles are lost and which are retained in a particular inbred line is largely a matter of chance. Typically in such inbred lines, the life span and fecundity of individuals are greatly reduced; in effect, aging is accelerated. Thus, inbred lines reveal the large number of deleterious alleles in natural populations. Because different alleles become fixed in different inbred lines, when two such lines are crossed, many of the deleterious alleles inherited from one parent are masked by normal alleles inherited from the other parent. As a result, hybrid populations formed by mating individuals from two inbred lines often live much longer than their parents, a form of hybrid vigor.

Because no two inbred lines are genetically identical, one might expect some to be tough survivors still alive and breeding at older ages and others to be more genetically inclined to flourish at younger ages. If aging were caused by antagonistically pleiotropic genes, the longer-lived lines should breed less prolifically at young ages, while the most fruitful lines in youth should be the least fruitful in old age, if only because they won't live that long. Usually, however, we find that a line either thrives early *and* late or else is a poor breeder at all ages. This pattern is counter to the prediction made by antagonistic pleiotropy, but may say more about the peculiar characteristics of inbred lines than about evolutionary theories of aging. Mutants become fixed in inbred populations and impair the body's general physiological condition, so that a line can neither reproduce early nor survive to reproduce in old age.

The genetic evidence doesn't clearly rule in favor of any evolutionary theory of aging. Rather, its message is mixed and somewhat contradictory. Clearly animal populations harbor considerable genetic variation. Much of this variation is hurtful to the body's functioning whether early or late in life, but some genes clearly exhibit antagonistic pleiotropy and support one evolutionary theory of aging. However, there is little evidence of genes that first become active late in life, and their absence is an argument against the validity of *any* evolutionary theory of aging.

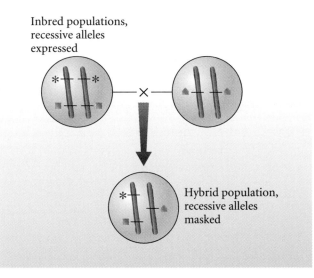

Inbred populations, recessive alleles expressed

Hybrid population, recessive alleles masked

At least some harmful recessive alleles (marked with symbols *, ■, and ▢) are likely to appear on both chromosomes in an inbred line. These alleles are masked by alleles with normal function in the hybrid population.

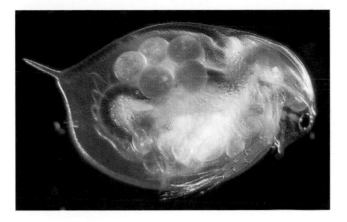

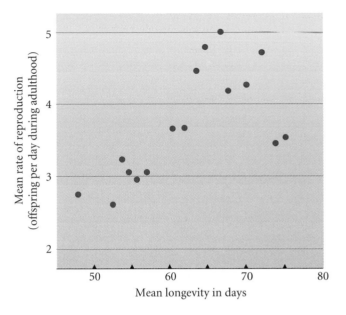

Above: The digestive tract and eggs developing in the brood patch are clearly visible in this water flea of the species *Daphnia magna*. This crustacean lives 2–3 months. Adults are 2 to 3 millimeters in length. Right: Longer-lived water fleas of the species *Daphnia pulex* also produce more offspring, at both early and late ages, than shorter-lived water fleas do, in contradiction to what the antagonistic pleiotropy hypothesis predicts. The data come from a study of all-female clones of *Daphnia pulex* in laboratory culture.

There is a way out of the impasse, and that is to suppose that aging is an inevitable result of "wear and tear," but that the rapidity with which it progresses is influenced by the body's ability to prevent and repair damage. Mechanisms of prevention and repair might function throughout the life of the individual, but no matter how well developed these mechanisms are, it is very likely that some damage escapes them. The unrepaired damage accumulates until a threshold is finally crossed and the physiological effects become pronounced enough to be noticed. As damage accumulates further, the body's ability to function deteriorates. The rate at which this damage accumulates and aging progresses depends on the effectiveness of the prevention and repair mechanisms, which are under the control of our genes. Think about it this way. An automobile will function well during the first year regardless of the quality of service it receives. Only after a few years do the frequency and quality of service make their mark on performance.

Certainly prevention and repair mechanisms will prolong life. However, they are also expensive to develop and maintain. They might reduce the resources that can be allocated to reproduction and thereby produce an apparent antagonistic pleiotropy, since we would live longer at the cost of bearing fewer children. Thus, "wear and repair" would cause apparent antagonistic pleiotropy, but without increasing variance in genetic expression with age—as much of the evidence seems to show. Genetic variation in repair mechanisms, then, provides a plausible explanation for variation in the course of aging.

We can reasonably assume that differences among species in the pattern of aging, particularly in the acceleration of mortality and decline in fecundity with age, have a genetic basis. Aging itself may not be caused by our genes, but genes may nonetheless regulate its expression and rate. Yet, we still have to explain why populations differ in their "aging" genes, and that leads us to consider the action of natural selection and other evolutionary mechanisms.

Genes and Aging

The Virginia opossum (Didelphis virginiana) *has become a popular subject of studies on aging in mammals because it has a short life span (1–2 years) for its body size.*

W e return now to the enigma posed at the beginning the last chapter: How can a feature of life that is so detrimental to the individual as aging be maintained by natural selection? And why does the rate of aging vary so much among species? To answer these questions, we need to understand how genes that reduce survival and fecundity at older ages can persist in populations when natural selection should weed them out. What we have learned about the genetic basis of aging suggests two possibilities. First, aging may be maintained against the tide of selection by mutation, which constantly creates new copies of harmful genes. Second, genes with bad effects in old age may have good effects expressed earlier in life. Under the right conditions, the good effects outweigh the bad, and the numbers of such alleles in populations are actually increased by selection.

What are the right conditions? This obviously depends on how good the good effects are and how bad the bad

7

The Evolution of Aging

effects are, but it also depends on how exposed the good and the bad are to natural selection. The bottom line is this: bad traits expressed later in life are not as readily removed from the gene pool of the population as are those expressed earlier in life. A gene may cause certain heart disease later in life, but if most people have already died of, say, infection or accident, then only a few people afflicted with the gene will survive long enough to develop the disease. And these people will have left as many offspring apiece as all the others who didn't have the gene but who also died younger anyway. Thus it is difficult for natural selection to eliminate the gene; we say that the strength of selection decreases at older age. To put the problem another way, so few individuals live to an old age that proportionately few copies of genes whose effects come late in life actually appear in the population, where they are exposed to natural selection. When a particular copy of a gene has no effect on the individual (because its bearer died of other causes before the gene was expressed), selection is blind to that copy of the gene.

The Theory of Life-History Evolution

The strength of selection is something that can be measured. Indeed, to understand why aging proceeds at different rates from species to species or even why it persists at all, we have to be able to quantify how strongly selection acts to remove harmful genes at different ages and in different populations. The science of doing just that is a part of the study of life-history evolution, which also considers questions regarding fundamental life stages such as the length of the development period and the age at sexual maturity, and looks at such issues as how resources (mainly time, energy, and nutrients) are allocated to self-maintenance, growth, and reproduction, and how the investment in reproduction is divided among males and females.

In the broadest sense, the life history of an individual is everything it is and does, including its decline in old age. This definition is too broad to be useful, and so the typical life history of a population of individuals is often presented as the results of all the "is and does" things: how long individuals survive and how sucessful they are at reproducing themselves. Survival and reproductive success are what really matter to evolution, because they determine the number of descendants left by an individual. To fill in the life table, population biologists calculate the average number of offspring produced at particular ages and the probabilities of surviving from one age to the next. These age-specific values, and additional values calculated from them, make up the life table of a population, which is illustrated by example in the accompanying box. Senescence manifests itself in the life table as decreasing fecundity, decreasing probability of survival, or both. In this sense, aging is a part of every individual's life history.

Two features of the life table are useful for studying the evolution of life histories, including aging. The first is that one may calculate the growth rate of a population whose individuals have particular life-table values. In the example in the box, the population will grow at an exponential rate of 0.185 per unit of time, say, per year. This is like an interest rate of 18.5%—high for a savings account but hardly unusual for populations of animals and plants. Even the population of the northern elephant seal, recovering from a drastic crash caused by hunting during the last century, achieved an exponential growth rate of more than 9% per year. Pheasants released on Protection Island in Puget Sound some years ago increased at a rate of 102% per year (more than double) until the population soon became too large for the habitat.

The second useful feature of the life table is that the values in it depend on how the individual organism functions in its particular environment. As a

Calculating Life-Table Entries

$\mathcal{T}$he population biologist starts off constructing the life table knowing two values, the survival rate (s_x) and fecundity (b_x). The value of each must be measured at each age for a population observed in the field or the lab. But once these two sets of values are available, all the other values can be calculated from them. The ultimate object is to calculate the growth rate of the population.

First note the difference in the table below between the survival rate (s_x) and the survival of individuals to age x (l_x): l_x is the proportion of newborn individuals that are alive on their xth birthday; s_x is the probability that those individuals will live to their next birthday. Of course, the value of l_x is found by multiplying together the values of s for all the years preceding x. In this life table, for example, $l_3 = 0.40 \times 0.70 \times 0.90 = 0.252$. In other words, about a quarter of all individuals live to see their third birthday.

We can interpret the numbers in each row of the life table as follows: at age 3, for example, 25.2% of a cohort of individuals lives to this age (l_x); 90% of them will survive to the next oldest age (s_x); on average individuals of age 3 will live 1.27 additional years (e_x); and each individual of age 3 bears an average of 2.5 offspring (b_x) that year.

A number of additional values can be calculated from the life table. One of these is the net reproductive rate (R_0), which is the average number of offspring per life span, calculated as the sum of the products of l_x and b_x, or $\Sigma l_x b_x = 1.8605$ in this example. A second is the average age at reproduction (T), which is the sum of the products of x, l_x, and b_x divided by R_0. In this example, $\Sigma x l_x b_x = 6.4631$, which divided by R_0 is $6.4631/1.8605 = 3.4738$.

Finally, one may estimate the exponential growth rate of the population reasonably closely by the expression $r = \log_e R_0/T = 0.179$. The actual value of r may be calculated by a more complicated mathematical procedure and for this life table is actually 0.185, which is not unlike the inflation rate in some developing countries.

Life Table for a Hypothetical Population

Age (x)	Survival Rate (s_x)	Survival (l_x)	Life Expectancy (e_x)	Fecundity (b_x)	$l_x b_x$	$x l_x b_x$
0	0.40	1.000	1.73	0.0	0.000	0.000
1	0.70	0.400	1.93	0.0	0.000	0.000
2	0.90	0.280	1.66	1.5	0.420	0.840
3	0.90	0.252	1.27	2.5	0.630	1.890
4	0.70	0.227	0.88	2.0	0.454	1.814
5	0.65	0.159	0.56	1.5	0.238	1.191
6	0.30	0.103	0.23	1.0	0.103	0.619
7	0.00	0.031	0.00	0.5	0.016	0.109
Totals		2.452			1.861	6.463

Elephant seals gathered on a beach on San Benito Island, Baja California, Mexico. In spite of being hunted close to extinction during the last century, the population has recovered at an astounding rate of about 9% per year.

consequence, life-table values differ between environments, as one would expect, but they are also influenced by genetic factors expressed in the phenotype of the individual. Therefore, life-table analysis enables us to assess the effect of a particular genetic change on evolutionary fitness by how much the change affects the survival rate and fecundity at each age.

The growth rate of a population may be calculated exactly from the survival rate and fecundity at each age, that is, from the life-table values. The relationship of population growth rate to s_x and b_x is somewhat complicated, but two basic points convey the essentials for understanding how patterns of aging are maintained by evolution. It may seem obvious that an increase in either survival rate or in fecundity will increase the growth rate of a population, which is equivalent to the number of descendants left by each individual. Thus, any change in the genetic makeup of the individual that increases its chance of survival or number of offspring at a particular age, relative to other individuals in the population, will be favored by natural selection: the proportion of such a favored individual's descendants will increase in the population as a whole.

What is less obvious is that equivalent changes in survival rate and fecundity at older ages have less effect on population growth rate. The reason is that at older ages less and less of the individual's reproductive potential is at stake. In the example described in the box, of the 1.86 offspring produced on average by each individual in the population, more than two-thirds are produced at ages 2, 3, and 4. Therefore, it stands to reason that a change in survival rate at age 1 will have more of an effect, whether good or bad, on lifetime reproductive success than will a change of similar magnitude at age 5. The same is also true of changes in fecundity at younger ages compared to older ages.

Without going into the complicated mathematics, we can set forth two general rules. First, the strength of selection on a change in fecundity at a given age is related to the proportion of individuals in the population that survive to that age, that is, to l_x. Second, the strength of selection on a change in the survival rate at a given age is related to the expected future reproduction at subsequent ages. One can see, therefore, that the strength of selection tends to depreciate with age. For example, selection created by a change in survival rate is more than 10 times stronger when the change occurs at age 2 than at age 5.

With the methods of life-table analysis, we can now assess the effect on evolutionary fitness (the exponential growth rate, r) of a change in any of the life-table entries. Consider a hypothetical population of nonsenescing individuals with an annual survival rate of 0.5 per year and an annual birth rate per individual of 1.0 beginning at age 1. Because only 1 individual in 1000 survives to age 10, we can truncate the life table at 10 years without affecting our calculations significantly. The exponential growth rate (r)

for this population is 0.103, indicating that births slightly exceed deaths and that the population is growing at a rate of about 10% per year.

Now let's see what happens when we change some of the life-table values. Case 1: If a mutation were to boost the fecundity of 1-year-old and 2-year-old individuals by 0.1 to 1.1, the value of r would increase by 0.020 to 0.123 and the mutation would increase in frequency relative to other alleles in the population. Case 2: If this same genetic factor also lowered the fecundity of 5-year-old and older individuals by the same amount (-0.1) that it raised the fecundity of younger individuals, then r would still increase, albeit by a smaller amount (by 0.015 to 0.118). Such a genetic factor clearly exhibits antagonistic pleiotropy and would also become fixed in the population. Thus, this genetic change would result in an apparent evolutionary acceleration of aging, in

Life Table for a Hypothetical Population without and with Aging

		Nonsenescing Population				Case 1		Case 2		Case 3	
x	s_x	l_x	b_x	$l_x b_x$	$x l_x b_x$	s_x	b_x	s_x	b_x	s_x	b_x
0	0.5	1.000	0.0	0.000	0.000	0.5	0.0	0.5	0.0	0.5	0.0
1	0.5	0.500	1.0	0.500	0.500	0.5	1.1	0.5	1.1	0.5	1.1
2	0.5	0.250	1.0	0.250	0.500	0.5	1.1	0.5	1.1	0.5	1.1
3	0.5	0.125	1.0	0.125	0.375	0.5	1.0	0.5	1.0	0.5	1.1
4	0.5	0.063	1.0	0.063	0.252	0.5	1.0	0.5	1.0	0.4	1.1
5	0.5	0.031	1.0	0.031	0.155	0.5	1.0	0.5	0.9	0.4	1.1
6	0.5	0.016	1.0	0.016	0.090	0.5	1.0	0.5	0.9	0.4	1.1
7	0.5	0.008	1.0	0.008	0.056	0.5	1.0	0.5	0.9	0.3	1.1
8	0.5	0.004	1.0	0.004	0.032	0.5	1.0	0.5	0.9	0.3	1.1
9	0.5	0.002	1.0	0.002	0.018	0.5	1.0	0.5	0.9	0.3	1.1
10	0.5	0.001	1.0	0.001	0.010	0.5	1.0	0.5	0.9	0.3	1.1
Exponential growth rate (r)				0.103		0.123		0.118		0.107	

the sense that the older members of the population would have lost some of their breeding capacity. Case 3: Let us now calculate the effect of an antagonistically pleiotropic genetic factor that increases fecundity by 10% to 1.1 at each age but reduces survival by 20% to 0.4 from ages 4 to 6 and by 40% to 0.3 from age 7 onward. With these changes in the life table, the exponential growth rate (r) is 0.107, an increase of 0.004. Thus, the new mutant, which accelerates aging, is selected nonetheless and will become fixed in the population. Even a fitness change of +0.4% is enough to cause evolutionary change.

Age and the Strength of Selection

Playing with the life table in this way soon makes it clear that when individuals stop breeding as frequently late in life or start dying a little sooner, these newly imposed disadvantages have less effect on fitness than similar changes early in life. As we have mentioned earlier, fewer individuals live to older ages and therefore fewer copies of genes expressed only at older ages are exposed to selection. With this conclusion, we have the foundation for most evolutionary theories of aging: deleterious mutations expressed at older ages are more difficult to remove by selection; deleterious pleiotropic effects expressed at older ages are more easily balanced by positive effects earlier in life.

One modifying factor is that some species become more prolific breeders with age as they continue to grow after the onset of reproduction. Many plants, fish, mollusks, reptiles, and others grow continuously, usually at a decreasing rate, throughout life. In these species, the decline in life expectancy with age is partly offset by the increase in fecundity, and so there is more selective weight put on what happens to older individuals. The greater fecundity

of some species with continuous growth may, in part, be responsible for their long life spans, although it is equally likely that their long lives are the consequences of the enhanced error-control and repair mechanisms, and the capacity for cell replacement, that may accompany continual growth. In general, however, as life expectancy and fecundity decline with age, so, too, does the total number of offspring an individual can expect to have in the future.

When the survival rate is changed up or down *before* the age of maturity, natural selection reacts to the change with the same strength regardless of the age at which the change first appears; the strength of selection begins to decline only after the age at which offspring are first produced. Accordingly, many biologists have predicted that senescence should begin only after the age at first reproduction in the population as a whole (an individual cannot put off aging by postponing or abstaining from reproduction; remember that selection works on the population as a whole). This prediction would hold true, however, only when the genes responsible for the survival rate decreasing with age were expressed at a single age or within a narrow range of ages. When a genetic factor influences survival at all ages after the onset of its expression, selection acts more forcefully on genes expressed earlier, even when they are first turned on before reproductive maturity.

Although the evidence is still accumulating, many genes that act on the processes of aging appear to be expressed throughout life, during youth and maturity both. Genes controlling the enzymes that repair and replace damaged DNA, for example, are probably turned on early in development, as are the genes controlling the production of substances that rid cells of free radicals. These genes act to counter processes whose ill effects may be apparent even before maturity and gradually accumulate throughout life. Furthermore, wear and tear begins when life begins, and it also may take a toll before maturity.

Regardless of when their effects first appear, the genes that influence a population's pattern of aging are most likely active throughout most of life. Thus, evolutionary theories of senescence do not say that aging can begin only after maturity. If it turns out that young organisms show no signs of aging, it will likely be because they have greater powers of regeneration and cell replacement than their elders, or because the harmful effects of wear and tear do not accumulate to debilitating levels until late in life.

Of all the conclusions to be drawn from evolutionary theories of senescence, perhaps one stands out: the strength of selection on a gene stands in direct relation to the proportion of individuals in the population that express that gene. We have seen that how many survive to the threshold of old age is determined primarily by how many die among the young. Where hazards to the young such as predation, bad weather, contagious disease, and accidents are few, many individuals live to old age; where death from such hazards is common, few make it past the prime of life. Therefore, if senescence creeps into a population because selection is too weak to weed out bad genes, then *the appearance and acceleration of aging should vary among species in direct relation to the mortality rate experienced by young adults.*

A direct relationship between aging and the death rate from external hazards is the most important single prediction from evolutionary theories of aging. It suggests that if the pattern of aging has a genetic basis, we should find that species living in dangerous habitats should show the bad effects of aging early and fast, independently of the underlying physiological causes that make cells and tissue deteriorate with age. We shall see shortly how well this prediction is borne out by observation and experiment.

Patterns and Predictions

The very fact of senescence neither supports nor refutes evolutionary theories of aging. If aging resulted solely from nongenetic wear and tear, the pattern it takes would be beyond the reach of evolution, yet we would surely enough age. So how do we tell for certain whether the pattern of aging has been modified by genes?

Regardless of what the specific "aging" genes turn out to be, all evolutionary models make two predictions that must hold true if evolution is acting on patterns of aging: they predict that (1) organisms breed less and die at higher rates as they age and (2) the acceleration of mortality resulting from aging will go up or down in synch with the minimum, baseline mortality rate experienced by young adults in the population. Both predictions are independent of the particular genetic mechanisms through which evolution modifies patterns of aging.

The first prediction is made by *all* theories of aging, whether they are evolutionary or nonevolutionary (like wear and tear). Hence, although we have abundant evidence confirming this prediction, it does not help us to distinguish among theories. Thus, we are left with one important prediction from evolutionary theories of aging, namely, that the rate of aging should vary in direct proportion to baseline mortality rates *independently of physiological differences between populations.*

Few data are available to test this prediction because patterns of aging are most often measured in the laboratory and estimates of deaths from accident, disease, or predation must be gotten in natural settings, where such information is difficult to obtain. At this point, we must rely on estimates of maximum life span for animals in captivity plus a few observations on mortality in the wild. As we have seen before, larger animals generally have lower mortality rates than smaller animals, and they age more slowly. Unfortunately, we can't use this correlation to distinguish evolutionary from nonevolutionary theories of aging because larger animals may suffer less wear and tear thanks to their lower rates of growth and metabolism.

The most convincing evidence that aging is under evolutionary control comes from comparing organisms having similar physiology but different rates of aging. For example, we generally assume that because birds fly they have lower mortality rates than mammals, and, indeed, among species of similar body size birds do have longer maximum life spans than mammals. It is not unusual for a sparrow to reach an age between 12 and 15 years, whereas few mice of similar body size can live longer than 3 years. In support of this point, the longevities of bats greatly exceed those of nonflying mammals of the same size. Although such comparisons support the idea that evolution modifies patterns of aging, we will need more detailed life tables of natural populations to provide convincing evidence of this type for evolutionary theories.

Long-term studies of natural populations are beginning to provide just the kind of data that we need to test the basic prediction of the evolutionary theory of aging. In a variety of species of birds and mammals, it has been possible to calculate the baseline mortality rates of young adults (A in the Gompertz aging equation) and the rate at which mortality increases with age (G in the Gompertz equation). From these values, we can estimate the age by which a certain fraction of the population would have died if deaths resulted only from aging and there wasn't any baseline mortality. Now, we may define the rate of aging as the inverse of the time required to reach this point. Suppose, for example, that 90% of individuals would die of old age by 5 years in one population and 10 years in another. We can see that aging is more rapid in the first population by looking at the inverse of these values: 1/5, or 0.2, per year and 1/10, or 0.1, per year, respectively. When we compare this rate of aging among species, we find that it increases in direct proportion to the baseline mortality, from about 1/50 per year for animals like elephants with a baseline mortality rate of 0.2% per year, to 1/10 per year for animals like small birds with a baseline mortality rate of 50% per year. The predicted relationship between the baseline mortality rate and the rate

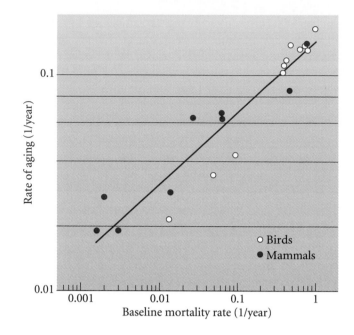

Species with a high baseline mortality rate will have a high rate of aging as well. The rate of aging is the inverse of the number of years that would be required for 90% of adult individuals to die from the causes of aging only. The baseline mortality is the rate for young adults.

of aging is thus evident in this broad survey of natural populations of birds and mammals.

While results from field studies are beginning to produce promising support for evolutionary theories of aging, scientists have tried to produce evolutionary change in the laboratory. Here the investigators themselves act as the selective force, choosing which individuals will survive to leave offspring. Their goal is to test ideas about the evolution of aging by attempting to modify patterns of senescence in laboratory populations. The approach is similar to that used by plant and animal breeders to produce such agricultural wonders as sweet corn and Holstein milk cows. The results are striking and reveal much about the evolution of aging, and its genetic basis, in laboratory populations of a few kinds of organisms.

Evolution in the Laboratory

Among the early attempts to modify the course of aging in laboratory populations were the experiments of David Mertz, at the University of Illinois (Chicago), on flour beetles *(Tribolium)*. Flour beetles normally live for up to a year as adults, but Mertz wanted to see if he could shorten that life span. In effect, he planned to accelerate the aging of flour beetles, and he planned to do so by shortening reproductive life.

Mertz began by setting up several experimental lines of beetles. Each new generation in a line was formed from eggs laid during the first 10 days of adult life. Mertz presumed that any changes in mortality rate that appeared after beyond 10 days would have no fitness consequences because the beetles were "post-reproductive" at those ages. Therefore, selection on genetic factors that accelerated aging would be relaxed and selection favoring increased early reproduction would intensify. The results of the experiments more or less conformed to these predictions. After 12 generations, fecundity during the first month had increased by 10%, to 460 eggs from 417, while longevity had decreased to 231 days from 271 in males, and to 207 days from 228 (not statistically significant) in females.

Much larger experiments with more complex de-

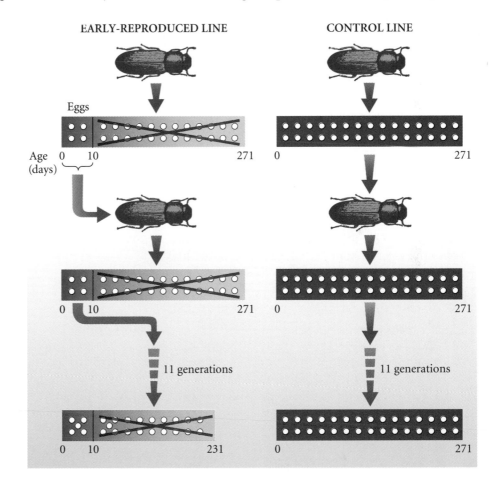

In his experiment, Mertz selected for early reproduction in flour beetles *(Tribolium)* and found a decrease in life span.

signs have been carried out on the fruit fly *Drosophila melanogaster*. Leo Luckinbill, at Wayne State University, established lines of fruit flies that were reproduced either early in life (in the first 2 to 6 days of adulthood) or late (after 22 days initially, but after 58 days following 16 generations of selection). The results were dramatic. In the late-reproduced lines, the maximum life span increased from about 35 days on average to more than 60 days. In the early-reproduced flies, the life span remained unchanged, suggesting that "natural" populations of these flies have short life spans and reproduce mostly at young ages.

An interesting aspect of Luckinbill's results was that flies selected for early reproduction spent a much longer period as larvae and pupae, before emerging as adult flies: 16 to 18 days instead of the normal 10 or 11 days. It would appear that flies that had longer development periods were able to start producing eggs sooner after emergence. Under usual circumstances no eggs are laid for the first few days after emergence as the reproductive system continues to mature and form eggs. Perhaps by remaining longer in the pupa, the flies could accomplish some of this development before emerging, so that flies fooled the investigators into believing that they were

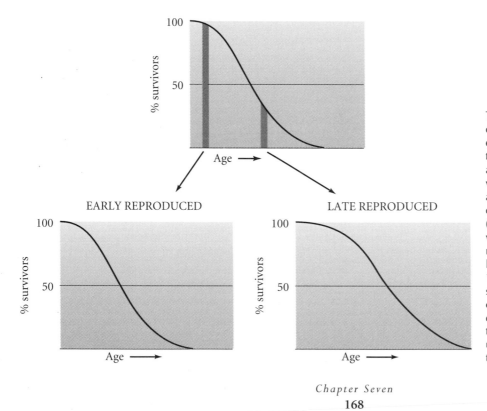

EARLY REPRODUCED

LATE REPRODUCED

The life spans of fruit flies can be changed by genetic selection. In this experiment by Michael Rose (similar to the one by Leo Luckinbill), young and old flies from a starting population were selected for breeding at different ages (vertical stripes). The life spans of those selected when young adults (early reproduced) become a bit shorter, while those selected in old age (late reproduced) became progressively longer lived, eventually reaching a 120-day record (35% longer than the starting point). Life spans in this and other studies described in the text can differ between experiments because the small size of the experimental populations, relative to human populations, gives rise to sampling errors.

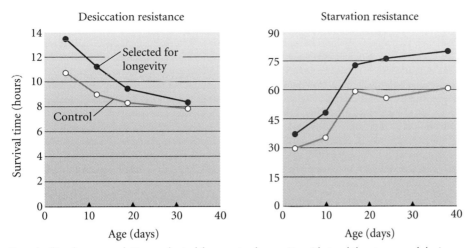

Desiccation resistance

Starvation resistance

Female flies from populations selected for greater longevity withstand the stresses of desiccation and starvation longer than control flies, regardless of the age at which they were compared.

"younger" than they actually were, counting from the beginning of larval development. In Luckinbill's experiment, early-reproduced lines were also more prolific breeders, by about 10% percent at early ages, suggesting antagonistic pleiotropy.

Michael Rose, of the University of California at Irvine, established lines of *Drosophila melanogaster* by collecting eggs for new generations initially at 28 days, and then, as longevity increased, at later and later times, until he could collect eggs from flies as old as 70 days. Compared to control lines of flies, which were not being selected, the average longevity of the late-reproduced flies increased to 43 days from 33 days for females and to 44 days from 39 days for males. Adult females laid a lifetime total of 1635 eggs on average in the control line and 1733 in the late-reproduced line, but this difference was not statistically significant. It was clear, however, that compared to control lines the selected lines reproduced slower at earlier ages and faster at late ages. Rose interpreted these results to mean that genes with antagonistic pleiotropic effects were being selected—that is, the flies were trading early reproduction for increased longevity and later reproduction.

Philip Service, then at Dalhousie University, and his colleagues examined some of the physiological changes that had taken place in Rose's late-reproduced lines. The longer-lived flies were significantly more resistant at all ages to desiccation, starvation (females only), heat stress, and the vapors of ethanol (grain alcohol). We might wonder whether declining resistance to these sorts of stresses is a normal part of aging in fruit flies, but this doesn't seem to be the case. The resistance to desiccation remains steady from "middle age" onward, and the resistance to starvation actually increases with age. Why, then, would the longer-lived flies have become more resistant to these stresses?

In a second study, Service and his colleagues measured the respiration rate (oxygen consumed per milligram of body mass per hour), activity (movement), and accumulation of fat deposits in the selected and control strains. Again the results were clear: flies selected for late reproduction had lower rates of respiration and activity at young ages and accumulated more fat than did the control flies. It is easy to see how the increased fat storage of selected flies might make them less vulnerable to starvation

The Evolution of Aging

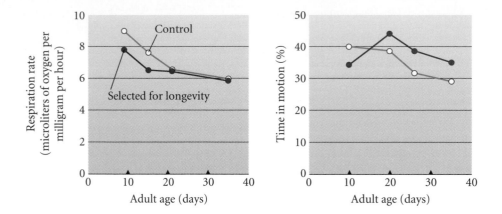

Flies from populations selected for greater longevity initially have both lower respiration rates and lower activity rates compared to flies from control populations.

and how their lower metabolism, by limiting the rate at which they use up food and water and produce heat, might give them greater resistance to the stresses of starvation, heat, and desiccation. These qualities also may have contributed to the greater longevity of the selected flies, although the causal connections are less direct because the flies were not exposed to stresses.

Following up on these results, Service, E. W. Hutchinson, and Rose conducted a pivotal experiment designed to evaluate the hypothesis of antagonistic pleiotropy. As we have seen, Rose's late-reproduced lines evolved to have a prolonged life span. This may have been accomplished in one or both of two ways: (1) it could be that the experiment causes deleterious mutations that are normally expressed at older ages to be eliminated, or (2) it could be that the experiment selects for pleiotropic genes with strongly beneficial effects at old ages and mildly deleterious effects at early ages. One sign of antagonistic pleiotropy was already apparent, in that the younger members of the selected lines were slow breeders in comparison to their counterparts in the

control lines, and Service devised this experiment to test whether the hinted-at antagonistic pleiotropy was supported.

The experimenters pulled a switch on the late-reproduced lines: they stopped selecting flies from those lines for late reproduction and instead began selecting them for early reproduction, a switch of the sort that plant and animal breeders call reverse selection. If, on the one hand, antagonistically pleiotropic genes had contributed to the slowing of aging observed in the first experiment, then this experiment should have led to a rapid acceleration of aging, toward the condition in the control population, as the advantages of breeding fast early in life come to dominate over the advantages of a longer life span. If, on the other hand, aging were caused by harmful mutations expressed late in life, the flies' life span would shorten only after enough such mutations had accumulated in the population. That accumulation would almost certainly have required more time than the length of the reverse-selection experiment.

The results of the experiment were somewhat complicated. The flies did breed faster when young, and they lost some of their resistance to starvation; however, their resistance to desiccation and ethanol vapors did not change. The flies had been kept crowded together at high density during the larval stage, and under these conditions the competition for food is likely to have a strong influence on larval development, adult size, and reproduction. When the experiment was repeated on flies raised at low density, and food was not a limiting factor, no changes were observed in either fecundity or resistance to starvation. Indeed, Rose had found earlier that flies raised at low density did not breed any slower at young age even when selected for increased longevity.

These experiments do not allow us to distinguish which of the two mechanisms, antagonistic pleiotropy or deleterious mutation, is responsible for the differences that we observe between populations in patterns of aging. Overall, the experimental evidence suggests that antagonistic pleiotropy may be most important under the competitive conditions of high density, but that the rate of aging also may be modified by other types of genetic factors. Even at high densities, the pleiotropic responses that we observe may have a simple physiological basis. It appears that the late-reproduced strains have lower metabolic rates, particularly at earlier ages, which might have been responsible for their lower rate of reproduction, slower aging (fewer metabolic byproducts produced; less wear and tear from activity), and greater resistance to stress.

If flies in selected populations actually achieved greater longevity by evolving to have lower metabolic rates, we have to ask whether the evolutionary responses to strong selection that we observe in the laboratory resemble the diversification of aging patterns that takes place in natural populations. Artificially selected animals and plants will respond to virtually any kind of selection by breeders. Chickens bred for high body mass may accumulate more fat rather than the muscle that farmers want, but they do achieve high mass. Selected for low mass, chickens

behave like anorexics who refuse to eat enough. They grow slowly because they are undernourished rather than because they have altered the controls over the growth process. Who knows what flies do when faced with similar situations?

One additional interesting experiment was performed by Larry Mueller, now at the University of California, Irvine. He had established two lines of flies: one in which individuals were allowed to reproduce only between 3 and 6 days of age and were maintained at a low population density; and another in which individuals were allowed to reproduce at any age, but were maintained at a high population density. After more than 120 generations, the early-reproduced flies produced few offspring at late age compared to the control lines, as one would expect, but they bred no faster at early ages either. Mueller then crossed several of the early-reproduced lines to obtain hybrids. The hybrids showed restored fecundity at the relatively late age of 4 weeks.

The inescapable conclusion is that only one mechanism could explain the loss of fecundity at older ages in early-reproduced lines: that is, these lines must have been accumulating harmful recessive mutations that were expressed late in life. Interestingly, different mutations would have accumulated in each of the separate experimental lines. When two of these lines were crossed, the harmful effects in one line would be masked by dominant alleles having normal expression in the other. Had the decline in fecundity late in life been due to genes with pleiotropic effects, then these genes would still have been present and expressed in the hybrid populations. Only in the unlikely circumstance that most pleiotropic genes were recessive, and that different ones had been selected in each experimental population, could they have been the cause of the observed results.

Scientists conducting laboratory experiments are able to investigate evolutionary changes in populations under highly controlled conditions. However, to date these experiments have studied only a nar-

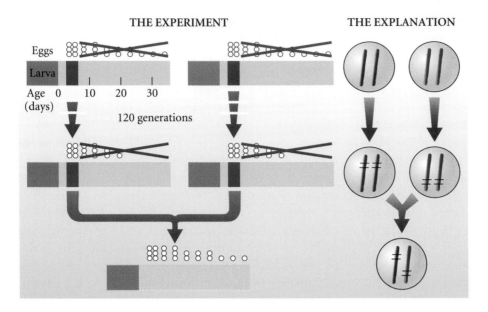

THE EXPERIMENT   THE EXPLANATION

In his experiment, Mueller found that the number of eggs laid per week by early-reproduced lines decreases between week 1 of adult life and week 4 compared to lines in which females are allowed to reproduce at all ages. However, when he formed hybrids between different early-reproduced lines, the eggs produced at 4 weeks of age were restored to its former number. These results suggest that the egg-producing ability of older flies in the selected lines had been curtailed by the accumulation of mutations that were masked in the hybrids.

row range of organisms, principally the fruit fly *Drosophila*, and so we may wonder about the generality of the results to other animals, including humans. Moreover, the evolutionary responses evoked in these experiments may not be representative of the responses that a natural population would display to a changing environment. As a general rule, the time it takes for a new trait to spread through a population depends on how much it increases the fitness of its bearers—in other words, on the strength of selection. In order to complete experiments in a reasonable time, even with fruit flies, one must exert extremely strong selective pressures on a single trait. But alleles favored by strong selection may differ from those favored by weak selection in ways that are manifested in aging.

It is often the case that strong selection produces organisms that meet the selection criterion (such as larger body size or greater egg production), but the same genes that have accomplished the selected change inevitably have other, damaging effects on fecundity, life span, disease resistance, growth rate, and so on. These bad effects are counteracted by the strong selection for the genes' beneficial effect. Under weak selection, such deleterious pleiotropic effects cannot be countered, and alleles of other genes may be favored, each with smaller effects on the trait in question but fewer harmful side effects. In addition, strong selection means that few animals meet the selection criterion, and the parental populations are often so small that there is an increase in inbreeding. As a result, a larger proportion of recessive alleles are expressed and become visible to selection.

Selection on Animals in the Wild

In natural environments, selection can favor only genetic factors without grave side effects. An organism in nature, therefore, cannot evolve a trait in response to one selective force that makes it more vulnerable to some other danger or reduces its reproductive rate. A poultry farmer might select a heavy meat-producing breed that can barely fly and could not escape predators. Such birds can be successful in the chicken yard because there are no predators. However, few highly selected domesticated animals or plants can make it on their own in the wild. Therefore, we would feel much more confident of our experimental results from selective breeding if we could observe similar responses in natural populations.

The life histories of animals and plants have been shown repeatedly to respond through evolution to changes in natural mortality. Hunting, whether by humans or by natural predators, reduces the average life expectancy of the prey and places an evolutionary premium on reproducing early in life. Often, one finds that animals in heavily hunted populations mature earlier and at a smaller size, and produce more young in each brood or litter, than animals in populations that are relatively unmolested by predators.

A particularly nice experimental study showing how predation could shape life histories was performed by David Reznick of the University of California at Riverside. Reznick worked on the island of Trinidad with guppies, which are small, tropical freshwater fish. Several of the island's streams had a series of waterfalls that prevented the large, predatory fish found in the larger expanses of water below from colonizing upstream stretches. Thus, portions of the upper reaches of the streams were like giant natural aquaria, into which Reznick could introduce guppies and different kinds of predatory fish and watch for changes in growth rate, age at maturity, and reproductive rate over ensuing generations. In one experiment, the guppies came from a population that had been subject to intense predation by the cichlid *Crenicichla*, a species of tropical fish that feeds on adults. As expected, these guppies spawned at an early age and allocated a large proportion of their re-

The Trinidadian guppy *(Poecilia reticulata)*. Several males are courting the larger and less brightly colored female. Guppies live about as long as mice and also show degenerative organ changes.

One of the experimental pools used by David Reznick in his study of the Trinidadian guppy. The pool, in a small stream in the Northern Range of Trinidad, is isolated from upstream and downstream stretches by small waterfalls that guppies and their predators cannot navigate.

sources to produce masses of numerous relatively small eggs. The guppies were introduced to a portion of a stream along with the predator *Rivulus*, which preys on smaller, immature guppies. The guppies quickly evolved to produce smaller numbers of larger eggs at an older age, just as predicted by life-history theory. Such selection for delayed maturity and decreased investment in offspring should also result in lower aging. This prediction has not yet been tested.

The Virginia opossum *(Didelphis virginiana)* has become a useful model for the study of aging in mammals because it has a short life span for a mammal of its body size. In most populations, the animals live less than 2 years; all opossums show signs of aging in their second year, in that they lose body mass and often develop cataracts in the lens of the eye. In addition, females show reproductive senescence in their second breeding year, unmistakeable in the atrophy of reproductive organs and reduced fertility. Steven Austad, now at the University of Idaho, has studied populations of opossums in coastal Georgia, where he has taken advantage of the very different predation rates in several populations: predation rates are much higher in mainland areas than they are on isolated islands off the coast, where predators are rare.

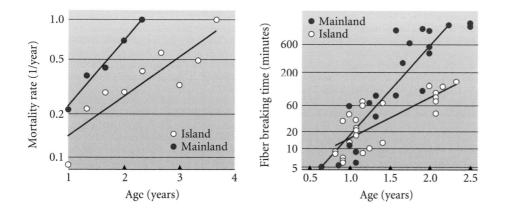

Left: The increase in mortality rate with age for island and mainland populations of opossums, fitted with Gompertz aging curves. Right: Collagen fibers take longer to break in older opossums of the mainland populations compared to island populations, a sign that aging is proceeding faster.

Remember that when baseline mortality rates are low, as in the Georgian island populations, selection to push back aging and prolong the natural life span is strong. Conversely, the higher mortality rates in mainland populations (mostly caused by predation) should relax selection against genes causing rapid senescence. Accordingly, Austad suspected that island opossums should experience a slower acceleration of mortality due to senescence than mainland populations.

Just as Austad had predicted, island populations, with their lower baseline mortality rates (A in the Gompertz equation), do indeed have a slower acceleration of mortality (the Gompertz parameter, G). These data confirm that opossums undergo the same declines in survival and fecundity with age observed in laboratory and field studies on other mammals, and that the rate of demographic aging is sensitive to environmental conditions that alter the death rate from predation or other extrinsic causes.

Next, Austad wanted to determine whether the increase in mortality rate with age might have resulted from physiological senescence. His method was to measure chemical and physical changes associated with aging in collagen fibers taken from the tails of animals of different ages caught in the wild. Collagen is a protein that naturally develops cross-links between molecules to form fibers. More and more of these cross-links form with age, resulting in a gradual loss of elasticity and resiliency. Austad was able to measure these changes by placing a fiber in a solution of urea under tension. The urea chemically breaks down the cross-links and thus reduces the fiber's mechanical strength until it breaks. The greater the number of cross-links, the longer the fiber takes to break. Austad found not only that cross-linkage increases with age in the collagen fibers of opossums, but that this sign of aging appears earlier in mainland than in island populations, matching the difference between the populations in demographic aging. It is one of the marvels of nature, of course, that evolution can transform differences in predation rates into differences in the age at which guppies mature and differences in the resistance to breaking of collagen fibers in the tails of opossums.

The Evolution of Aging

Evolutionary theories of aging have helped biologists to resolve the dilemma of how a population can maintain a seemingly harmful trait in the face of natural selection. In addition, these theories let us understand why species vary in their patterns of aging. Experimental studies, particularly with the fruit fly *Drosophila*, demonstrate convincingly that laboratory populations can respond to selection in such a way that processes of aging are indeed altered, and there is some evidence of similar responses in natural populations.

Our interpretation of the most current information is this. Aging itself is largely induced by general biochemical and mechanical wear and tear, that is, by factors in both the internal and external environments. There is also strong evidence that populations accumulate deleterious mutations whose effects are not expressed until later ages. These mutated genes may produce their protein products throughout the lifetime of the individual, but the effects of these genes are cumulative over time, so dysfunction does not appear until late in life, if ever. The evidence for antagonistically pleiotropic genes is weaker. Although some experiments with fruit flies seem to suggest that such genes exist, in that long life goes with a less reproductively active youth, other interpretations are possible. It may be, for example, that changes in the general level of metabolic activity are altering the rates of both fertility and aging. Or, the balance between early fecundity and aging might also depend on the outcome of the need to allocate energy and other resources between maintenance and repair mechanisms and reproductive function. The general absence of aging in young organisms, especially before they begin reproducing, may reflect the fact that the effects of harmful alleles, environmentally induced damage, and wear and tear are cumulative and do not appear until late in life. The freedom of youth from aging may also result from the cell proliferation taking place in the tissues of growing organisms. Because new cells are being created rapidly at this age, others that are damaged through wear and tear, accidents, and somatic mutation can be readily replaced, and the organism continues to function normally.

Although aging may be environmentally influenced, we are convinced that the *rate* of aging is under genetic control, probably through various cellular mechanisms of maintenance and repair, as well as cell turnover within tissues. It seems likely to us that most of the differences that have evolved between populations in rate of aging can be traced to maintenance and repair mechanisms.

Maintenance and repair mechanisms are expensive, and the degree to which they are developed should depend on how much they are likely to prolong the lives of individuals in a population. Where death from accident, predation, or disease is high and few individuals make it to old age, maintenance and repair are of little use. Where the probability of death from these extrinsic causes is low, maintenance and repair may prolong the lives of many that survive to old age and may therefore be strongly selected. Thus, we see differences among populations in how they balance the inevitability of wear and tear against genetic mechanisms to reduce the impact of that deterioration on the individual. The germ line itself is a special case: it is prevented from aging within the lifetime of the individual primarily by cell lineage selection.

Given these conclusions, what are the prospects for prolonging our own life span and increasing the quality of life at older ages? The processes responsible for aging will never be stopped, because they appear to be largely a consequence of life itself. Aging is therefore a natural process that may be limiting but is not necessarily immediately debilitating or even life threatening. From a genetic standpoint, the first goal for ameliorating human aging should be to understand the biochemical consequences of the most harmful genes well enough to identify their presence early in life and alter their expression. In many cases, genetic screening and counseling could reduce the frequency of exceptionally harmful genes within the population. Unfortunately, numerous deleterious mutations, each with small effect, will not yield to such a strategy because they are too difficult to identify and work with.

A second goal should be to understand the cellular mechanisms of maintenance and repair well enough to invent means of enhancing them. Programs to boost these mechanisms may ultimately be as simple as regularly taking antioxidants, but a wide variety of such mechanisms undoubtedly remain to be discovered, and many of these should prove possible to enhance by some form of therapy.

We may, eventually, be able to manipulate some genetically determined aspects of aging and so, eventually, extend the maximum life span of our species.

We can, however, obtain much more dramatic and immediate results from reducing various detrimental impacts on health and survival arising from the environment. Whereas a part of the aging process results from the biochemical processes normally present in all cells, a second component comes from sources of damage outside living cells and tissues. We have seen how the use of sunscreens that block ultraviolet radiation has reduced the prevalence of skin cancer, and how the decrease in smoking in the United States has reduced the incidence of lung and cardiac diseases. We live in dangerous environments. Recognizing the dangers and taking action to reduce them could produce tremendous public health benefits and extend the average human life span.

Old age—like youth—can be a time of new beginnings.

*N*o demographic projection can be made with more certainty than the continued aging of the human population. As medical technology has spread and standards of living have improved, everywhere around the world the numbers of older people are increasing to unprecedented levels. During the last 40 years, the average life expectancy at birth of the world's population has increased by 35%, from about 46 years in 1950 to about 63 years in 1990. In the United States, during that same period, the proportion of the population that is 65 years or older grew from 8.1 to 12.6%. By 2020, this fraction will increase to about 17%—every sixth individual in the country will be over the age of 65 years.

This shift in the population structure raises many questions about the quality of life of older generations, the increasing average costs of health care, and the societal changes that will accompany this shift. Once considered a privilege or a stroke of good fortune, reaching old age

8

A Look at the Future

in reasonable health is now considered by many a birthright to be supported by society as a whole and by governmental policy. It is impossible for us to predict the precise patterns of aging 20 or 50 years from now, or society's response, except to say that, as our average ages increase, life will be different than it is now. Even without a crystal ball, though, we can make some general observations that bear on the future of aging and the graying of the human population.

As a Population, We're Getting Older

Most demographers agree that life expectancy at birth will continue to increase throughout the world and that the fraction of the population reaching 65 years of age is the most rapidly growing age group everywhere, regardless of whether the birth rate is high or low. The demographic consequences of aging patterns are shown by mapping the age structure of a

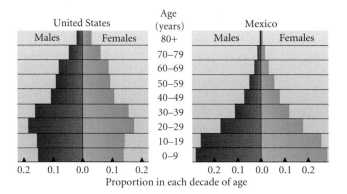

Proportions of the 1985 population of the United States and Mexico in each 10-year age class. The markedly pyramidal shape in the case of Mexico reflects the high birth rate of the population. The baby-boomer bulge is apparent in the age structure of the population of the United States. The graph also shows that more women than men reach old age.

population, that is, the fraction of the population in each age group. Consider the United States and its neighbor Mexico. The population of the United States has relatively more young adults and middle-aged adults than children. Other industrialized countries, such as Canada and the nations of Europe, have similar age structures. In contrast, Mexico is typical of many developing nations in that the fraction of the population under the age of 15 is almost twice as large as in the United States. These young individuals will maintain Mexico's high population growth rate as they enter their peak reproductive years. Nonetheless, the representation of older individuals in this population will also increase, so that by 2020 one in 14 will be over age 65, about twice the current level. While this fraction is less than half of that in the United States, the number of elderly will nonetheless be huge—about 10 million.

In the developed countries, an impressive number of individuals will reach even more advanced ages. In the United States, the proportion of individuals over 85 years will increase from the present-day 3 million, or 1.3% of the population, to over 15 million by the year 2050. While it is heartening that so many of us will live so long, we must remember that as more and more of us escape the dangers of youth and young adulthood, more of us will fall victim to the diseases that plague the senescent years. Heart attacks, strokes, dementia, cancer, diabetes, and other consequences of aging have now become the primary causes of death in the United States and Europe. Clearly, as the body ages it becomes less able to resist pathogens and to repair damage, and so the likelihood of succumbing to one of these disorders increases. In addition, as we have seen, some types of damage and deterioration accumulate with age, making the body's task of self-maintenance all the more difficult. Are we trading earlier, and usually quicker, deaths from contagious diseases for prolonged suffering in old age? A recent drawing in *The New Yorker* shows a middle-aged man sitting at a bar and lamenting to his friend, "The problem with doing things to prolong your life is that all the extra years come at the end, when you're old."

More people are surviving to old age, but do people who now reach 65 or 85 years of age have the same survival rate as did the few who survived to these ages a century or two ago? Those of you who have strolled through old cemeteries may have been struck not only by the innumerable lives cut short in childhood and youth, but also by the fortunate few who achieved relatively old ages. Colonial New England had its share of tough octogenarians. Our ancestors had to run a gauntlet of pathogens as children and young adults, but, once having survived the common infectious diseases, they seem to have had good prospects for reaching old age. Given a healthy environment, this has apparently always been so. From the days of the Roman Empire, early in the second century, we have, for example, Pliny's ringing praises of the healthy nature of his summer home in the Apennines:

> Hence the number of elderly people living there—you can see the grandfathers and great-grandfathers of people . . . and hear stories and tales of the past. . . . a visit here is like a return to another age.

These inhabitants of the Apennines enjoyed long lives because they had access to good food and clean water, and because they enjoyed a respite from epidemics and warfare.

Of course, improved medical care now extends the lives of those afflicted with the degenerative diseases of advanced age. Between 1900 and the present, the further life expectancy of Americans reaching 65 years of age has increased from 11 to 15 years in men, and from 12 to 19 years in women. Moreover, most afflictions of the elderly have decreased in prevalence somewhat, in spite of the fact that individuals with weak constitutions, who in former times might have died of pathogenic disease, now survive to advanced age. Whether the maximum life span of humans is likely to increase in the future is much more difficult to predict. We might find it encouraging that the oldest humans have lived during this century, and living contenders are undoubtedly closing in on the record of 120 years shared, at the time of writing, by Shigechiyo Izumi and Madame Jeanne Calment. The present mark will not stand long.

This rosy picture may, however, be somewhat misleading. Even if survival in old age had not improved at all, the smaller human population and higher mortality of children and young adults would have made a 120-year-old less probable a hundred or a thousand years ago. Poor record keeping would just about guarantee that we wouldn't know about such a long-lived person, anyway. Of course, the number of extremely old people is increasing steadily, and, just by chance, individuals will occasionally reach record longevities. What concerns each of us individually, however, is our personal prospect for achieving old age. Will some breakthrough of science or medicine allow humans to routinely live to 100, 120, or even 150 years? Some scientists think so. After all, a change in a single gene can greatly extend the life span of that favorite roundworm *Caenorhabdites elegans,* and relatively few generations of selection can increase (or decrease) longevity in the common fruit fly *Drosophila melanogaster.* Why not in humans? Our own thoughts on this issue are mixed. Worms and flies may not be good models for aging in mammals because of tremendous differences in body plan and physiology. Yet our understanding of the factors that impinge on aging offer hope that we will find ways to prevent and treat the illnesses of aging.

Postponing Senescence

Whether one develops some life-threatening affliction at older age depends in part on one's genetic constitution, in part on one's lifelong exposure to certain environmental factors, like cigarette smoke, and in part on the sheer luck of avoiding accidents.

Studies of coronary heart disease have identified three major risk factors—cigarette smoking, high blood pressure, high serum cholesterol—and numerous minor risk factors, such as obesity, inactivity, and stress. Yet, all these factors together account for only about 40% of the incidence of coronary heart disease in the population as a whole. When it is so difficult to determine what puts an individual at risk, prevention cannot be guaranteed. We can, however, reduce risk considerably by avoiding the factors that encourage it. If you want a long, healthy life, eat well, don't smoke, exercise regularly but moderately, stay out of the sun, and, to hedge your bets, take supplements of the antioxidants vitamins C and E. Preventive measures, while reducing the afflictions of old age in the population as a whole and extending life expectancy, can accomplish only a limited amount.

For disease that originates outside the body, it is relatively easy to identify the causative agents, such as pathogens and toxins, and do something about them. Most of the diseases of old age, however, result from the malfunctioning of the body itself, and their causes are rooted in the failure of defense and self-maintenance systems to function properly after a lifetime of hard work. Some of these problems are simply built into the system, like the development of rheumatoid arthritis and other autoimmune diseases as the immune system becomes sensitive to some of the body's own proteins.

Many problems of old age result directly or indirectly from changes in gene activity that could be controlled by taking drugs or otherwise manipulating external influences. Dramatic examples are the consequences of estrogen loss at menopause, which alters the activity of genes throughout the female reproductive system. The bone loss, uterine atrophy, and most other effects of menopause can be retarded or even prevented by maintaining estrogen levels through replacement therapy. The supplemental estrogen activates the transcription factors that regulate gene activity. The onset of Alzheimer disease at later ages may also be viewed as an outcome of altered gene activity. The mystery of that disease is what causes the gene activity in particular cells to change.

The example of the honey bee shows that the same set of genes can be programmed by diet to yield adults with very different life spans. In our own species, too, the activity of a large number of genes can be influenced by the external environment. You will all remember that the age of onset of Alzheimer disease is delayed in individuals who have more years of higher education. Diet influences gene activity in the liver, muscle, and brain, and hormones do so in innumerable examples. In the future, many powerful approaches for modifying human aging will employ external influences to intervene in the activity of genes—turning off genes with adverse effects and keeping necessary genes active. This type of genetic engineering is, however, very different from the much more difficult task of replacing defective or damaged genes.

If the course of aging and its lethal results were determined strictly by genetic factors, two courses of action would be open to us. One would be to turn to the newly invented techniques of genetic engineering, to modify the activities of existing genes or to replace damaged ones. The other would be to employ the ancient techniques of selective breeding, also known as eugenics.

Manipulating Our Genes

Eugenics is the science of improving the genetic makeup of a population, particularly by allowing the production of only genetically superior offspring. For millennia humans have applied eugenics to plant and animal breeding: we define the superior qualities, such as high milk production, and carry out the breeding and selection to improve the genetic stock accordingly. During the early part of this century, many people considered applying eugenic ideas to the human population. This line of thinking is now properly considered elitist, and it often had ugly racial overtones. Needless to say, many people who espoused eugenics painted the ideal genetic constitution in their own image.

Even if eugenic methods were put into practice, they could do little to increase maximum life span. The few humans who reach very old age make up such a small fraction of the total population that increasing their breeding rate would have little effect on the frequency of longevity genes in the population as a whole. Besides, if antagonistic pleiotropy applied, these individuals would actually produce fewer offspring than the population average, and one would have to severely curtail breeding in everyone else to have any impact at all. Most telling, by the time a person's longevity is known, he or she is most likely past the reproductive years. This, of course, could change in the future, as we are better able to predict an individual's longevity in advance.

The genetic engineering of human beings may be in the offing as a way to combat aging, although, complex as it is, the technology will be a long time in coming. Genetic engineering includes a variety of techniques, such as introducing new genetic sequences into an individual, introducing foreign cells with desirable genetic sequences into particular tissues, modifying hormonally or otherwise which genes are expressed and when, and providing gene products when a defective gene fails to make them. These are powerful methods, but if aging is controlled by many genes, expressed at different times, genetic engineering becomes a bit like trying to keep winter at bay by gluing the leaves back on the trees.

There has been considerable excitement about the recent identification of mutants of the human *BRCA1* gene that increase susceptibility to breast and ovarian cancers. Once we understand how this gene acts, that understanding may lead to treatments that substitute for the proper functioning of the gene. Lest expectations be raised too much, however, we note that delivering an artificial gene product exactly where it is needed at exactly the right moment may be nearly impossible. Moreover, only about 5 to 10% of breast cancers are the result of known inherited susceptibilities, leaving the remainder of the cases unexplained. The genetic approach will take us only so far—how far we don't yet know.

Our identification of mutant alleles of the *BRCA1* gene has made it possible to screen women for the presence of the mutant gene; women who are revealed to have a mutant allele can take steps to improve their chances of detecting a cancer early. Moreover, genetic screening could eliminate some of the practical obstacles to selective breeding—the presence of the gene can be spotted before the carrier reaches the age of reproduction—and it raises the possibility that genetic counseling could be used to prevent the births of individuals carrying rare diseases caused by a single mutation. Ordinarily, selection on rare recessive genetic factors such as the *BRCA1* gene is impractical, simply because most of the genetic variation is hidden. The *apoE-4* allele associated with Alzheimer disease, for example, is carried in a single dose (heterozygous) by 1 in 10 individuals in most populations. Thus, only about 1 in 100 children inherits two of these alleles and is at higher risk of developing the disease, and many of these individuals will die from other causes at an earlier age. When such a small percentage of the genes in the population are exposed because they cause disease, early genetic screening would be required to identify potential carriers of the trait.

Even genes that are at first normally functioning may suffer damage during the course of life from such physical factors as ultraviolet light and x-rays and such chemical factors as oxygen radicals, and even such biological factors as viruses that invade cells and alter their genetic machinery. Many types of cancer appear to result from such genetic change. No matter the precise agent that produces these mutations, they are difficult to prevent because they may crop up at random in only a few cells, and, of course, they may affect any gene. The only possibilities open to us may be to reduce the mutagenic factors themselves or to bolster the body's mechanisms for recognizing and repairing the damage.

Genetic Screening and Ethical Questions

Since 1950, women in the United States have tended to have their children at increasingly later ages. In 1985, one-quarter of all children in this country were born to mothers over the age of 30 and almost 1% to mothers over the age of 40. With older age at maternity come a higher proportion of babies with various defects, including Down syndrome. Thus, a shift in the maternal ages of childbearing is making genetic screening for birth defects ever more important.

The point of genetic screening and counseling is to provide prospective parents with information that can help them make informed decisions about childbearing. This is, of course, different from eugenics. Couples are not coerced to refrain from breeding or, if they have the "right" genes, to produce large numbers of progeny. When prospective parents carry genetic traits that would be harmful to their children if passed on, they may choose to refrain from reproducing, employ artificial insemination from a noncarrier donor, or adopt children instead. The sickle-cell trait, for example, is not seriously life-threatening when it is inherited from only one parent. When present in both copies of a gene, however, it causes a potentially lethal anemia. Simple tests can determine whether parents are carriers of the trait. When both turn out to be carriers, the chance of a child inheriting the disease is one in four. The information is clear; the choice is up to the parents.

Once a child is conceived, the embryo may be tested for the presence of a number of genetic factors. Prenatal screening for Down syndrome and other birth defects is now common—and was taken advantage of by about 10% of prospective parents in 1993. Some choose to abort their severely deformed fetus, whereas others use the information to prepare for the special care needed. We can anticipate that some prospective parents will want to know whether they carry genes for Alzheimer disease, just as some are already being tested for early-onset fatal diseases like the rare genetic disorders in blood lipids. For some parents, the decision may be fairly straightforward. It makes little sense to bring a child into the world with a life expectancy measured in days or months, or a future of total dependency and an unknowable quality of life.

In other cases, the choices are more difficult. Even children born with Down syndrome may live into their 40s or 50s; they appear to enjoy their lives, and they may bring tremendous warmth and love to a family. But, what about genes that predispose individuals to Alzheimer disease, a horrible end to what may otherwise be a normal, happy, and productive life? What about genes that predispose females to breast cancer? Would you knowingly expose a daughter to that risk, or would you choose to abort the fetus and hope that the next child conceived didn't carry the genetic defect?

Here is where the application of scientific knowledge is placing us on moral thin ice. As the map of human genes expands and as we learn more about the large number of harmful alleles, our ability to detect these potential defects increases, and the number and difficulty of choices will increase as well. We could choose not to seek information about specific genes we may carry, take our chances in the genetic crap shoot, and deal with the consequences as they come. Or we could choose to know our genetic makeup and struggle to make decisions beforehand. It is our guess that almost everyone carries a gene that would bring harm in one environment or another.

Aging, Human Population Growth, and Society

There is no question that a shift in age structure toward the elderly will have a strong impact on the growth rate of the human population. Simply put, old people don't have children, and men and women in their reproductive years are becoming a smaller proportion of the population. Moreover, as a population ages, more of its economic resources are devoted to caring for the elderly and become unavailable for child rearing. Old people do not produce children, but they do use resources that could otherwise be devoted to the young.

When men and women wish to maintain or improve their standard of living, they will often choose to have fewer children, and the absolute growth rate of a population will slow down. It is not surprising that the lowest birth rates in the world are found in Europe and North America, where people enjoy long lives, but where care of the elderly absorbs an increasing share of personal wealth, and where women and men are well educated and make conscious choices about family size. In many developing nations, education has lagged behind improvements in public health and medical care. The result has been extremely rapid population growth and all the social, economic, and environmental problems that follow. It is a double burden for society to have to support growing proportions of children and elderly at the same time.

Numerous books have been written on the social consequences of aging, and many of the issues will be familiar to you through either reading or personal experience. The crux of the matter is that as science and technology improve, and we gain greater control over our lives, we are also forced to make increasingly difficult decisions. The aging of the human population has made genetic counseling, genetic engineering, abortion, care of the elderly, termination of life, responsibilities of families and society toward the elderly, and the economics of health care into major ethical, social, legal, and political issues. These are not likely to be resolved easily if only because each individual is unique and our individual experiences with these issues differ so widely.

One real danger arising from the aging of the population is the inevitable generational gap in our perceptions. Older men and women would like to enjoy their golden years with the support that they have earned from society and their families through hard work and rearing their offspring. Many younger people, used to being cared for by their parents and having less experience with elderly relatives living in their homes, see the increasing dependence of the elderly as a burden. As the numbers of elderly grow, so too does their political power and the potential for conflict over the distribution of money and other societal resources. Of course, many young people realize that they will someday be old, but foresight is even less clear than hindsight. Besides, one of the blessings that makes our younger years so enjoyable is that we aren't preoccupied with aging and death.

Much of the "debate" about care of the elderly focuses on the narrow issues of health and dependency. These are important issues, but we shouldn't neglect the tremendous opportunities afforded to both individuals and society by increasing longevity.

Age and Quality of Life

Society admires the team with the winning season or the athlete who holds the world record. When it comes to aging, the world record is held by the man or woman who lives the longest. Living well is also important, of course, but one cannot play down society's preoccupation with longevity. Our fear of death is great, especially when we have long years to contemplate death and watch as it makes its way

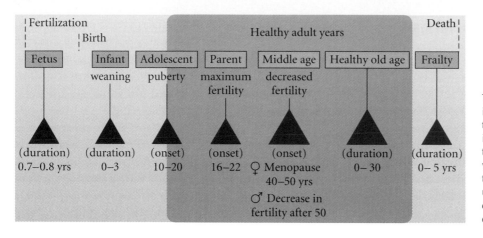

| Fertilization | Birth | | | Healthy adult years | | Death |

| Fetus | Infant | Adolescent | Parent | Middle age | Healthy old age | Frailty |

weaning puberty maximum decreased
fertility fertility

(duration)	(duration)	(onset)	(onset)	(onset)	(duration)	(duration)
0.7–0.8 yrs	0–3	10–20	16–22	♀ Menopause 40–50 yrs	0–30	0–5 yrs
				♂ Decrease in fertility after 50		

The phases of life history, including aging, vary widely among individuals. In this diagram, the width of the triangles indicates the range of years. Most in the United States will enjoy many years of healthy aging before entering the phase of frailty. Even then, individuals differ in the duration of serious disability before the natural event of death.

through our own generation. Yet, why should one want to live a long time if the quality of those extra years is low?

As biologists, we reemphasize here that the course of aging, like that of earlier development, is not rigidly determined and shows a great deal of flexibility. Starting from the beginning, weaning can occur soon after birth or be delayed for 3 to 5 years, as is the custom in many traditional societies. Puberty can begin as early as 10 years or as late as 20. After puberty, the healthy phase of adult life can be as short as 30 years for someone who dies prematurely of a heart attack or cancer or as long as 100 years or more. Madame Jeanne Calment, the French woman who at 120 may be the oldest person alive, was living independently until only a few years ago.

These observations on the plasticity of human life phases hint that there is no general ticking time bomb causing our cells to self-destruct at any particular age. Even if aging brings an increasing risk of dysfunction for molecules, cells, and organ systems, the risks are statistical rather than absolute.

Many approaches will be found to reduce risks of cancer, heart attacks, osteoporotic fractures, and other major causes of disability during aging. Even Alzheimer disease may eventually be conquered, or at least slowed so that its consequences are negligible during the life spans of most individuals. Slowing these diseases is a major priority of biomedical research on aging. A 20% reduction of hip fractures, for example, would save at least $50 billion in medical expenses by 2010.

Nonetheless, despite these and other expected medical advances, death is inevitable and medical intervention has so far proved to be ineffective against many of its causes. Our preoccupation with a long life might more productively shift to a preoccupation with a higher quality of life in old age. Of course, preventing an unpleasant old age starts at home with a sensible life style early in life. The responsibility then extends to society as a whole, which must develop the will to reduce toxins and other insults in the environment, help reduce stress at work and in social and family settings, and encourage public health and preventative medicine, including the ensuring of access for the less fortunate members of society. There is a lesson to be learned from the dental profession, which has basically eliminated tooth and gum disease among young people who have regular checkups and take preventative measures. Most of us will retire with a full set of teeth.

The well-being of society can benefit tremendously from the growing proportion of older age classes. Many people retire from their jobs in their late 60s, but they could still have a significant role to play in one another's lives and the lives of younger generations, and in sharing their collective wisdom with society as a whole. It is important that the experience of age tempers and directs the energy of youth; the combination is powerful for individuals and for society as a whole.

Here are both the opportunity and responsibility of old age: to stay engaged in life, family, and society to the fullest extent possible. As time goes by, our prospects of living to old age and enjoying a decent quality of life may depend less on biology and more on social and economic factors. We hope, and we will ourselves strive to see, that the value of human life continues to increase with advancing age.

Further Readings

General Books

Buss, Leo W. 1987. *The Evolution of Individuality*. Princeton, New Jersey: Princeton University Press. A lucid account of the evolution of development patterns, including a chapter on August Weismann's insights about the separation of the soma and the germ line.

Comfort, Alex. 1979. *The Biology of Senescence*, 3d ed. Edinburgh and London: Churchill Livingstone. A classic book by the author who also brought us *The Joy of Sex*.

Finch, Caleb E. 1990. *Longevity, Senescence, and the Genome*. Chicago: University of Chicago Press. An encyclopedic treatment of the processes of aging throughout the animal kingdom, with detailed accounts of the physiological and molecular mechanisms of aging and speculations on how patterns of senescence have changed during evolutionary history.

Hayflick, Leonard. 1994. *How and Why We Age*. New York: Ballantine Books. A look at the biology of aging and prospects for the future by a leader in research on the cell biology of aging; you will note the lack of evolutionary and comparative perspectives in this treatment.

Medawar, Peter B. 1952. *An Unsolved Problem of Biology.* London: H. K. Lewis. This classic book is the beginning of modern considerations of the evolution of senescence.

Rose, Michael R. 1991. *Evolutionary Biology of Aging.* New York and Oxford: Oxford University Press. An excellent, comprehensive treatment of evolutionary thinking applied to the phenomenon of aging, with explanations of the genetic bases of aging and accounts of selection experiments designed to test evolutionary theories of aging.

Stearns, Stephen C. 1992. *The Evolution of Life Histories.* Oxford, New York, and Tokyo: Oxford University Press. A clear and thorough treatment of the evolutionary modification of such traits as age at maturity and reproductive rate, including a chapter on reproductive life span and aging, as well as a general explanation of evolutionary analysis.

The Human Side of Aging

Abeles, Ronald P., Helen C. Gift, and Marcia G. Ory, eds. 1994. *Aging and Quality of Life.* New York: Springer.

Cockerham, William C. 1991. *This Aging Society.* Englewood Cliffs, New Jersey: Prentice Hall. Social aspects of aging in the United States.

Cole, Thomas R. 1992. *The Journey of Life: A Cultural History of Aging in America.* Cambridge and New York: Cambridge University Press.

Cole, Thomas R., and Mary G. Winkler, eds. 1994. *The Oxford Book of Aging.* Oxford and New York: Oxford University Press. Human thinking about aging in literature and poetry.

Frieden, Betty. 1993. *The Fountain of Age.* New York: Simon and Schuster. A noted feminist and author explores life in old age, taking a positive view of the possibilities.

Keith, Jennie, and others. 1994. *The Aging Experience: Diversity and Commonality Across Cultures.* Thousand Oaks, Calif.: Sage Publications.

Moody, Harry R., 1992. *Ethics in an Aging Society.* Baltimore: Johns Hopkins University Press.

Sapolsky, Robert M., 1994. *Why Zebras Don't Get Ulcers: A Guide to Stress, Stress-Related Diseases, and Coping.* New York: W. H. Freeman.

The Biology of Human Aging

Aiken, Lewis R. 1995. *Aging: An Introduction to Gerontology.* Thousand Oaks, Calif.: Sage Publications.

Cavanaugh, John C. 1990. *Adult Development and Aging.* Belmont, Calif.: Wadsworth. Physiological, psychological, and social aspects of adulthood and aging.

Coni, Nicholas, William Davison, and Stephen Webster. 1992. *Aging: The Facts,* 2d ed. Oxford and New York: Oxford University Press. A concise look at all aspects of human aging, with data primarily from the United Kingdom.

Crews, Douglas E., and Ralph M. Garruto, eds. 1994. *Biological Anthropology and Aging: Perspectives on Human Variation over the Life Span.* New York: Oxford University Press.

Holliday, Robin. 1995. *Understanding Ageing.* Cambridge: Cambridge University Press.

Maddox, George L., ed. 1995. *The Encyclopedia of Aging.* New York: Springer Publishing Company. A good, succinct source of information on all issues related to aging, from *abilities* to *World Health Organization,* with *arthritis, cognitive processes, gene expression, life extension, nutrition, sexuality,* and much more, in between.

Suzman, Richard M., David P. Willis, and Kenneth G. Manton. 1992. *The Oldest Old.* New York and Oxford: Oxford University Press.

Sources of a More Technical Nature

Carey, James R., Pablo Liedo, Dina Orozco, and James W. Vaupel. 1992. Slowing of mortality rates at older ages in large medfly cohorts. *Science* 258:457–461 (October 16, 1992).

Rose, Michael R., and Caleb E. Finch, eds. 1993. *The Genetics of Aging,* special issue of *Genetica* 91(1–3). This issue includes a variety of technical articles, many of them easily accessible to the lay reader, covering a variety of genetic aspects of aging research.

Schneider, Edward L., and John W. Rowe, eds. 1990. *Handbook of the Biology of Aging,* 3d ed. San Diego: Academic Press.

Wallace, Douglas C. 1992. Mitochondrial genetics: a paradigm for aging and degenerative diseases? *Science* 256:628–632 (May 1, 1992).

Williams, George C. 1957. Pleiotropy, natural selection, and the evolution of senescence. *Evolution* 11:398–411. This classic paper introduced the concept of antagonistic pleiotropy.

Recent Scientific American *Articles on Aging and Related Topics*

Boon, T. Teaching the immune system to fight cancer. 268(3):82–89 (March 1993).

Capecci, M. R. Targeted gene replacement. 270(3):52–59 (March 1994).

Cohen, J. S., and M. E. Hogan. The new genetic medicines. 271(6):76ff. (December 1994).

Garnick, M. B. The dilemmas of prostate cancer. 270(4):72ff. (April 1994).

Horgan, J. Eugenics revisited. 268(6):122ff. (June 1993).

Perls, T. T. The oldest old. 272(1):70–75. (January 1995).

Rustang, R. L. Why do we age? 267(6):130ff. (December 1992).

Selkoe, Dennis J. Amyloid protein and Alzheimer disease. 265(5): 68–78 (November 1991).

Welch, W. J. How cells respond to stress. 268(5):56ff. (May 1993).

The entire September 1993 issue, vol. 269(3), is devoted to the immune system.

Sources of Illustrations

Cover
William Rubell/Woodfin Camp & Assoc.

Frontispiece
Hans Baldung Grien, *The Three Ages and Death,* Prado, Madrid, Spain. Giraudon/Art Resource

Opposite page 1
William Rubell/Woodfin Camp & Assoc.

Page 2
Carl Cordonnier/Dailylife and the Ipsen Foundation

Page 3
Science Photo Library/Custom Medical Stock

Page 6, top left
Redrawn from H. B. Jones, "A special consideration of the aging process, disease, and life expectancy," *Adv. Biol. Med. Phys.* 4: 281–337 (1956).

Page 6, bottom right
J. R. Carey, P. Liedo, D. Orozco, and J. W. Vaupel, "Slowing of mortality rates at older ages in large medfly cohorts," *Science* 258: 457–461 (1992).

Page 8
George Dunnet

Page 9
Art Wolfe/Tony Stone Images

Page 11
Anthony Bannister/Natural History Photo Agency

Page 12
Brian Kenney/Planet Earth Pictures

Page 13, top left
From Jarmila Kukalova Peck, "Ephemeroid wing venation based upon new gigantic Carboniferous mayflies and basic morphology, phylogeny, and metamorphosis of pterygote insects," *Canadian Journal of Zoology* 63: 933–955, Figure 1.

Page 13, bottom right
Michal Jazwinski, Louisiana State University

Page 14
Art Wolfe, Inc.

Page 15
Andrew Neal/Planet Earth Pictures

Page 16, left
Richard Grosberg

Page 16, right
Redrawn from a drawing supplied by Richard Grosberg, University of California, Davis

Page 18
Graphische Sammlung Albertina

Page 22
Kurt Randerath et al., "Age- and tissue-related DNA modifications in untreated rats," *Carcinogenesis* 7(9) (1986).

Page 23
Hilton Mollenhauer, USDA Research Unit, College Station, Texas

Page 25
NIBSC/Science Photo Library/Photo Researchers

Page 28
Robert Becker/Custom Medical Stock

Page 29, top left
Adapted from L. Hayflick, "Cellular aging." In *Handbook of the Biology of Aging,* 1st ed., C. E. Finch and L. Hayflick, eds., Van Nostrand, 1977, p. 162, Figure 1.

Page 29, bottom right
Redrawn from D. Rohme, "Evidence for a relationship between longevity of mammalian species and lifespans of normal fibroblasts in vitro and erythrocytes in vivo," *Proceedings of the National Academy of Sciences* 78: 5009–5013 (1981).

Page 31
Robert Moyzis, *Scientific American*, July 1994, p. 14.

Page 32, left
Chip Clark

Page 32, right
Adapted from V. J. Maglio, "The evolution of mastication in the Elephantidae," *Evolution* 26: 638–658 (1972).

Page 33
Redrawn from M. L. Pollack, C. Foster, D. Knapp, J. L. Rod, and D. H. Schmidt, "Effect of age and training on aerobic capacity and body composition of master athletes," *J. Appl. Physiol.* 62: 725–731 (1987).

Page 36
American College of Rheumatology

Page 39, left
Redrawn from R. G. Gosden, *The Biology of Menopause: The Causes and Consequences of Ovarian Aging.* Academic Press, New York, 1985. Based on data from E. B. Hook, "Rates of chromosome abnormalities at different maternal ages," *Obstet. Gynecol.* 58: 282–285 (1981).

Page 39, right
Hattie Young/Science Photo Library/Photo Researchers

Page 41
U. Eichenlaub-Ritter, A. C. Chandley, and R. G. Gosden, "The CBA mouse as a model for age-related aneuploidy in man," *Chromosoma* 96: 220–226, Figure 2 (1988).

Page 42
Redrawn from A. Guyton, *Textbook of Medical Physiology,* 6th ed., Saunders.

Page 43, top
Redrawn from a figure in *The Columbus, Ohio, Dispatch,* November 19, 1991.

Page 43, bottom
From National Center for Health Statistics, National Hospital Discharge Survey, 1974–79.

Page 44
J. P. Deslypere, J. M. Kaufman, T. Vermeulen, D. Vogelaers, J. L. Vandalem, and A. Vermeulen, "Influence of age on pulsatile luteinizing hormone release and responsiveness of the gonadotrophs to sex hormone feedback in men," *J. Clin. Endocrinol. Metab.* 64: 68–73 (1987).

Page 46
Catherine Karnow/Woodfin Camp & Assoc.

Page 51
Adapted from a figure in David Crews, "Animal sexuality," *Scientific American* 270(1): 111 (January 1994).

Page 53
Adapted from B. E. Henderson, B. C. Pike, and R. K. Ross, "Epidemiology and risk factors," in *Breast Cancer: Diagnosis and Management,* G. Bonadonna, ed., Wiley and Sons, New York, 1984, pp. 15–33.

Page 55
James Stevenson/Photo Researchers, Inc.

Page 56
From Figure XVI-2 in A. M. Hartman and A. M. Goldstein, "Melanoma of the skin," Section XVI of *Seer Cancer Statistics Review, 1973–1990*, Washington, D.C.: USDHEW, NIH Pub No. 93–2787.

Page 57
J. M. Labat/Auscape

Page 59
Redrawn from R. H. Weindruch and R. L. Walford, "Dietary restriction in mice beginning at 1 year of age: Effect on lifespan and spontaneous cancer incidence," *Science* 215: 1415–1418 (1982).

Page 60
Adapted from a figure in M. S. Brown and J. L. Goldstein, "How LDL receptors influence cholesterol and atherosclerosis," *Scientific American* 251(5): 61 (November 1984).

Page 65
From H. Braak and E. Braak, "Neuropathological staging of Alzheimer-related changes," *Acta Neuropath* 82: 239–259, p. 243, Figure 1.

Page 66
From P. Hof and J. H. Morrison, "Cellular basis of cortical disconnection in Alzheimer disease and related dementing conditions." In *Alzheimer Disease*, R. D. Terry, R. Katzman, K. L. Bick, eds., Raven Press, New York, 1994, p. 205, Figure 4.

Page 67
Dennis J. Selkoe, Harvard University

Page 68
Comstock

Page 69
Redrawn from E. H. Corder et al., "Gene dose of apolipoprotein E type 4 allele and the risk of Alzheimer's disease in late onset families," *Science* 261: 921–923 (13 August 1993).

Page 70
Based on data from Yaakov Stern et al., "Influence of education and occupation on the incidence of Alzheimer's disease," *Journal of the American Medical Association* 271(13): 1004–1010 (6 April 1994).

Page 73
From Figure 1 in Hideo Uno et al., "Hippocampal damage associated with prolonged and fatal stress in primates," *Journal of Neuroscience* 9(5) (May 1989).

Page 74
Tui de Roy/AUSCAPE Int.

Page 79, left
John Cancalobi/VIREO

Page 79, right
Phillip Coffey, Jersey Wildlife Preservation Trust

Page 80
Jack Kelly Clark/Comstock

Page 81, left
Bill Patterson

Page 81, right
John M. Dean

Page 82
Frans Lanting/Minden Pictures

Page 83
Chuck Huntington

Page 84
Frans Lanting/Minden Pictures

Page 90
Jean-Paul Ferrero/AUSCAPE Int. Adapted from S. N. Austad and K. E. Fischer, "Mammalian aging, metabolism, and ecology: Evidence from the bats and marsupials," *Journal of Gerontology: Biological Sciences* 46(2): B47–53 (1991).

Page 92
Adapted from R. W. Hart and R. B. Setlow, "Correlation between deoxyribonucleic acid excision-repair and life-span in a number of mammalian species," *Proceedings of the National Academy of Sciences U.S.A.* 71(6): 2169–2173 (1974); and K. Y. Hall, R. W. Hart, A. K. Benirschke, and R. L. Walford, "Correlation between ultraviolet-induced DNA repair in primate lymphocytes and fibroblasts and species maximum achievable life span," *Mechanisms of Aging and Development* 24: 163–173 (1984).

Page 93
George Lepp/Comstock

Page 94
C. A. Henley/AUSCAPE Int.

Page 96
Art Wolfe, Inc.

Page 100
Chip Clark

Page 101
From A. Burt and G. Bell, "Mammalian chiasma frequencies as a test of two theories of recombination," *Nature* 326: 803–805 (1987).

Page 102
Frans Lanting/Minden Pictures

Page 103
From R. E. Ricklefs, "Fecundity, mortality, and avian demography," in *Breeding Biology of Birds,* D. S. Farner, ed., National Academy of Sciences, Washington, D.C., 1973, pp. 366–435.

Page 104
Reed Bowman

Page 107, left
From P. A. Prince, A. G. Wood, T. Barton, and J. P. Croxall, "Satellite tracking of wandering albatrosses *(Diomedia exulans)* in the South Atlantic," *Antarctic Science* 4(1): 321–336 (1992).

Page 107, right
From P. Jouventin and H. Weimerskirch, "Satellite tracking of wandering albatrosses," *Nature* 343(6260): 746–748 (1990); and H. Weimerskirch, M. Salamolard, F. Sarrazin, P. Jouventin, "Foraging strategy of wandering albatrosses through the breeding season: A study using satellite telemetry," *Auk* 110(2): 325–342 (1993).

Page 108
Doug Wechsler

Page 109
Adapted from C. Groot and T. P. Quinn, *Fishery Bulletin* 85 (1967).

Page 110
Peter Kresan

Page 111, left
Doug Wechsler

Page 111, right
From R. Karban, *Population Ecology of Periodical Cicadas,* Ph.D. dissertation, University of Pennsylvania, 1982.

Page 114
Comstock

Page 115, top left and right
Jeremy Jackson

Page 116
From S. R. Palumbi and J. B. C. Jackson, "Aging in modular organisms: Ecology of zooid senescence in *Steginoporella* sp. (Bryozoa; Cheilostomata)," *Biological Bulletin* 164: 267–278 (1983).

Page 118
Joseph Collins/Photo Researchers

Page 121, left
Dwight Kuhn

Page 121, right
W. P. Wergin and E. H. Newcomb, University of Wisconsin/ Biological Photo Service

Page 126
Peter Ginter/Bilderberg Archiv

Page 128
Pasteur Institute

Page 130
Stephen Dalton/Natural History Photo Agency

Page 132, top left
Robert Brons/Biological Photo Service

Page 132, top right
John Tower

Page 132, bottom
From J. E. Fleming, E. Quattrocki, G. Latter, J. Miquel, R. Marcuson, E. Zuckerkandl, and K. G. Bensch, "Age dependent changes in proteins of *Drosophila melanogaster*," *Science,* p. 1158 (1986).

Page 134
Custom Medical Stock

Page 136
Adapted from Table 24.4 in P. J. Russell, *Genetics,* 2d ed., Scott Foresman, Glenview, Illinois, 1990.

Page 139
From R. Plomin, M. J. Owen, and P. McGuffin, "The genetic basis of complex human behavior," *Science* 264: 1733–1739 (1994).

Page 142
Adapted from T. H. Clutton-Brock, S. D. Albon, and F. E. Guinness, "Reproductive success in male and female red

deer." In *Reproductive Success: Studies of Individual Variation in Contrasting Breeding Systems,* T. H. Clutton Brock, ed., University of Chicago Press, Chicago, 1988, pp. 325–343.

Page 151
Mark Wexler/Woodfin Camp & Assoc.

Page 152
Sinclair Stammers, Science Photo Library/Photo Researchers

Page 153
From Figure 7-6 of J. W. Fristom and M. T. Clegg, *Principles of Genetics,* 2d ed., Chiron Press, New York, 1988.

Page 155, left
From Figure 7-1 of J. W. Fristrom and M. T. Clegg, *Principles of Genetics,* 2d ed., Chiron Press, New York, 1988.

Page 157, left
Clyde E. Goulden

Page 157, right
From G. Bell, "Measuring the cost of reproduction. II. The correlation structure of the life tables of five freshwater invertebrates," *Evolution* 38: 314–326 (1984).

Page 158
Art Gingert/Comstock

Page 162
Comstock

Page 166
Data from Table 3.1 in C. E. Finch, *Longevity, Senescence, and the Genome,* University of Chicago Press, Chicago, 1990, and other sources.

Page 169
Adapted from P. M. Service, E. W. Hutchinson, M. D. Mackinley, and M. R. Rose, "Resistance to environmental stress in *Drosophila melanogaster* selected for postponed senescence," *Physiological Zoology* 58: 380–389 (1985).

Page 170
Adapted from P. M. Service, "Physiological mechanisms of increased stress resistance in *Drosophilia melanogaster* selected for postponed senescence," *Physiological Zoology* 60(3): 321–326 (1987).

Page 173
Dave Reznick, University of California at Riverside

Page 174
Helen Rodd

Page 175
From S. N. Austad, "Retarded senescence in an insular population of Virginia opossums *(Didelphis virginiana),*" *Journal of Zoology, London* 229: 695–708 (1993).

Page 178
Gary Chapman/Louisville Courier Journal

Page 180
Data from Nathan Keyfitz and Wilhelm Flieger, *World Population Growth and Aging: Demographic Trends in the Late Twentieth Century,* University of Chicago Press, Chicago and London, 1990.

Index

Cancer *(cont.)*
   endometrial, 54
   and mutation, 22
   prostate, 54
   skin, 55
   stomach, 93
   uterine, 53
Carbonyl group, 25
Cardiovascular disease, 144
Carey, J., 80
Catalase enzyme, 146
Cell aging, 28
Cell culture, 113
Cell differentiation, 30, 49
Cell division and cancer, 55
Cell organelles, 121
Cell proliferation, 14, 124
Centenarians, 82
Cerami, A., 26
Cerebral cortex, 64
Cerebrovascular disease, 67
Chloroplast clone, 121
Cholesterol, 61, 62, 143, 182
Chromosome, 41, 98
   abnormal number, 37
   sex, 93
Cicada, periodical, 111
Cigarette smoking, and heart disease, 182
Clone, 13
   aging in, 122
   asexual, 112
   aspen, 116
   cell, 120
Codon, 129
Cohen, D., 68
Cohort, 77
Collagen, 26, 175
Colonial animals, 115
Color blindness, inheritance of, 150
Common garden experiment, 137
Contraceptive, oral, 54
Coral, 116
Coronary heart disease, risk factors, 182
Corticosteroid, 9, 37, 71, 72, 73, 94, 112
Corticosterone, 71, 73
Cortisol, 71, 72, 94
Cost of meiosis, 98
Creosote bush, clone, 13, 15
Cross-linkage, 26
Crossing-over

frequency of, 101
   genetic, 98, 99
Cushing's disease, 9
Cytosine, 20, 129

daf-2 mutant, 151
Darwin, C., 7
Dauer stage, 151
Death, programmed, 110
Death rate, 76
   human, 2
Deleterious alleles, 156
Deleterious mututations, 143
Dementia, 63
   early-onset, 67
   and education, 69
   in elderly, 180
   multi-infarct, 64
Demographic aging, 175
Desiccation resistance, 169
Development
   and aging, 15
   and life span, 91
Diabetes, 144
   adult-onset, 57
   in elderly, 180
   non-insulin dependent (type II), 26, 57
   type II, 26
Diabetes mellitus, 58
Didelphis virginiana, 174
Diet
   and cancer, 53
   and fertility, 59
Diet restriction, and aging, 58
Differentiation, cell, 30, 49
Diploid chromosome number, 38, 98, 117
Diploid egg, 117
Disease
   cerebrovascular, 67
   and evolution of sex, 100
   genetic, 150
   vascular, 60, 63
Divergence, genetic, 114
Dizygotic twins, 138
DNA
   damage to, 102
   double helix, 21
   I-spot, 21

Other Books in the Scientific American Library Series